HISTORIC ALAMANCE COUNTY

A Biographical History

by William Murray Vincent, PhD

Commissioned by the Alamance County Historical Museum

Historical Publishing Network
A division of Lammert Incorporated
San Antonio, Texas

ACKNOWLEDGMENTS

The author would like to express his appreciation to the following staff members of the Alamance County Historical Museum for their kind assistance in the production of this book: Kevin Johnson, Debbie Strickland, and Laurie Smith. A special debt of gratitude is owed to Bennie Catoe who typed and edited the manuscript. Some documentary photographs and historic post card images were drawn from the personal collections of Giles Mebane, Jane Moore, Julia Jordan, and Grover Moore. Barry Black and Colin Hart of Historical Publishing Network assisted with the production of the book. Any errors in fact in the text are solely the responsibility of the author.

First Edition

Copyright © 2009 Historical Publishing Network

ISBN: 9781893619982

Library of Congress Card Catalog Number: 2009924208

Historic Alamance County: A Biographical History

author:	William Murray Vincent
cover artist:	Mort Künstler
contributing writers for "Sharing the Heritage":	Susan Cumins
	Doris Kraus

Historical Publishing Network

president:	Ron Lammert
project managers:	Barry Black
	David White
administration:	Donna M. Mata
	Melissa G. Quinn
	Evelyn Hart
book sales:	Dee Steidle
production:	Colin Hart
	Craig Mitchell
	Charles A. Newton, III
	Roy Arellano
	Joshua Johnston
	Glenda Tarazon Krouse

PRINTED IN KOREA

CONTENTS

Illustration from "The Beasts of Carolina," a series of drawings contained in the 1709 London edition of John Lawson's A New Voyage to Carolina. *The plate depicts a whitetail deer stag attacked by a bobcat.*

"THE FLOWER OF CAROLINA"

Located in the central Piedmont of North Carolina, the land that has become Alamance County was traditionally seen as an area of natural abundance and agricultural promise. The first Europeans to leave records of their observations of the region were impressed by its potential and bounty. When the explorer John Lederer entered what is now Alamance County in June 1670 he observed that the woods were "full of fallow deer (and) there was great variety of excellent Fowl, as wilde Turkeys, Pigeons, Patridges, Phesants, &c." (Lederer, 1672)

Some thirty years later, in 1701, when the English surveyor and naturalist John Lawson visited the region he called it "the Flower of Carolina" and claimed he "had never seen 20 miles of such extraordinary rich land, lying all together, like that betwixt Hau-River and Achoneechy Town." "No man", he said, "that will be content within the Bounds of Reason, can have any grounds to dislike it (for) here the country becomes more clear'd of Wood, (and) becomes more healthful to the Inhabitants...There (is) rich land enough to contain some Thousand Families; for which Reason, I hope, in a short time, it will be planted." (Lawson, 1967)

Within this area between the Haw and Eno Rivers Lawson thus saw great potential for building and settlement: besides the open grassy savannahs of "the Haw Old Fields", the area boasted abundant water resources, splendid oak and hardwood timber reserves, and great outcroppings of granite and stone, which were particularly evident along the Haw River watershed. A natural fault line, running east to west throughout the region, created a variance in local land elevations, which allowed area creeks and rivers to flow rapidly with a fair exchange of water volume. This was an ideal situation for the development of water-powered grist and saw mills. Finally, the area was readily accessible to potential settlers: since the seventeenth century Native Americans had established a network of trails throughout the territory, and these trails extended into Virginia and northward as far as Chester County, Pennsylvania. In the coming years these trading paths would provide entry for settlers coming from the north, and supported their settlement and internal movement once they reached the lands of Alamance County. Paradoxically, then, the accomplishments of local Native Americans in establishing trading paths also sealed their ultimate displacement by people of European descent.

Fault line and rapids on the Haw River near Glencoe Mill Village, central Alamance County.

PHOTO BY KEVIN JOHNSON.

NATIVE AMERICANS AND CONTACT IN ALAMANCE

In the 1750s when European settlers first began to arrive in the Carolina Piedmont they found it occupied by several small Indian tribes who shared a common culture and similar Siouan language dialects. Archaeological and linguistic evidence suggests that the ancestors of these Native Americans had themselves migrated into the region, coming from the west and crossing the North Carolina mountains several centuries before Columbus arrived in the Americas. Once in the Piedmont, these Siouan-speakers supplanted and merged with an older Woodland culture dating to 1000 B.C. The existence of Clovis and Hardaway-type projectile points found in southern Alamance County suggests an even more ancient aboriginal presence in the Carolina Piedmont, however, and Paleo-Indians probably lived here as early as 11,000 B.C.

By the mid-1600s the region came to be dominated by the Siouan-speaking Occaneechi, whose language may have served as a lingua franca for much of the Carolina Piedmont. The Occaneechis' dominance resulted from their intense involvement with the deerskin trade, which they controlled by force from a fortified island stronghold strategically located on the Roanoke River near the present Virginia/North Carolina border. From this village Indian hunting parties penetrated deep into North Carolina, where the fertile Haw River Valley was a favorite hunting ground.

The island village of the Occaneechi was visited in 1670 by the explorer John Lederer and again in 1673 by fur traders James Needham and Gabriel Arthur. These early contact explorers state that the Occaneechi maintained and reinforced their dominant role in the trade network through a combination of warfare and intimidation. Thus the Occaneechi earned a fierce and pugnacious reputation, which ultimately led, in 1676, to an eruption of armed hostilities with Nathaniel Bacon's colonial militia.

Following their battle with Bacon, the Occaneechi were greatly reduced in number and could no longer defend their island village on the Roanoke. By 1677 the survivors abandoned the Roanoke River site and retreated southward to the central North Carolina Piedmont villages of the O'enock, a related Siouan group. Once in the area, the Occaneechi quickly established their major headquarters on the Eno River near present Hillsborough, North Carolina. This village, known as

Remnants of Indian Trading Path, northern Alamance County.

PHOTO BY KEVIN JOHNSON.

Reconstruction of typical Siouan winter dwelling showing years of wear.

PHOTO BY KEVIN JOHNSON.

Typical Piedmont North Carolina projectile points, stone ax, and celts. Collection: Alamance County Historical Museum.

PHOTO BY KEVIN JOHNSON AND LAURIE SMITH.

Achoneechy Town in the colonial period, but referred to today as the Fredericks/Wall Site, has been the focus of intense archaeological investigations since 1983 (see Dickens et. al., 1987). By the 1690s Achoneechy Town had become the largest Siouan settlement in the Carolina Piedmont, and its population, numbering several hundred, eclipsed smaller Siouan settlements located along nearby tributaries of the Haw.

By the early 20th century descendants of the Occaneechi were largely concentrated in the northern Alamance County community known as Little Texas. Over the years processes of acculturation led the Occaneechi to live lifestyles similar to those of their African-American and Scots-Irish neighbors. Despite culture loss and intermarriage with outsiders, however, some members of the Little Texas community clung to a self-ascription as Native Americans.

In 1934, an unsuccessful effort was made by some residents of Little Texas to have the federal government provide an Indian school for the children of the area. Although an agent of the Bureau of Indian Affairs visited northern Alamance County, no assistance or formal recognition was received. Some fifty years later in 1984, members of the Little Texas community, together with people from the Burnetts' Chapel area of southern Alamance County, formed the Eno-Occaneechi Indian Association. The goals of the association were the preservation and teaching of Indian heritage, coupled with official recognition as a tribal people. To these ends, an annual Pow-Wow was inaugurated and a petition for official state recognition was submitted to the North Carolina Commission on Indian Affairs in January 1990. This recognition was granted to the Occaneechi Band of the Saponi Nation on February 4, 2002.

Typical Siouan summer dwelling, Occaneechi Tribal Center.

PHOTO BY KEVIN JOHNSON.

EARLY SETTLEMENT PATTERNS

By the middle of the eighteenth century population growth in Pennsylvania and the Virginia backcountry began to create prohibitively high local land prices. As a result, many young families began to look south for land and opportunity. By the 1750s travel into the southern backcountry and what became Alamance County was facilitated by the creation of the so-called Great Wagon Road which largely followed existing Indian trading paths that extended from Philadelphia into the Carolina Piedmont. Persons entering Alamance on the Great Wagon Road initially followed an eastern fork in the road which carried them south through portions of the Shenandoah Valley into Mecklenburg County, Virginia and eventually to present-day Vance County, North Carolina and Orange County. By the late 1750s, however, a more westerly route came to be favored, and brought settlers bound for Carolina across Virginia's Dan River into modern Caswell County, northwest Alamance and present-day Guilford. Additionally some early English settlers entered the region from then more populated eastern North Carolina communities near Edenton, Bertie County, and the Roanoke River

Reconstructed palisaded Native American village, Occaneechi Tribal Center, northern Alamance County.

PHOTO BY KEVIN JOHNSON.

Occaneechi tribal members with State Highway Historical Marker, Hillsborough N.C.

COLLECTION: OCCANEECHI TRIBAL COUNCIL.

Pow-Wow at Occaneechi Tribal Center.

COLLECTION: OCCANEECHI TRIBAL COUNCIL.

Valley. A small group of Welsh settlers also immigrated to northern Alamance County from Pennsylvania's "Welsh Tract" along the Delaware River.

By far the greatest percentage of immigrants into Alamance was of three distinctive ethnic and religious groups: Scots-Irish Presbyterians, German Lutherans, and English and Irish Quakers. Within these groups families often moved in stages: it was a common practice for men to go together to the place of settlement in the fall of the year, where they cleared land and often constructed makeshift

On Sunday, February 8, 1701, an adventurous Englishman named John Lawson entered "Achoneechy Town" at about three o'clock in the afternoon. He was greeted by the Indians with presentations of bear meat and venison, and was given lodging in the "king's Cabin" (Lawson 1967:61). There he also acquired an Indian guide, known as Enoe Will, who conducted him eastward to the English. Before reaching Achoneechy Town, Lawson had crossed "the famous Hau-River, by some called Reatkin. It is called Hau-River from the Sissipahau Indians who dwell upon this stream, which is one of the main branches of the Cape-Fear."

The Indians Lawson saw in 1701 were accustomed to regular visits by Virginia traders who had penetrated farther into the Carolina Piedmont following the destruction of the Occaneechi Roanoke River stronghold in 1676. By the early 1700s the introduction of European trade goods, disease, and alcohol began a period of cultural demise for the Piedmont Siouans, whose populations rapidly declined. These problems were further exacerbated beginning in 1711, when a decade of intercultural conflict with invading Tuscarora peoples created additional cultural stress.

As a result, in 1713, several Siouan-speaking tribes, including the Occaneechi, Tutelo, and Saponi, signed a treaty with Virginia's Lieutenant Governor Alexander Spotswood that formalized their relationship with the province. The Indians agreed to leave North Carolina and relocate along the Meherrin River, near the present-day town of Lawrenceville, Virginia. There they would live in the shadow of Fort Christianna, an outpost to be built by a trading company and manned by colonial rangers. In return for their promises to help defend the frontier and pay tribute to Williamsburg, the natives were to receive protection, trade rights, a reservation, and instruction in "civilization" and Christianity. To these ends, a school and a minister were provided for the Indians' instruction. In 1716 a visitor to the settlement found native children sitting attentively in a classroom under the watchful eye of an English tutor (Beaudry 1981: 2-13).

The experiment was short-lived, however, and by 1717 Fort Christianna was officially closed. Competing trade interests led to the abolishment of the trading company, and by the 1720s, the Christianna Indians found themselves harassed by nearby settlers, attacked by northern war parties, and abandoned by colonial officials. In 1728 they marched back into the Carolina Piedmont along the old Indian trading path to join other refugees heading south toward the Catawbas. Their stay in the Catawba Nation proved to be as brief as the Christianna experiment, and by 1733, they were back in Virginia, from whence they eventually scattered in several directions including Greensville County, Virginia. Moravian records indicate that a palisaded Indian village was located on the Haw River as late as 1756 (Fries 1922: 165). Local tradition holds that when William Braxton received a land grant in the Snow Camp area of Alamance County in 1756, there were Indian "wigwams" still standing along nearby Piney Creek.

Recent research (Hazel 1987: 1991) has suggested that, about the time of the American Revolution, a core group of Occaneechi descendants migrated from Greensville County, Virginia, to northern Alamance County, where they subsequently obtained title to land and formed an endogamous and racially distinctive community known as "Little Texas." During the 1800s, the Little Texas families were almost invariably listed on official lists as "Free Colored" or "Mulatto," although at least one member of the community, Abner Burnette, was listed in the 1860 census as Indian. Despite how the Little Texas community was perceived by outsiders within the largely biracial population of Alamance County, however, there seems to have been a persistent belief by members of the community that its members were largely of Indian descent. [Troxler and Vincent, 1999: 22-23]

19th Century lithograph depicting travel along the "Great Wagon Road".

COLLECTION: ALAMANCE COUNTY HISTORICAL MUSEUM.

dwellings. By early spring they retrieved their families who then entered Alamance with modest housing already in existence and land ready to plant. Households usually moved south in groups related by kinship, ethnicity, religion, and common origins. Once in Alamance the groups fanned out along the rich tributaries of the Haw, which provided a resource for the development of grist and saw mills.

The nature of these immigration patterns meant that Alamance came to be settled in a distinctive manner: Scots-Irish Presbyterians tended to settle east of the Haw River, Quakers settled the southernmost region of what became Alamance County, and German Lutherans settled to the west of the Haw River. By the 1740s Scots-Irish Presbyterians were living at Hawfields, Stony Creek, and Cross Roads, and it is known that Presbyterian ministers visited these areas as early as 1743, and again in 1751 and 1755. By about 1750 Quakers dominated the Cane Creek settlement in southern Alamance County. This largely Irish Quaker settlement was supported by at least two local grist mills, operated by Simon Dixon and Thomas Lindley, and had two Quaker meeting houses known as the Spring and Cane Creek meetings. In 1748 a small party of Germans scouted Alamance County for land on which to settle their Pennsylvania families. They found a small contingent of

German speakers already living along the present-day Alamance-Guilford line, and, in the ensuing ten-year period between 1759 and 1769, more than eighty men of German heritage established households in the Alamance and Stinking Quarter Creek areas west of Haw River. By far the majority of these German settlers came south from the port of Philadelphia, however some are also known to have come to Alamance County from German settlements located near Charleston, South Carolina and the so-called Germanna colony of Virginia. By 1753 courts were describing the waterway along which these German settlers lived as the "great Allemanze" perhaps derived from the term "allemance" or "allamance" denoting an area inhabited by Germans. Curiously the term Alamance may also stem from the Siouan word "alamanche" meaning "place where water flows through blue clay banks."

WHEN ALAMANCE WAS ORANGE

In response to the dramatic influx of settlers into the Carolina backcountry in the mid 1700s the legislature of the colony of North Carolina created a new

county in 1752. As originally established, Orange County encompassed large portions of modern-day Orange, Chatham, Alamance, Caswell, Rockingham, Lee, Randolph, Guilford, Person, and Durham counties, and, by the late 1760s, Orange came to be the most populous county in the colony. Present Alamance County was situated at the geographic heart of this new county, which the Haw River effectively bisected from east to west.

In 1752 the first county courthouse was situated on Back Creek about half way between the present-day towns of Mebane and Haw River. It remained in use until March 1754, but within a year, by 1755, the county seat was moved east to the Eno River, to a place soon to be known as Hillsborough. This action was directly related to the creation of Rowan County from a portion of Orange in 1753. The division effectively stripped from the former Orange County large tracts of land to the south and west so that the Back Creek courthouse site was no longer centrally located. Hillsborough on the Eno would then become the county seat of old Orange, which included all of today's Alamance County. Not until 1849 was a new county called Alamance officially created from the westernmost half of old

Period charcoal drawing showing Cross Roads Presbyterian Church as it appeared in the mid-1800s.

COLLECTION: CROSS ROADS PRESBYTERIAN CHURCH.

Period photograph of Nick's Store Building, the oldest commercial structure in Graham, N.C. The building was constructed in 1851 and originally housed McLean and Hanner Mercantile Company.

COLLECTION: DR. DURWARD STOKES.

Original Alamance County Courthouse, constructed in 1851 by brothers John and Samuel McClain and John and William Denny.

COLLECTION: DR. DURWARD STOKES.

Orange, and the Alamance County seat of Graham was established. The town of Graham was named for William Alexander Graham (1804-1875) under whose administration as Whig party governor the campaign to create Alamance came to fruition.

RESENTMENT AND THE WAR OF REGULATION

One factor influencing the settlement of Alamance during the 1750 to 1760 period was the ready availability of arable land at reasonable prices. By 1760 "eight pounds and four shillings Virginia currency, or about six pounds sterling, would buy 640 acres of 'good' land" (Troxler and Vincent, 1999: 58) in Alamance territory. This meant that average land costs in this portion of the so-called Granville tract were about five shillings per acre. Reasonable land prices were offset, however, by the dishonest way in which Granville lands were administered and sold, the difficulties of obtaining certified land title, and the unfair way in which taxes were levied. Additionally, the ability of local government officials to "distrain" or seize movable property, such as cattle or grain, in lieu of cash tax payments proved a hardship for many backcountry farmers. A 1743 law granting voting rights only to persons owning fifty acres or more effectively disenfranchised many small land owners in Alamance territory. Perceived linkages between a dominant class of landed local officials and an eastern oligarchy centered in Edenton and

New Bern also fueled local resentment. The 1766 legislative decision to establish a capitol for the colony in the tidewater community of New Bern exacerbated the tension between the rural backcountry and the more prosperous coastal areas. Public resentments grew with the construction of Tryon Palace and the heavy poll taxes required to support its building and maintenance.

Against this backdrop of corruption, insecure land tenure, unfair taxation, and general disorder a self-styled "Regulator" movement arose in the Alamance area. By the fall of 1766 a circular, known as the "Regulator Advertisement," was printed decrying "abuses of power" and expressing the need for "judicious inquiry" in the form of organized citizen meetings. During the ensuing months several such meetings were indeed held, whereupon participants agreed not to pay unlawful taxes and to "bear testimony against such abuses."

Escalating tensions between local Regulators and government officials culminated in September 1770 with the so-called Hillsborough Riots. Over a several day period Regulators disrupted the Hillsborough court, "insulted some gentlemen of the bar," whipped several justices of the peace, and demanded greater representation on juries and in the affairs of the colony. A result of this insurrection was the passage in January 1771 of the Johnston Riot Act, which defined the felony of riot and authorized prosecution of those involved in riotous acts. A further consequence was the arrest of Herman Husband, who was widely viewed as a leader of the Regulator movement.

Regulator reaction to these events was rapid: more than 2,000 men assembled with the stated goal of marching on New Bern and confronting royal governor Tryon. In reaction to these actions Tryon was authorized to lead a militia force into the Carolina interior, and by May 1771 he was camped along Alamance Creek near the community of Bellemont. Just a few miles away, along the old Trading Path, a group of some 1,000 Regulators lay in wait.

Following a series of exchanges between the two sides, including a reading of the Riot Act by Tryon, the battle between the Regulators and the North Carolina militia under royal Governor Tryon began on May 16, 1771. The battle commenced a little before noon and continued for about two and a half hours. At its conclusion about 61 members of the militia forces were wounded and upwards of three hundred Regulators were said to be injured. Nine men on each side were killed. Six prisoners taken by Tryon's forces were also executed at Hillsborough on June 19, 1771. These events would help to set the stage for a fulminating conflict that exploded ten years later in 1781 as the Southern Campaign of the American Revolution.

ALAMANCE AND THE SOUTHERN CAMPAIGN OF THE REVOLUTION

By 1781 General Nathaniel Greene had taken command of the Continental Army in the South and his forces were entrenched in Piedmont North Carolina. His English protagonist, General Charles Lord Cornwallis, had also brought an impressive force consisting of both loyalist militia and provincial corps into the central North Carolina community of Hillsborough. This British-led presence was bolstered by the forces of Banastre Tarleton, whose camp was located near present day Tarleton Avenue in Burlington, and whose forces consisted of 200 cavalry,

John Allen Log House (ca. 1780), currently located at Alamance Battleground State Historic Site.
PHOTO BY KEVIN JOHNSON.

Lieutenant – colonel Banastre Tarleton, a leader of the British forces in Piedmont North Carolina.

FROM: BENSON LOSSING'S PICTORIAL FIELD-BOOK OF THE REVOLUTION IN THE CAROLINAS AND GEORGIA, 1850.

Early 20th century postal card depicting a scene from the Battle of Alamance.

COLLECTION: JANE MOORE.

150 men of the 33rd Regiment, and over one hundred German Jaegers. Word of Tarleton's presence also brought the forces of General "Lighthouse" Henry Lee's legion into the Alamance area. This action led to the conflict known locally as "The Hacking Match," or Pyle's Massacre, in which, in a bloody confrontation, Lee's forces defeated a group of loyalists headed to meet and join Cornwallis. Important battles also occurred in March 1781 at Clapp's Mill near the confluence of Beaver and Alamance Creeks and at Weitzel's (Whitsell's) Mill in present Boone Station Township. These events would culminate with the Battle of Guilford Courthouse on March 15, 1781. Following the heavy fighting there, both Cornwallis and his adversary Greene would seek solace for their wounded among the Quakers of Guilford and the southern Alamance communities of Snow Camp and Cane Creek.

Less than six months after Cornwallis' stay in Snow Camp a battle was fought at nearby Lindley's Mill on September 13, 1781, which proved to be one of the deadliest of the Piedmont campaign. When fighting stopped some 200 men were left dead or dying, many of whom were buried in mass graves at the battle

Early 20th century postal card depicting the monument erected on May 29, 1880 to commemorate the Battle of Alamance (1771).

COLLECTION: JANE MOORE.

site and Spring Meeting House. The casualties and insults suffered by Cornwallis and the loyalist forces during this 1781 Southern Campaign undoubtedly influenced the outcome of Yorktown and the Revolutionary cause as a whole.

REVIVALISM IN ALAMANCE

In the immediate aftermath of the Revolutionary War a spiritual evangelicalism gripped much of central North Carolina and the central Alamance area. This emphasis on spiritualism may have been influenced, in part, by an influx of Baptists and Methodist Protestants in the immediate post-Revolutionary period. Many scholars have also argued that the spiritualism of a growing African-American population had an impact: by 1830 enslaved people made up thirty-seven percent of the population of the northern Alamance area and twenty-eight percent of the population of Southern Alamance.

African concepts of spiritual ecstasy and notions about spiritual homecoming—sometimes referred to as "going over home"— came to be incorporated as fundamental parts of the Baptist and Methodist faith experience. Shouting and various physical displays of religious fervor were often coupled with foot washing and the laying on of hands. These practices were particularly prevalent at area camp meetings and revivals.

Burlington's First Baptist Church, a Neo-Classical Revival structure erected in 1922-1923.

POSTAL CARD COLLECTION: JANE MOORE.

Postal card depicting the Alamance Cotton Factory as it appeared in 1837. Inset is a photograph of mill owner E.M. Holt.

COLLECTION: ALAMANCE COUNTY HISTORICAL MUSEUM.

Revival Meeting, Cross Roads Presbyterian, ca. 1870.

COLLECTION: ALAMANCE COUNTY HISTORICAL MUSEUM

One such service, held in March 1801 at Cross Roads Presbyterian Church is generally regarded as formative in the spread of the Great Awakening in the South. This event promoted the penchant for revivals and protracted meetings that came to be important parts of the spiritual and social life of the Carolina Piedmont until the early part of the twentieth century.

NEW BEGINNINGS

In 1800 North Carolina had the lowest per capita wealth of any state in the nation. With little industry, limited commerce, and poor transportation, the Piedmont was largely a region of yeoman farmers, and the state as a whole was known as the "Rip Van Winkle State." These depressed conditions created pressures for out-migration, and, between 1815 and 1850, fully one-third of the area's population emigrated to Tennessee, Ohio, Arkansas, and beyond.

Against this economically depressed backdrop a small group of citizens was determined to chart a new course for the state. Chief among these was Archibald DeBow Murphey, a state senator (1812-1818) and judge who lived along the Haw River. Murphey championed a system of public education, internal improvements, and constitutional reforms unparalleled in the state's early history. Murphey's proposals would lead to the development of the state's modern network of roadways and his insistence upon educational reform helped to establish a statewide system of standardized public instruction, including state schools for the hearing and sight-impaired. Importantly, Murphey drew around him a group of citizens who sought to widen the horizons of the area beyond its agricultural base.

Among these supporters of Murphey was Edwin Michael Holt, a fourth-generation descendant of one of the area's pioneering German families. In 1837, in partnership with his brother-in-law William Carrigan, Holt launched one of the area's first industries, a textile mill known as the Alamance Cotton Factory. Initially organized as a spinning operation, the mill was converted in 1853 when looms were purchased from

Archibald DeBow Murphey, age 28.

COLLECTION: ALAMANCE COUNTY HISTORICAL MUSEUM

the North, and the mill began production of woven cotton goods known as "Alamance Plaids." These materials have the distinction of being the first colored cotton fabrics manufactured in the American South. By 1900 members of the extended Holt family operated 24 mills in the local area. Several of these early mills were eventually incorporated into the consolidation of Burlington Mills, founded in 1924. Under the capable leadership of J. Spencer Love, who capitalized on the success of man-made fibers like rayon, the company changed its name to Burlington Industries in the 1950s. By the 1970s the

Lewis W. Hine photograph of doffers tying threads at a Southern cotton mill, January 19, 1909.

ARCHIVES: LIBRARY OF CONGRESS.

Lewis W. Hine photograph of child laborers, December 1908. In the 1880s child workers In Alamance County textile mills were paid approximately five cents per day.

ARCHIVES: LIBRARY OF CONGRESS.

company operated plants in several states and some twenty foreign countries, and the business employed more than 26,000 people. In the 1980s changes in the industry and competing market forces wreaked havoc with Burlington Industries, which eventually declared bankruptcy. When it emerged from bankruptcy, Burlington Industries merged with the former Cone Mills and several subsidiary corporations to form the International Textile Group.

Another area textile success story began in 1896 when Daisy Hosiery Mill was opened by W. C. Thurston and associates. Within a few years this operation was purchased by brothers Ben and W. H. May whose May Hosiery brand soon became nationally known. By the 1950s more than fifty hosiery mills were in operation in Alamance County. Many were small family operations; others, like the May-McEwen-Kaiser group and Kayser-Roth were internationally known.

The proliferation of hosiery mills inaugurated an era of economic prosperity in Alamance County, and Burlington came to be known as "The Hosiery Center of the South." A further innovation occurred in 1959, when pantyhose—then called 'pantilegs'—were developed locally by the Gant family and Glen Raven Mills. Glen Raven Mills has also cemented its reputation through the production of

canvas-type materials, and its Sunbrella© brand is now internationally known. Copeland Fabrics, located in Hopedale at the confluence of Stony Creek and Haw River, is now a major producer of drapery and upholstery-weight fabrics.

THE COMING OF THE RAILROAD AND THE CIVIL WAR

An outgrowth of Archibald Murphey's progressive plans for the state was Whig support in the 1840s and '50s for an expansion of railroads into the North Carolina Piedmont. Earlier, an 1828 meeting at William Albright's home in southern Alamance is generally regarded as the first public meeting to promote railroads in North Carolina. Whig Governor William A. Graham and party member Giles Mebane were instrumental in the passing of legislation in 1849 creating the North Carolina Rail Road Company and providing charter for construction of a railroad linking western portions of the state with the Goldsboro terminus of the Wilmington and Weldon Railroad. The eventual construction of the new line through central Alamance County gave rise to Burlington and Gibsonville and helped shape Mebane, Haw River, and Graham by shifting the area's demographics and ensuring that the late nineteenth century manufacturing plants clustered in those areas.

Construction of the railroad through Alamance County began in 1851, although trains did not begin regular runs through the area until 1856. Some local persons responsible for grading the line included Benjamin Hurdle, Thomas Sellars, and Solomon Dixon. Many of the men who built the railroad and maintained it were enslaved residents of the area, hired for designated periods of time. Benjamin Trolinger of Haw River, a member of the railroad's Board of Directors, was a major contractor for the road, doing more than $70,000 of the work from 1852 to 1856 and selling the company

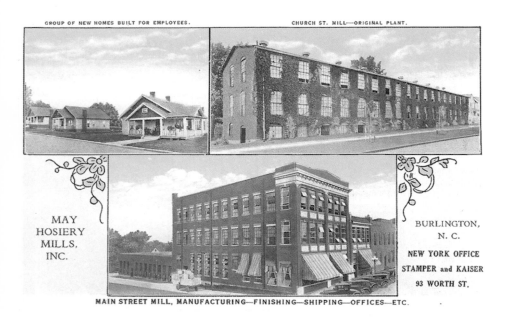

GROUP OF NEW HOMES BUILT FOR EMPLOYEES.   CHURCH ST. MILL—ORIGINAL PLANT.

MAY HOSIERY MILLS, INC.

BURLINGTON, N. C.

NEW YORK OFFICE STAMPER and KAISER 93 WORTH ST.

MAIN STREET MILL, MANUFACTURING—FINISHING—SHIPPING—OFFICES—ETC.

Early 20th century postal card depicting Daisy Hosiery Mill (1896), top right, and its successor, May Hosiery Mill. At left are bungalow-type houses constructed in Burlington, N.C. for mill employees.

COLLECTION: JANE MOORE.

Women seated along Burlington's Main Street wearing nylon stockings produced by May Hosiery during World War II.
COLLECTION: ALAMANCE COUNTY HISTORICAL MUSEUM.

some land on which it built its Company Shops. His graceful railroad bridges over the Haw River and Back Creek soon became the best-known landmarks along the railway line.

19th century lithograph showing a steam locomotive crossing the railroad bridge at Haw River, N.C. The image is incorporated on personalized checks used by E.M. Holt in the 1880s.
COLLECTION: ALAMANCE COUNTY HISTORICAL MUSEUM.

On January 30, 1856 the first train passed along the entire route from Goldsboro to Charlotte. Soon thereafter, company officials began plans for a repair station, to be located approximately midway along the line. Known as Company Shops, the repair station was largely completed by 1859. As the location of the railroad company's office and maintenance operation Company Shops became a center of activity in the latter half of the nineteenth century. Because engineers, mechanics, and other skilled employees were needed, the shops attracted workers from ten states and several foreign countries. This lent a dis-

tinctly cosmopolitan air to the railroad town and had a marked effect on the development of the community.

At the advent of the Civil War, Charles F. Fisher, president of the North Carolina Rail Road Company began to recruit along the railroad route. On June 1, 1861, his force, which became the 6th NC Regiment, came to train in a field just east of the Shops. Today, Alamance County is closely associated with "Fisher's Regiment," or "The Bloody Sixth," but local men served the Confederacy in many other regiments as

well, in particular the 1st, 2nd, 8th, 13th, 14th and 15th N.C. Regiments. Throughout the war the railroad proved to be a lifeline of communications, supplies, and manpower. Near the end of the war it was from Company Shops that Confederate General Joseph E. Johnston boarded a train that would take him to Bennett Farm near Durham and his fateful surrender to Union General William Tecumseh Sherman.

By the close of the Civil War, Company Shops became the center of furor over buried Confederate treasure, estimated to include over $500,000 in gold. During the last chaotic days of war in North Carolina gold coins, bullion, treasury funds, and other valuables were shipped through the town. Much of the treasure disappeared in the panic and some was reportedly buried along the tracks near Company Shops. Some treasure was also recovered: on May 4, 1865 Union occupation forces including Companies B and K of the 10th Ohio Volunteer Cavalry reportedly dug up about $100,000 in gold, which had been buried in boxes and sacks near the Shops. Nevertheless, even when Company Shops formally became Burlington on February 8, 1887, the rumor of its ties to buried Confederate gold persisted.

The Burlington train depot as it appeared about 1900.
POST CARD COLLECTION: JANE MOORE.

The Railroad Hotel, ca. 1900. Called "extravagant" by its critics, the hotel served the town of Company Shops (later Burlington) from the 1850s until the building burned in 1904.

COLLECTION: ALAMANCE COUNTY HISTORICAL MUSEUM.

Alamance County klansman as depicted in A Fool's Errand, by Albion W. Tourgee, 1879.

Colonel Charles F. Fisher, president of the North Carolina Rail Road Company. Burlington's Fisher Street bears his name.

COLLECTION: ALAMANCE COUNTY HISTORICAL MUSEUM.

RECONSTRUCTION

In Alamance County the violence associated with the Civil War did not end in 1865. In the immediate Reconstruction period secret organizations such as the White Brotherhood and the Invisible Empire found a foothold in Alamance County, and they began to employ violence in an attempt to reestablish the hierarchy and control to which their membership had long been accustomed. Organized from the old formerly established elite, members of the 'Klan' in Alamance County initially targeted whites—those perceived as "carpetbaggers" and those whose agendas were aimed at redressing the previous disenfranchisement of local blacks. By 1868, however, Klan violence spread to the area's black population. Caswell Holt, a literate former slave of textile pioneer E. M. Holt, was shot and whipped, and former slaves Daniel Jordan and Nathan Trollinger were whipped and physically mutilated. This white-on-black violence peaked on the night of February 20, 1870 when Wyatt Outlaw, a Graham town councilman, leader of the Union league and a black Republican, was lynched on courthouse square in Graham. Several months later, Republican State Senator John Walter Stephens was murdered by Klan members in neighboring Caswell County.

POSTBELLUM AGRICULTURE AND NEW INDUSTRY

As the county's textile industry expanded through the first half of the twentieth century its agricultural base also continued to grow. While several large-scale dairy and grain farm operations came to dominate the southern Alamance landscape, tobacco became the area's premier cash crop. By 1949 more than 6,700 acres of county lands were devoted to the production of tobacco. The crop was largely farmed in the county's northernmost half where deposits of Congoree Loam provided a soil conducive to the cultivation of the plant. The tobacco grown in the local area was also marketed here: major warehouses came to be located in Mebane and Burlington, and for many years autumn tobacco sales boosted the area's economy.

In the second half of the twentieth century concerns about tobacco's effects on health dealt a major blow to local tobacco farming and the industry in general. By the 1990s the production of tobacco was reduced by two-thirds from its peak at

KIRK-HOLDEN WAR

As a result of Klan violence, North Carolina Governor William W. Holden declared Alamance to be in a state of insurrection, and on March 7, 1870 martial law was implemented in the area. Occupation of Alamance and Caswell Counties began on July 6, 1870, with troops stationed in Company Shops under command of Colonel George W. Kirk, a former Union officer from Tennessee. Once in Alamance County, Kirk's forces arrested eighty-two men believed to be connected to Klan violence; another nineteen men were taken into custody in Caswell County. On July 16, 1870 these men were placed in the Caswell County jail, the location designated by Governor Holden for the so-called "Klan Trials."

Within hours, on the morning of July 17, 1870, a writ of habeas corpus was secured for several of these men by Alamance County attorney Edward Parker. The writ was signed by the state's chief justice, Raymond M. Pearson. The next day, Alexander McAlister, a Company Shops merchant and former Confederate officer, volunteered his services and delivered the writ to Colonel Kirk who was camped near the Alamance/Caswell county line. The colonel refused to accept the writ, stating that he was acting under legal orders from the governor and would yield his prisoners to no other authority.

Conservatives then sought relief in the federal courts by bringing charges of militarism against Holden and Kirk. The charges were supported by tales of outrage and indignity committed by Kirk's occupation forces. Most serious of these charges was the report that Kirk's troops had hanged by the neck two white Alamance County citizens, William Patton and Lucien Murray, in an attempt to elicit information about the Klan. These charges, coupled with Holden's apparently unconstitutional suspension of the writ of habeas corpus, led U. S. Judge George W. Brooks to again issue writs for the prisoners' release. President Grant advised Holden to bow before the federal courts, and by late August of 1870, the prisoners were freed. On November 10, the governor formally ended the "Kirk-Holden War" by declaring that Alamance and its neighboring counties were no longer in a state of insurrection.

Holden and his Republican Party lost more than the dispute over the writ, however, because in the midst of the furor and resentment over the Kirk-Holden War, the Conservatives carried the fall election and achieved firm control of the state legislature. The Conservative Party secured a two-thirds senatorial majority, with which they quickly moved to impeach Governor Holden for his anti-Klan activities. On December 14, 1870, upon favorable recommendation of the state's judiciary committee, the House of Representatives adopted the following resolution by a vote of 60 to 46: "That William W. Holden, Governor of the State of North Carolina, be impeached of high crimes and misdemeanors in office...."

With impeachment proceedings under way, Holden was forced to relinquish his office and Lt. Governor Tad Caldwell was elevated to that post. Holden's trial, which began on February 2, 1871, lasted forty-four days. On March 22, 1871, the Senate, by a vote of 36 to 13, passed a resolution removing Holden from the office of governor and disqualifying him from ever again holding "any office of honor, trust or profit under the State of North Carolina."

A significant postscript to this history of the Klan is furnished by the persistent determination of Holden's friend, Judge Albion Tourgee, to root out perpetrators of Klan violence in his district. In 1873, Tourgee urged criminal indictment of those responsible for the murder of Wyatt Outlaw and others in Alamance County. These efforts succeeded when the Grand Jury of Alamance "presented bills of indictment against 63 members of the Klan for felony and 18 for the murder of Outlaw." Within a few days following the indictment, Conservative legislators successfully presented a bill in the state legislature to repeal the law under which most of the indictments had been secured. In less than three weeks, this bill became law and negated 63 felony indictments in Alamance County.

Conservatives next prepared to utilize a nationally popular "amnesty and Pardon" program in behalf of the Ku Klux Klan, following a precedent already established by federal authorities. A bill was soon introduced into the North Carolina legislature granting pardon and amnesty for all crimes committed in behalf of any secret organization. Within a year the bill was passed, thus extending full protection to Klan members. Significantly, any question of amnesty or pardon for ex-governor Holden was excluded, as were all matters connected with Republican railroad projects developed during Holden's administration. (Troxler and Vincent, 1999: 331-332)

mid-century. In 1995 less than 2,300 acres of Alamance were devoted to tobacco farming, and the majority of the area's tobacco warehouses had closed.

The decline of the tobacco industry brought many former tobacco farmers into the wage force within the county's furniture and bedding industry. This process centered in the Mebane area where, in 1881, two brothers, Stephen A. White and D. A. White, organized White Brothers Furniture Company. Until its closing in March 1993 White Furniture was known as one of North Carolina's oldest continuously operated furniture factories. Former farmers also found employment at Mebane Royall Company (now Kingsdown Mattress Company), which was founded in 1928 from the merger of Mebane Bedding Company (1904) and Royall and Borden Mattress Company (1886) of Goldsboro. A

Former slave dwelling and miller's house located at "Poplar Grove", a tobacco plantation in northern Alamance County.

PHOTO BY KEVIN JOHNSON.

former Mebane Royall employee, L. P. Best, founded Craftique in October 1945. From its inception Craftique has been noted for its high-end eighteenth century mahogany reproductions. More recently the firm developed the 'Thomas Day' line, a group of furnishings based on the works of a well-known nineteenth century free black cabinetmaker from nearby Caswell County.

Typical tobacco field, Pleasant Grove Township, northern Alamance County, 1937.

COLLECTION: ALAMANCE COUNTY HISTORICAL MUSEUM

Rural mail carriers leaving downtown Burlington, ca. 1900.

POSTAL CARD COLLECTION: JANE MOORE.

"Putting-in" tobacco, early 20th century photograph, Pleasant Grove, northern Alamance County.

COLLECTION: ALAMANCE COUNTY HISTORICAL MUSEUM.

Streetcars were the first form of public transportation in Alamance County. The streetcar line operated from 1911 until 1923 and served the towns of Burlington, Graham and Haw River.

COLLECTION: ALAMANCE COUNTY HISTORICAL MUSEUM.

TRANSPORTATION AND PUBLIC SERVICES

The early twentieth century also witnessed advancements in transportation and public services in Alamance County. Electricity was introduced to Burlington in 1902, and by 1911 an electric streetcar operation was inaugurated. By 1913 the line extended from Burlington to Graham and Haw River. Under the name Piedmont Power and Light Company the streetcar system operated until 1924 when growing automobile ownership made the streetcar line obsolete. In addition to generating power for trolley cars, Piedmont Power and Light Company also produced electricity for home and business use. In 1921 electric streetlights were installed in Burlington, and the service was extended to Graham in 1923. By 1924, when C. E. Scott became general manager of Piedmont Power, there were about 3,300 private electrical customers in the county.

One year later, in 1924, Piedmont Power and Light became a division of the North Carolina Company, and on July 21, 1927, Southern Public Utilities Company, known today as Duke Energy, purchased the stock and assumed control. By 1950 more than 20,000 customers from throughout the county were being served. Today, Duke Energy supplies not only electricity, but fiber-optic applications, which allow home computers to be connected worldwide with Internet services.

Gas service was introduced to Burlington on September 4, 1926, and within two years more than fifteen miles of gas main were installed. By 1928 approximately 450 customers were being served. By 1950 about 2,000 customers in Burlington and Graham received piped natural gas, and bottled propane was being supplied to more than 2,500 local farms.

C. A. Lea opened a local taxi company in 1921, which was begun with a single 1919 Hudson automobile. As the company grew, it eventually located on West Front Street near the present Boston Sandwich Shop. The cab company had a convenient telephone number—777—which led to a popular local expression: "Call a three seven." In 1927 Lea introduced the concept of rental cars to the area when he opened U-Drive-It car rental agency. Lea also opened an area bus line in 1931. By the mid 1940s, the bus and taxi companies were operating more than 30 vehicles for public transportation, and these conveyances covered an excess of 3,000 miles per day. In 1945 Lea sold his operations to W. R. Massey and R. C. Baylor. Within a short time, Massey and Baylor sold the taxi company; however, they continued for many years to operate the bus line as M&B Transit.

By the 1950s, Burlington became a major juncture point for three intersectional bus routes: Charlotte to Norfolk, New York to Florida, and Norfolk to Memphis and the Pacific Coast. In the peak year of 1949, more than eighty motor coaches per day made stops in Burlington as they traveled to destinations across the United States. By the 1980s, however, this service had dramatically declined due to the popularity of aviation and the private automobile.

R. W., James A., and John Barnwell organized Barnwell Brothers Trucking Line in 1930 with the purchase of a single GMC straight truck. Within days of purchasing the vehicle, James A. Barnwell and Robert Preddy delivered the first truckload of textiles from the local area to New York City. By 1940, Barnwell Brothers had become one of the two largest trucking firms in the South and was operating fifty straight trucks, 150 tractors, and 180 trailers.

In 1942 the company merged with Horton Motor Lines, as well as several smaller firms including Southeastern Motor Lines, Moran Transportation Company, and McCarthy Freight Systems. The newly merged company became known as Associated Transport, Inc. By 1950 Associated Transport owned thirty-eight terminals scattered along the eastern seaboard and was operating more than 3,000 trucking units in thirteen eastern states. In 1975, during a period of financial difficulty, Associated Transport merged with Eastern Freightways. After filing for Chapter 11 bankruptcy protection, the merged firm closed on April 1, 1976. The Burlington terminal was subsequently sold and became an outlet shopping mall. (Troxler and Vincent, 1999: 395-396)

Burlington's Main Street looking south, ca. 1930.

POSTAL CARD COLLECTION: JANE MOORE.

Burlington's Main Street looking west from Front Street, ca. 1930.

POSTAL CARD COLLECTION: JANE MOORE.

The Alamance Hotel was erected in 1925 in downtown Burlington.

POSTAL CARD COLLECTION: JANE MOORE.

Stainback General Store, Cross Roads Community, northern Alamance County. This 19th century store, which operated sporadically until the 1970s, was typical of the general stores found In many rural areas of the county.

COLLECTION: ALAMANCE COUNTY HISTORICAL MUSEUM

"Fountain Place", an early Burlington planned subdivision was developed between 1917 and 1940 by Walter E. Sharpe in a cow pasture formerly owned by Joseph and Christian Isley. Many houses were designed by George Foxworth, Burlington's first licensed architect.

POSTAL CARD COLLECTION: JANE MOORE.

Burlington's Piedmont Hotel. The building was constructed in 1906 to house the Piedmont Trust Company. The upper floors contained the hotel rooms.

POSTAL CARD COLLECTION: JANE MOORE.

WATER FOR ALAMANCE

Many municipal improvements occurred during the period between 1919 and 1944 when Earl Horner served twelve consecutive terms as mayor of Burlington. During his tenure city streets were paved, sidewalks and streetlamps (1921) were installed, and a major program of sewer upgrades was completed. In 1919 Burlington inaugurated its first water filtration plant using water diverted from Stony Creek. Eventually a thirty-foot dam with hydro pump was constructed, thereby creating City Lake at Carolina. By 1949 Burlington was supplying almost three million gallons of water per day to its own citizens and an additional 300,000 gallons daily to the town of Graham. This was a vast improvement over the city's initial water service, a "community well" dug in 1888 in the vicinity of Burlington's Front Street.

As the area's population grew dramatically in the mid-twentieth century, the county and various municipalities undertook programs to impound water from a number of area streams to create additional lakes and reservoirs. In 1953, J. D. Macintosh, Jr. was hired as city manager in Burlington and, with the help of city council member Allen Cammack, a bond referendum was eventually passed to create a new lake north of the city of Burlington. In 1959 Lake Burlington was completed; it was later re-named Lake Cammack in honor of the councilman who led efforts to ensure adequate water for the area. The county's water supply was further enhanced with the impoundment of the Quaker and Back Creek watershed near Mebane, thereby creating Quaker Lake, and the completion in 1981 of Lake Macintosh located south of Burlington.

NEW INDUSTRIES IN THE POST-WORLD WAR II ERA

On February 17, 1942 the Federal Government, under the auspices of the U.S. Defense Plant Corporation, purchased the former Johnson Rayon Mill located in Burlington's east end and leased the property to Fairchild Engine and Airplane Corporation. The company was charged with construction of airplanes to be used for training airmen to operate aerial bombers during World War II. Due to the scarcity of aluminum during the war years the planes were constructed via a patented process

Female employees constructing engines for the AT-21 airplane, Fairchild Plant, ca. 1943.

COLLECTION: ALAMANCE COUNTY HISTORICAL MUSEUM.

Twin-engined AT-21 gunner, one of several training planes constructed at Burlington's Fairchild Plant between 1942 and 1944. The plane was used to train crews for B-25 and B-26 twin-engined bombers.

COLLECTION: ALAMANCE COUNTY HISTORICAL MUSEUM.

ALAMANCE COMMUNITY COLLEGE

In the late 1950s, Alamance County remained a largely rural area with an economy dominated by Western Electric and the various textile industries located in the county's municipalities. Following the Korean War, employment was high, yet there was a shortage of trained workers for highly skilled jobs. Industrial education came to be promoted as one key to attracting industry and securing a good future for the citizens of Piedmont North Carolina. Alamance Community College "was born forty years ago as a result of a figurative collision between pressing economic and employment needs and a community of civic-minded individuals determined to overcome those needs."

In 1957 Governor Luther Hodges secured from the North Carolina General Assembly an appropriation of $500,000 per institution to establish a series of industrial education centers throughout the state. Wallace Gee, a prominent local business executive with close political involvement with the Hodges Administration, lobbied early for Burlington as the site for the state's first industrial education center. With the support of Dr. L. E. Spikes, then superintendent of the Burlington City Schools, and J. W. Pierce, an engineer from Western Electric, an extensive survey of local industry was conducted showing community support for such a training center. As a result, in 1958 the Burlington-Alamance County Industrial Education Center (IEC) was established by the Burlington City Schools, and, by 1959, construction of the original building, located on Vaughn and Camp Roads, was completed. To direct the new IEC, Dr. Spikes hired an experienced educator from North Dakota, Ivan E. Valentine, who remained with the program until 1962, when Dr. William E. Taylor was named director and subsequent president.

Wallace Gee Building, Alamance Community College.

PHOTO: WILLIAM VINCENT.

In the 1950s, Western Electric was the county's largest employer with a payroll numbering more than 5,000 persons. Early in the history of IEC, Western Electric provided untold hours of employee time and vast amounts of donated equipment and surplus parts to the nascent industrial education center. Other local industries also fostered the growth of IEC: Kayser-Roth Hosiery provided both equipment and instructions for the hosiery looping classes, while Major Dye Works and Puritan Finishing Mills—begun by Tate Horton and J. Nimrod Harris—provided instructors in knitter fixing and industrial chemistry. Help also came from other area mills, including Travora and Glen Raven.

IEC was separated from the Burlington City School system in 1963, and the following year the institution was granted full status as a technical institute. To reflect these developments the education center's name was changed to Technical Institute of Alamance (TIA); however, the facility remained in its original building on Vaughn Road. TIA was accredited by the Southern Association of Colleges and Schools in 1969.

By the early 1970s, growth of the school's curriculum and increased enrollment pressures necessitated that the school move from its cramped location on Vaughn Road. At that time, Governor Robert Scott owned a tract of fifty acres adjacent to the interstate highway near Haw River, while Scott's aunt, Mrs. Elizabeth Scott Carrington, owned about sixty-six acres of land adjacent to her nephew's home. Mrs. Carrington suggested a land exchange between the family members, to be followed by donation of the interstate property for the new facility. These transactions were accomplished, and the Haw River land was donated in 1971. In 1972 a bond referendum for construction of a new campus passed by a 78.8 percent majority, and ground was broken for the new facility in 1974. The new Haw River campus had opened by 1976, and the following year the former Glen Hope School Building was also purchased from the City of Burlington to create an adjunct Burlington campus. By 1976 the institute was granted technical college status and its name changed to Technical College of Alamance. In 1988 the technical college was granted license as a community college and became known as Alamance Community College. Today the college serves hundreds of students each year. In addition to core classes in the trades, the college offers program in adult basic and continuing education, a science and humanities curriculum, computer programming, and college transfer courses, which are taught in cooperation with the faculty of the University of North Carolina at Greensboro. (Troxler and Vincent, 1999: 398-99)

called Duramold, which used laminated and molded wood for much of the plane's undercarriage and superstructure. The resulting airplane, called the AT-21 Gunner, was a twin-engine plane intended for use in training crews for the B-25 and B-26 bombers. With a wingspan of fifty-three feet and an overall length of almost thirty-eight feet, the plane had a top speed of about 210 miles per hour.

In May 1943 the first plane was flown from the Burlington Fairchild plant, which had its own airstrip, formerly known as Huffman Field. Contemporary news reports indicate that 15,000 people flocked to the airstrip to witness the plane's maiden flight. North Carolina Governor J. Melville Broughton was the featured speaker, and another special guest was Adolphus Drinkwater. Forty years earlier Drinkwater had witnessed and described the Wright Brothers successful flight at Kitty Hawk. Production of the plane was short-lived, however, and by October 1944 the Fairchild plant ceased its operations.

Despite its limited period of operation, the aircraft plant greatly changed the Alamance County area. Not only did the plant bring to the county immigrant workers from diverse ethnic and religious backgrounds, it created new housing and residential areas in what became known as Fairchild Heights. Due to the shortage of male labor during the war years, many women entered the workforce at the aircraft factory. These women worked on assembly lines, tested landing gear, and built and installed aircraft engines. They were in the vanguard of a nascent social movement for women's rights and gender equity pay scales.

Following the closing of the Fairchild plant in 1944 the property was purchased by the Firestone Corporation, which immediately began production of ninety-millimeter cannons and artillery shells in the former aircraft bays. This operation, too, was short-lived, and munitions production ceased with the conclusion of World War II in August 1945. Some seven months later, in March 1946, the plant was leased to Western Electric Company, ostensibly for the manufacture of telephones.

Between 1951 and 1953 Western Electric constructed several new buildings at the site, and the plant was eventually used for the assembly and testing of the Army's Nike Ajax guided missile system. In August 1963 the plant was named the Tar Heel Missile Plant. At its peak the plant employed over 3,000 individuals, and the site grew to include more than twenty-six buildings.

In the 1970s the signing of the Strategic Arms Limitations Treaty between the United States and the Soviet Union necessitated a reduction in the Cold War arms race. The treaty dealt a major blow to Western Electric. Employment at the plant began to decline, and AT&T took over the buildings. AT&T remained on the site until 1992 when it moved to Greensboro, North Carolina.

Burlington's Rainey Hospital, ca. 1916.

MEDICAL SERVICES

Prior to World War I medical care in the county was largely dependent upon the family doctor. In the late 1800s local physicians like Dr. B. A. Sellars and Dr. William Rainey Holt received their training at Philadelphia's Jefferson Medical College, a subsidiary of the University of Pennsylvania. Area residents also traveled to nearby mineral springs for various water cures. One of the most popular of these was Rockingham Mineral Springs, later known as Lenox Castle. Owned by Archibald Murphey, the 1,650-acre property was located near High Rock Road and NC87 near the Caswell County line, and included a "house of entertainment," baths with "patent showers," a post office, a store, and various residential cabins for patients. Area residents also sought cures at Kimesville and Buffalo Lithia Springs in Virginia.

In 1916 Dr. Rainey Parker constructed the private Rainey Hospital in east Burlington. Surgical services offered at the hospital complemented the more general medical care available at community health clinics such as the one operated by the Scott family at Union Ridge. Other local clinics included the Java C. Wilkins Clinic in Haw River, the Mebane Clinic, and the Hub Clinic near Altamahaw,

opened by Dr. Charles Kernodle, Sr. In 1922 Dr. R. E. Brooks joined the staff at Rainey Hospital, which further expanded in 1927 when Dr. George Carrington became a full partner. In 1937 Rainey Hospital became Alamance General Hospital, and by 1950 the hospital had grown to a 65-bed facility. By that time the hospital services included an emergency room and limited trauma facilities.

At a cost of $1.2 million in 1951 Alamance County opened a new hospital on Graham-Hopedale Road. Known as Alamance County Hospital, the facility operated for about ten years in conjunction with the old Alamance General, which was itself replaced in 1961 with the construction of Memorial Hospital of Alamance, located on Heritage Road near Edgewood Avenue. The two hospitals—"County and Memorial"—co-existed as separate entities until 1986 when their operations were formally merged. Plans were soon developed to close both hospitals upon completion of a new hospital. When the old hospitals closed in July 1995 the former County Hospital building reverted to county ownership and has been converted to office space for the Department of Social Services and other county agencies. Memorial Hospital was razed and a new retirement community, the Village at Brookwood, was developed on its site.

On July 30, 1995, a new hospital complex known as Alamance Regional Medical Center (ARMC) opened to the public. Located on Huffman Mill road, the 238-bed all-private-room facility offers state-of-the-art diagnostic and treatment, including magnetic imaging, nuclear medicine facilities, and cardiac and oncology centers. The hospital services are supplemented by the Edgewood Campus facility and the newly constructed Kernodle Clinic located adjacent to the medical center complex.

ELON UNIVERSITY

On September 2, 1890, Elon College officially joined the list of four-year liberal arts colleges in the state. Today, Elon

In 1919, upon graduation from Elon College, Warrentown native Thomas Edward Powell, Jr. joined the college faculty as instructor in biology and geology. He was made a full professor in 1923 after obtaining his M.A. degree from the University of North Carolina. This was later supplemented by a Ph.D. in biology from Duke University.

Thomas E. Powell, Jr. (1899-1987).

ARCHIVES: CAROLINA BIOLOGICAL SUPPLY COMPANY.

Impressed with the difficulty of obtaining specimens for scientific laboratory work, in 1927 Powell founded the Carolina Biological Supply Company, a mail-order biological supply company that he initially operated on a part-time basis. Working out of a small woodshed beside a pond in Elon College, the energetic young professor managed to gross $2,000 in the first year of operation, despite the Depression. Encouraged by this success, he soon erected a 20' x 40' laboratory building on a few acres of land boasting several natural springs. With a few college professors and students as part-time employees, the business grew steadily, and in 1934 Powell left teaching to devote himself full-time to the presidency of Carolina Biological Supply Company, a position he held until 1977. The facility eventually grew to include over 140 acres and more than a dozen buildings, although the original springs and pond remain as a source of specimens and water used for culturing microorganisms. As the years passed, the company progressed into physics, mathematical applications, computers, and videotaped scientific films and lectures.

As a hybrid scientist-businessman, Powell was one of the more outstanding entrepreneurs North Carolina has produced. His company eventually established a division, Powell Laboratories in Gladstone, Oregon, which now supplies biological specimens to western states. Collection stations were also established in Louisiana (Waubun Laboratories, Inc.), Texas (Rana Laboratories), and Maine, which allow the company to control the collection and preservation of specimens through local sources nationwide. These laboratories are today part of a worldwide biological supply network.

Over the years, a number of Powell's eight grandchildren became involved in various company subsidiaries. Granite Diagnostics, with a lab in Burlington and a 1,500-acre animal facility in Mecklenburg County, Virginia, produces sterile blood media for medical and educational laboratories. Bobbitt Laboratories manufactures plastic teaching models and electronics, and Wolfe Sales imports microscopes and related supplies for classroom use. Omni Resources imports maps from around the world and produces geologic teaching supplies. Warren Laboratories in Warrenton, North Carolina, includes 2,500 acres of land devoted to production of genetic corn.

In 1969 three of Dr. Thomas E. Powell, Jr.'s sons—James, Edward, and John—formed Biomedical Reference Laboratories, a medial diagnostic testing firm. The firm was initially located in the former Rainey Hospital building on Rainey Street. In 1982, the company was one of three testing labs the Hoffman-LaRoche Company united to form Roche Biomedical Laboratories, which by 1989 was one of the four largest medical testing labs in the nation. During the early 1980s, the corporate headquarters were located on a sixty-acre tract on York Road, and, in 1984, the company acquired the former Kayser-Roth office building on Maple Avenue in downtown Burlington, which was used as the company's financial and billing facility. Subsequently, Roche Biomedical Laboratories also acquired the former Federal Building and extended operations into other downtown structures including the old JC Penney building, the former First Federal Savings and Loan building, and Rose's. The company's major acquisition was the 1929 Atlantic Bank and Trust tower, which had previously been occupied by Security National Bank and NCNB. The multistoried building became the company's headquarters and the centerpiece of a major corporate campus in downtown Burlington. In 1996 Roche-Biomedical Laboratories substantially completed an operational consolidation it undertook on April 28, 1995, when the company merged with National Health Laboratories Holding, Inc. The newly merged company, known as Laboratory Corporation of America (LabCorp), resulted in the formation of the nation's largest reference laboratory for molecular diagnostic testing. LabCorp currently offers more than 1,700 different clinical trials, from routine blood analysis to more sophisticated technologies. The company performs diagnostic tests nationwide for physicians, managed care organizations, hospitals, and industrial companies. On August 5, 1997, the company announced that it is the first commercial reference laboratory to offer HIV genotyping using GeneChip DNA probe assays and trials based on polymerase chain reaction.

In 1999 Dr. James Powell, M.D., announced his resignation as president and CEO of LabCorp, which is now headed by David P. King. Powell announced the founding of a new firm named AutoCyte, also based in Burlington. The new company concentrates on PAP smear diagnostics and their standardization (Troxler and Vincent, 1999: 392-393)

Alamance Building, Elon University.

PHOTO: KEVIN JOHNSON AND DEBORAH STRICKLAND.

Dr. William S. Long, first president of Elon College (now Elon University).

COLLECTION: ALAMANCE COUNTY HISTORICAL MUSEUM.

University boasts an enrollment of 4,950 undergraduates, 500 graduate students, and an expanding curriculum that includes a Law School and a graduate Business program.

Founded by the Christian Church in the South in 1899, the school traces its origins to the incorporation of Graham Institute in 1851, later chartered as Graham College in 1859. Following a disastrous fire on July 22, 1892, which destroyed the Graham

facility, a decision was made to move the school to Mill Point, a small railroad freight station located in Boone Station Township. The station was established near the juncture of two wagon roads that served cotton mills in Altamahaw and Ossipee.

Because the newly selected site contained massive oak trees, the name Elon— a derivation of the Hebrew word for 'oak'—was chosen for the school, which received its formal charter on March 11, 1889. The college's initial land holdings consisted of 86.81 acres acquired at a total cost of $281.50. Twenty-five acres located on the north side of the railroad tracks were reserved for the physical plant of the school itself. Eighteen lots west of campus were reserved for businesses, while the remaining forty lots on the eastern and northern side of campus were offered to the public as residential lots. Dr. William S. Long served as the college's first president.

Elon admitted its first black students in 1963. Eugene E. Perry, of the class of 1969, was the first African American to receive an undergraduate degree from Elon College. Under the capable leadership of presidents James Earl Danieley, James Fred Young, and Leo Lambert Elon University has greatly expanded its physical plant, and has gained a national reputation as one of the premiere educational institutions in the south.

DESEGREGATION AND ADJUSTMENTS IN RACE RELATIONS

Until the 1950s dual systems of racially segregated public schools were maintained throughout the South under a "separate but equal" doctrine established by the Supreme Court in 1896 in *Plessy v. Ferguson.* Almost 60 years ago, on May 17, 1954, in the case of *Brown v. Board of Education,* the Supreme Court rejected the separate but equal ruling and directed that blacks were to be admitted to public schools "on a racially non-discriminatory basis with all deliberate speed." In 1964 Congress passed a Civil Rights Act with provisions to withhold federal funds for education in school districts where racial discrimination continued to be practiced.

McCray School, constructed in 1915 for use by African-American children in northern Alamance County.

PHOTO: WILLIAM VINCENT.

While token integration was implemented in some of North Carolina's largest municipalities as early as 1957, in 1962 the school system in Alamance County remained uniformly segregated. Beginning in the fall of 1963, however, Dr. Brank Proffitt, superintendent of Burlington City Schools, instituted a plan to integrate Burlington schools by setting up a gradual program of year-by-year integration working from the primary grades through the senior high level, with full integration to be achieved by the fall of 1970.

While initially successful, the integration process was marred in May 1969, when tensions between the black and white

The publication of Alex Haley's *Roots* in 1976, and the subsequent televised miniseries of the same name, brought national attention to Alamance County as the location of ante- and postbellum events described by the Pulitzer Prize-winning author. During 1974 Haley's research into his family history brought him to Alamance County, where he learned that his maternal great-grandfather Tom (Murray), born in 1833, had lived as a slave on the Andrew Murray plantation, located in the northeastern section of the county near Cross Roads Presbyterian Church. Haley's research was corroborated by oral history accounts provided to him by Effie Murray White, a 93-year old woman whose parents had also been slaves on the Murray farm. In his research Haley was also aided locally by Dr. Willard Goley and descendants of the Murray plantation family, including Ila Murray Bryan, Alice Anderson Barnes, Louise Sellars Gillespie, Claude Vincent Long, and Blanche Vincent Long.

In *Roots*, Haley describes his great-grandfather as a slave blacksmith (Haley 1976: 497) whose iron-working skills were well-known throughout the county. These facts are verified by Murray family tradition and indirect evidence. In the period prior to the Civil War, the brothers Andrew and Eli Murray operated an extensive wagon-making factory and iron foundry on their plantation; this operation required the skills of expert iron-mongers and wheelwrights, most of whom were slaves, and the factory was known throughout the Piedmont region as a supplier of large utility vehicles (Anderson 1985: 74; 97). In *Roots*, Haley also states that Tom (Murray) eventually married a Holt slave named Irene before moving to Henning, Tennessee, following emancipation.

In 1977 Haley returned to Alamance County, where he appeared at a fund-raising event for the Alamance County Historical Museum. On November 13, 1977 Haley also participated in filming a documentary in Alamance County titled, "Roots: One Year Later." The film focused on the Murray family, black and white, and was televised to a national audience on ABC television in January 1978. A traveling photographic exhibit titled "Roots Country," produced by Pat Shaw Bailey, was also exhibited throughout North Carolina. [Troxler and Vincent, 1999: 407-408]

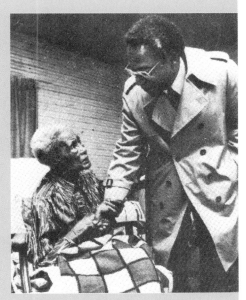

Alex Haley talking with Effie Murray White at her home near Cross Roads, northern Alamance County, 1974.
PHOTO: TIMES-NEWS COLLECTION: PAT BAILEY, ALAMANCE COUNTY HISTORICAL MUSEUM.

Alamance County Public School Teachers, 1914.
COLLECTION: ALAMANCE COUNTY HISTORICAL MUSEUM.

communities resulted in violence. Following protests over cheerleader try-outs at Williams High School (in which no black students were elected to the squad), on the evening of May 16, a riot broke out on Rauhut Street in northeast Burlington. Efforts of the entire 90-man Burlington police force, plus 156 members of the National Guard, one hundred state highway patrolmen, and members of the SBI and the local sheriff's department were required to quell the disturbance. More than 25 rioters were arrested, several persons were wounded, and Leon Mebane, a fifteen-year-old black student from Turrentine Junior High, was killed by gunfire.

The following evening, on May 17, a curfew order was issued for all of Alamance County and its municipalities. More than 400 National Guardsmen and eighty members of the highway patrol

Jack O'Kelly (1925-1983), civil rights advocate and member of Alamance County Board of Commissioners.

were called in to enforce the curfew, which was not lifted until Monday, May 19.

Over the ensuing summer racial dialogue was improved through the formation of a Human Relations Council, comprised of prominent black and white community leaders. When school opened in the fall of 1970, Jerome Evans, former football coach at Jordan Sellars was named head football coach at Walter Williams. Evans would become the first African American in the South to serve as head coach of a previously all-white school. Later that year, Sonia McIntyre would become the school's first black valedictorian.

In the years following the Burlington riot, full integration of both city and county schools was achieved, and racial cooperation in Alamance County improved. In 1972 noted educator and civil rights advocate Jack O'Kelley was appointed as the first black commissioner of Alamance County. In 1974 he was elected to a second term by a tremendous majority. O'Kelley would serve on the County Board of Commissioners for more than ten years and was board chairman at the time of his death on May 2, 1983. In 1978, O'Kelley was honored by the Alamance County Committee on Civic Affairs as its "Man of the Year."

Alamance County educator Donna Oliver was named the North Carolina "Teacher of the Year" in 1986. The following year she became the first African American to be named National Teacher of the Year. That same year, Oliver's daughter, Rachael Oliver, was crowned Miss Black America.

CURRENT TRENDS

The last two decades of the twentieth century witnessed a dramatic increase in the residential population of Alamance County. New housing starts along the county's eastern, western and southern borders have produced subdivisions whose residents are employed both within the county's broadened industrial base and in neighboring areas such as the Research Triangle. These "bedroom communities," coupled with a number of retirement villages such as Twin Lakes, Oak Creek, Hawfields Presbyterian Home, Cedar Ridge, and the Village at Brookwood, have introduced the county to a population whose traditional heritage lies outside the Piedmont regions.

The 1980s and 90s saw major growth in locally owned businesses, including Copland Fabrics and Glen Raven Mills. Recently, several successful "homegrown" businesses, such as Byrd Foods, Stadler Hams, Shoffner Industries and Roche Biomedical Research, have been purchased by firms from outside the local area or have merged with companies of national and international standing. Industrial recruitment has brought to the area a number of multi-national corporations such as Honda, GKN, and Konica.

During the last thirty years, the county has also made strides in preserving its cultural heritage. In 1976 both the Alamance County Historical Museum and Cedarock

"Oak Grove", plantation home of Michael Holt, now the Alamance County Historical Museum.

Reconstructed summer kitchen located at "Oak Grove" plantation, now the Alamance County Historical Museum.

Captain James and Emma (Holt) White house, Graham, N.C., now headquarters of the Alamance County Arts Association.

PHOTO: KEVIN JOHNSON.

Historical Park were organized as an outgrowth of the Bicentennial Celebration. Today there are also historical museums in Graham, Mebane, and Haw River and the Scott Family Collection, housed at Alamance Community College, is an important repository of local and state history.

The Alamance County Historic Properties Commission, also founded in 1976, has been largely responsible for the restoration of historic properties such as the McCray School. The commission has supported architectural surveys of the county and has assisted in placing monuments at several historic sites, including the Battle of Clapp's Mill, Pyle's Defeat, and the Charles Drew Memorial. Historic District Commissions have been created in the cities of Burlington and Graham. Burlington's "Main Street Program" resulted in the restoration of a number of municipality's business facades; the restoration of the former Atlantic Bank Tower, funded by Roche Biomedical Research, received national attention. Burlington's former engine house, built as a part of Company Shops in the 1850s to provide maintenance for train engines, is now the local Amtrack Station. The 18,000 square foot facility also houses the North Carolina Railroad Company's 'Whistlestop Exhibit,' including a model of Company Shops. Our restored 1910 Dentzel Menagerie Carousel, featuring 46

hand-carved animals, is the centerpiece of the 76-acre City Park and is a favorite of children and adults alike. Other important sites include the newly restored Caboose Museum and train depot.

In 1995 NationsBank completed a major restoration and adaptive reuse of the former James and Mary Elizabeth Holt Williamson house, and the local Arts Council has restored the former residence of James and Emily Holt White as a new home for the arts. In 1996 the county completed a major exterior restoration of the county courthouse. Preservation

North Carolina announced plans in 1997 for the restoration of Glencoe Mill Village, which today includes a textile heritage museum, restored mill housing and streetscape, and proposed commercial and retail space. The historic former textile mills at Saxapahaw have been transformed into upscale apartments and set the standard for adaptive reuse and the transformation of former commercial spaces into residential uses.

The historically biracial makeup of the county's residential population is itself rapidly changing. Today the county's growing Hispanic and Asian populations have created educational needs that must be met by the recently merged Alamance-Burlington School System, which unified in the 1996-1997 school year to promote standardized quality education for the county's rural and urban populations. As we move into the first decade of the new millennium the increased ethnic diversity of the county and the citizens' growing awareness of their complex heritage and common destiny will add richness and texture to the tapestry that is Alamance County. The lives of our citizens, recorded in these pages and woven into history, will underpin a new generation of achievement and progress.

Restored streetscape, Glencoe Mill Village.

PHOTO: KEVIN JOHNSON.

JAMES A. BARNWELL

James Alexander Barnwell was born August 5, 1904, on a tobacco farm in the Cross Roads Community of Alamance County. He was the son of Bettie (Anderson) Barnwell and Alexander ("Zan") C. Barnwell (b. 1861), whose Irish ancestors settled in the Quaker Creek area of Pleasant Grove Township in the 1780s. The couple had four additional children: Robert William (b. 1889); John Henry (b. 1899); Anderson Hall (b. 1901); and Mary Elizabeth (b. 1909).

A graduate of Burlington High School and the University of North Carolina, James began his business career in 1929 when, with his brothers Robert and John, he formed Barnwell Warehouse and Brokerage Company. In the early 1930s a fourth brother, Hall, joined the firm as a warehouse man and dispatcher.

Beginning with a single GMC truck, James Barnwell and Robert Preddy are credited with driving the first load of textiles shipped by truck from the south to New York City. From this small beginning, the warehouse business expanded and was transformed by the 1920s into Barnwell Brothers Trucking Line, a pioneer in the field of motor transportation. The firm quickly grew into a major business, providing valued service to the textile industry in Alamance County and operated from a major terminal located on Highway 70, then the main traffic artery across North Carolina.

On December 20, 1942 tragedy struck the company when a fire broke out at the terminal, destroying the firm's offices, along with all the loading docks and many trucks. With an estimated loss exceeding half a million dollars the blaze was, at the time, said to be the most destructive fire ever to hit Alamance County.

Following the fire, the terminal on North Church Street was rebuilt. In 1942 Barnwell Brothers joined Horton Motor Lines and five smaller carriers to become Associated Transport, Inc., one of the leading motor transport lines in the nation and the largest common carrier in the world at that time. By 1965 the company operated in 13 states and had more than 3,000 units on the highway on any given day. It was then that the operation moved to a new, ultramodern terminal on I-85 south of Burlington. The company continued to operate until 1976, when the terminal site became an outlet mall.

Jim Barnwell remained a member of the executive committee of Associated Transport throughout his life, but retired from active management of the firm some years after the merger. During his later career he developed several other businesses in the area, including Tire Sales Company and Huffman Oil Company.

James A. Barnwell.

Barnwell served as Commissioner of the 5th North Carolina Highway Division under Governor Kerr Scott (1949-1953) and was instrumental in that administration's effort to pave "farm to market" secondary roads. He also served on the Board of Trustees of Alamance County Hospital and was a local director of North Carolina National Bank.

In 1934 he married Cornelia Vincent (b. 1907) of Pleasant Grove Township, the daughter of Daisy Murray (1879-1967) and Ralph Waldo Vincent (1878-1944). James and Cornelia Barnwell had two children: Dorothy (Barnwell) Kerrison (b. 1938) and James A. Barnwell, Jr. (b. 1940). James A. Barnwell, Sr. died at 69 on April 5, 1974.

John and Elizabeth Berry.

JOHN BERRY

John Berry, prominent architect, builder and politician, was born in Hillsborough, North Carolina in 1798. On March 6, 1827 he married Elizabeth Ann Vincent, daughter of Thomas and Elizabeth Cooksey Vincent of the Cross Roads Community of northern Alamance County. The couple had eight children, including two sons (one of whom became a prominent physician), and six daughters, several of whom studied at the Pratt Institute in Philadelphia. During the Civil War, Berry served with the Orange Guards, and it was from this service that he acquired the title "Captain," which he retained for the duration of his life.

Berry began his professional career in the early 1820s in partnership with John A. Faucett, a local carpenter. By 1860 Berry had become one of the wealthiest citizens of Orange County, and he was the owner of 45 slaves, most of whom were skilled laborers. Among these were slave masons and brick makers, as well as a highly competent slave carpenter named "Joe," and a tinner called "Ned."

By 1831 Berry is known to have owned a substantial library of architectural books from which he drew inspiration. These included Owen Biddle's *Young Carpenter's Assistant*, from which Berry adopted Federal-style motifs and stairway plans; Asher Benjamin's *American Builder's Companion and Practical House Carpenter*; and Minard Lafever's *Young Builder's General Instruction* with its emphasis on Greek Revival designs. Some evidence suggests that Berry acquired several of these volumes from Hillsborough resident Francis Lister Hawks, the grandson of John Hawks, who was the English architect of Tryon Palace. Berry's familiarity with the contents of these books gave his buildings a certain academic correctness and style lacking in many of the vernacular buildings of nineteenth century Piedmont North Carolina.

During the early 1800s Berry constructed a number of significant buildings in his native Hillsborough: these include the Masonic Hall (1823-25); St. Matthews Episcopal Church (1825-26); the masterful Greek Revival Orange County Courthouse, completed in 1845, and "Burnside" (1835), the residence of Paul Cameron. Other important buildings constructed by John Berry throughout the state include the Caswell County Courthouse (1831-33); the main building of Wake Forest College (1835-37); the Oxford Orphanage (1855-57); and Smith Hall (1850-51), now Playmakers Theatre, on the campus of UNC—a neo-classical temple which he constructed from a plan drawn by famed New York architect A. J. Davis.

Tradition has it that when Berry took jobs distant from his Hillsborough headquarters he moved his workmen, tools, equipment, and even his family to the construction site. In doing so he made use of large utility wagons manufactured by his wife's Murray relatives on their plantation in Cross Roads. Large canvas tents—some as large as 30' x 50'—were transported to the construction sites, where they were erected for housing Berry's slave laborers.

William James Bingham.

Captain Berry was also active in politics, serving five terms as state senator (1848-1866) and one term in the North Carolina House of Representatives (1862). From 1850 to 1862, he was a trustee of Wake Forest College. John Berry died of pneumonia in 1870 at his Hillsborough residence, called "Sunny Side." He and Elizabeth (Vincent) Berry are buried in the cemetery of Hillsborough's First Presbyterian Church.

WILLIAM BINGHAM

William Bingham, author and educator, was born in Hillsborough, North Carolina on July 7, 1835. He was the eldest son of William James Bingham, headmaster of the Hillsborough Academy, and Eliza Alves (Norwood) Bingham. Bingham was

William Bingham.

named for his paternal grandfather, who was a schoolmaster and professor at the University of North Carolina.

At the age of ten, William Bingham moved with his family from Hillsborough to Oaks, a rural community south of Mebane. Educated at his father's classical academy, he remained on the family farm until 1853 when he entered The University of North Carolina, from which he graduated with first honors in 1856. Soon thereafter his father employed him as a teacher, and in January 1857 he was made full partner in the school, under the firm name W. J. Bingham and Sons. That same year, William's younger brother, Robert Bingham, also became a partner in the academy.

Bingham remained with the school for the duration of his life, initially concentrat-

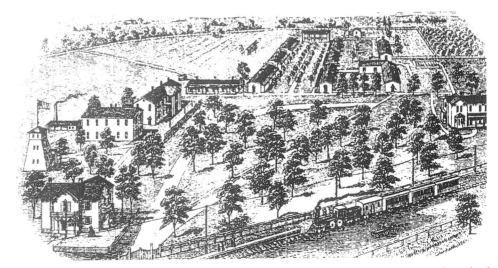

The Bingham School, ca. 1870, located on the outskirts of Mebane, N.C. Note proximity of the campus to the tracks of the North Carolina Railroad. William Bingham's residence appears at far right.

Robert Bingham.

ing upon the preparation of more advanced pupils for college. His father's failing health and his brother's service during the Civil War eventually made him, by 1861, the dominant figure in the school's management. By 1863 he became headmaster and, one year later, in 1864, he succeeded in obtaining a special thirty-year charter for the school from the North Carolina General Assembly. Under its provisions, students of the Bingham School would be exempt from conscription until the age of eighteen but would receive military training and be liable for mobilization as a separate unit in case of military emergency. As headmaster, Bingham became an *ex officio* colonel in the state militia, and his instructors were likewise given military commissions. Bingham moved the school from the Oaks to Mebane (1864), and a substantial campus was erected along the tracks of the North Carolina Railroad.

With the aid of his brother-in-law, Stuart White, and a cousin, William B. Lynch, Bingham operated the school throughout the Civil War, except for a brief period during Stoneman's Raid, when the student body was called to active duty. During this period Bingham wrote and published a Latin grammar (1863) and an edited translation of Caesar's *Commentaries* (1864). By the late 1870s, both books were being used as textbooks in almost every state in the Union, and the volumes remained in print for over twenty-five years. Bingham also wrote an English grammar (1867), as well as a series of Latin readers. He was also

noted as an accomplished public speaker, pianist, and organist. He died on February 18, 1873, after petitioning the state senate to reopen the University of North Carolina in the aftermath of Reconstruction.

Bingham was survived by his wife, Owen White (whom he had married in 1856), and their six children. Bingham's nephew, Robert Worth Bingham (1871-1937), who was born in Mebane, became owner of the Louisville, Kentucky *Courier-Journal* newspaper, served as president of the Associated Press, and in 1933 was appointed ambassador to Great Britain. In 1916 Robert Worth Bingham married Mary Lily Kenan Flagler, the widow of railroad magnate Henry Flagler. She died one year later in 1917; her will left Bingham $5 million and endowed the Kenan professorships at the University of North Carolina.

DON BOLDEN

Don Bolden, journalist, newspaper editor, and historian, was born in Burlington on January 19, 1933, the son of Ralph and Mary Lee (Stadler) Bolden. He graduated from Burlington High School in 1951 and the University of North Carolina School of Journalism in 1955. While at UNC he was a member of Kappa Tau Alpha, honorary journalism fraternity.

Bolden's journalism career began in 1948 while still in high school, when he took a part-time job with the Burlington *Times-News*. In 1955 he was hired for a regular staff position as a sports writer. Over time, Bolden served as city reporter, telegraph operator, and he held various editing positions, including managing editor. He was named executive editor in 1982 and served in that capacity until his retirement on January 1, 2000. At that time Bolden had 51 years of service with the Burlington *Times-News* organization. Now in retirement, he continues to write a weekly column published each Sunday. During his tenure as editor, Bolden initiated the Newspaper in Education program at the *Times-News*.

Bolden is the former president of the Associated Press News Council, and, in 1998, he was named the first recipient of

the R. C. Hoiles Award, an honor given to an associate of Freedom Communications who best exemplifies the ethical standards of the company's founder. In 1987 his journalism career carried him to the Oval Office of the White House when he covered the National Teacher of the Year presentation awarded to Burlington teacher Donna Oliver by President Ronald Reagan.

In 1990 Don Bolden was named "Alamance County Citizen of the Year." In 2003 he was also named "Alamance County Boy Scout Man of the Year." That same year, Bolden received the Distinguished Service Award from Elon University.

Bolden has served on the board of the Alamance County Chamber of Commerce, the board of directors of the Alamance County Historical Museum, and the board of Crimestoppers. For 25 years he has been a member of the board of directors of Elon Homes for Children and has twice served as chairman. For a number of years Bolden has also served as chairman of the advisory board of the School of Communications at Elon University.

Bolden has written five books on Alamance County history. In the 1980s he published two volumes titled *Alamance in the Past*. A third book, entitled *Alamance: A County at War* was published in 1995 and won the History Award Medal from the Daughters of the American Revolution. In 2002 Bolden published a photographic history of the county entitled *20th Century Alamance: A Pictorial History*. In 2006 *Remembering Alamance: Tales of the Railroad, Textiles and Baseball* was published. Bolden has also written a 100-year history of Elon Homes for Children and a history of Burlington's First Baptist Church. With W. B. Teague Bolden worked to develop Alamance County's War Memorial Monument, located in Graham.

Bolden has served as moderator of the Mt. Zion Baptist Association, and, for twenty years, he was a director of *The Biblical Record*, the state Baptist newspaper. In 2001 he received the North Carolina Baptist Heritage Award for his service to the denomination.

Bolden is married to Billie Faye Johnson,

a former teacher employed by the Burlington City Schools.

WILLIAM GARL BROWNE, JR.

In 1993 renovations at the Orange County Courthouse in Hillsborough uncovered historical graffiti consisting of the signatures of more than fifteen men who lived in the mid-nineteenth century. The series of signatures, together with the date 1855, were found beneath 150 years of paint and plaster, and were apparently etched on fresh whitewashed plaster using a stylus pencil dipped in some indelible liquid such as indigo.

Among the signatures recorded on the courthouse wall is that of the nineteenth century portrait artist, William Garl Browne, Jr. (1823-1894), who gained fame both before and after the Civil War through his depictions of General Zachary Taylor and many prominent southerners. Among those North Carolinians who sat for Garl Browne were textile pioneer Edwin Michael Holt and his wife Emily, whose original portraits by Browne presently hang in the parlor of the Alamance County Historical Museum. The Holt portraits were donated to the museum in 1982 by E. M. Holt's great-great grandson, Thomas Cheatham.

The artist William Garl Browne, Jr., came to America in 1836 at the age of 13. Born in Leicester, England, he was the son of W. G. Browne, a well-known English landscape and genre painter whose works were frequently exhibited at London's Royal Academy.

Within four years of arriving in America, at the age of seventeen, the younger Browne exhibited two portraits at Washington's National Academy in the spring of 1840. About 1846 he moved his studio from New York City to Richmond, where he soon established himself as the foremost portrait artist in eastern Virginia. Within a year, in 1847, Browne's fame enabled him to take a trip to Mexico to paint commissioned portraits of Zachary Taylor and other heroes of the Mexican-American War. These portraits were exhibited to much acclaim in both Richmond and Philadelphia in the fall of 1847.

During the 1850s Browne traveled extensively throughout the upper South, painting numerous portraits in Maryland, Virginia and the Carolinas. During these years he visited "Blandwood," the Greensboro home of Governor John Motley Moorehead, where he painted portraits of the governor and several members of the Moorehead family. About the same time, Browne also spent several months at "Fairntosh," the Durham County plantation estate of Duncan Cameron, widely believed to be the wealthiest man in North Carolina in the mid-1800s. While at "Fairntosh," Browne produced an excellent portrait of Duncan Cameron, as well as several miniature portraits of the allied Cameron/Bennehan families.

About 1856 Browne returned to New York City, where he made his residence until the fall of 1865. Following the Civil War, Browne returned to the South, where, in 1876 at the age of 53, he married Mary McFeely of Charleston, S.C. For a while the couple lived in Charleston and later in Columbia, S. C., and, from 1887, the couple made their residence in Richmond.

Throughout his married life, Garl Browne continued to travel throughout the south seeking portraiture commissions. The fall of 1879 found him again in the Piedmont of North Carolina, where he revisited "Blandwood," the former Governor Moorehead house, then occupied by Morehead's daughter, Emma, and her husband, Julius Gray. While at "Blandwood," Browne painted portraits of Mr. and Mrs. Gray and was introduced to their friends, Mr. and Mrs. E. M. Holt of Alamance. In November, Browne traveled from Greensboro to the Holt home, where his portraits of the Holts were completed on December 5, 1879. Mr. Holt was 73 at the time of the portrait was completed and Mrs. Holt was 71.

Portraits by William Garl Browne, Jr. are found in numerous museums and private collections throughout the country. Major

Captain James N. Williamson, age 43, as depicted in an original oil painting by William Garl Browne, Jr.
COLLECTION: ALAMANCE COUNTY HISTORICAL MUSEUM.

Mary Elizabeth (Holt) Williamson, age 38, daughter of textile pioneer E.M. Holt. Original oil portrait by William Garl Browne, Jr.
COLLECTION: ALAMANCE COUNTY HISTORICAL MUSEUM.

collections housing portraits by Browne include Valentine Museum in Richmond, the Metropolitan Museum of Art in New York City, and the Smithsonian's National Portrait Gallery in Washington, D.C., where a Garl Browne portrait of President Rutherford B. Hayes is prominently displayed. Portraits by Browne are also in the collections of Virginia Military Institute, Wake Forest University, the University of North Carolina, and the North Carolina Division of Archives and History.

ELIZABETH (SCOTT) CARRINGTON

Elizabeth Hughes Scott was born October 3, 1902, one of fourteen children of Robert Walter and Elizabeth (Hughes) Scott. Her childhood was spent on her father's Melville Farm, south of Haw River. She attended the nearby Hawfields Public School and graduated from Flora McDonald College in 1924. She then attended the University of Pennsylvania Hospital School of Nursing from which she earned the R.N. degree in 1926 and a master's degree in 1940. For eleven years, from 1929 to 1940, Elizabeth Scott served as instructor in the University of Pennsylvania School of Nursing, where she also worked as Operating Room Supervisor.

On March 1, 1941 Scott married George Lunsford Carrington, M.D. (1893-1972), a distinguished surgeon who was a native of Durham with degrees from Duke University, Johns Hopkins Medical University, and the School of Medicine at Yale. In 1924 Dr. Carrington came to Burlington and entered into partnership with Dr. Ralph E. Brooks in the operation of the Alamance General Hospital (formerly Rainey Hospital). Mrs. Carrington's extensive nursing training made her invaluable as an assistant to her husband, particularly in the late 1940s when the war effort resulted in a statewide nursing shortage.

In 1954 Major L. P. McLendon, then head of the Medical Foundation of North Carolina, asked Mrs. Carrington to serve on a volunteer committee to assist in formulating plans for a new four-year nursing school to be established at the University of North Carolina-Chapel Hill. Carrington served as chairman of the committee for many years during which time she was a successful fund raiser and advocate for the program. Under her leadership, the nurses' training program at Chapel Hill came to be recognized as one of the foremost in the South.

In 1972 at the death of Dr. Carrington, the George and Elizabeth Carrington Fund was established to further improve the teaching program at the University of North Carolina School of Nursing. Mrs.

Elizabeth (Scott) Carrington.

Carrington continued her work with the school, and, in 1969, the new two-million dollar building of the School of Nursing at Chapel Hill was named the Elizabeth Scott Carrington Hall. *The Carrington Quarterly*, a publication of the School of Nursing, was also named in her honor.

In 1974 Mrs. Carrington donated approximately 60 acres of land in the Hawfields area to what was then known as the Technical Institute of Alamance. The site now serves as the primary campus of the Alamance Community College, the successor to the former T.I.A.

In 1983 the University of North Carolina conferred upon Mrs. Carrington the honorary degree of Doctor of Laws and bestowed upon her its prestigious Distinguished Service Award. She died ten years later on October 8, 1993.

STALEY ALBRIGHT COOK

Staley Albright Cook was born in southern Alamance County on December 6, 1895, the son of George Henry and Viola (Albright) Cook. His given name was derived from an uncle, Dr. W. W. Staley, who was second president of Elon College (1894-1905) and a minister of the Christian church in Suffolk, Virginia.

During World War I, Cook served as a member of the 30th Division and saw action in France and Belgium. Immediately after the war, he enrolled at Northwestern University in Evanston, Illinois, from which he received a degree in journalism. On August 1, 1920 he married Grace Lillian Lane, by whom he had two daughters: Nora Lee and Nancy Lane.

In 1920 Cook joined the staff of the Burlington *Daily Times-News*, where, for the next fifteen years he rose through the ranks as reporter, managing editor, chief editorial writer, and chief executive of the company. In 1957 he was named editor and general manager of the publication. Throughout this period Cook's perceptive editorial skills led to the newspaper's reputation as one of the state's best regional papers.

Cook served one term in the North Carolina House of Representatives, during which time he was co-sponsor of North Carolina's original unemployment service law. By gubernatorial appointment he also became a member of the advisory committee of the State Unemployment Compensation Board. In 1950 he was named to the State Board of Conservation and Development, and his leadership in this position helped to make the Alamance Battleground a state historic site. One year earlier, in 1949, he collaborated with Walter Whitaker and A. Howard White in writing and publishing the *Centennial History of Alamance County*.

Staley Albright Cook.

Cook was a long-time chairman of the board of trustees of Alamance General Hospital, and, for five years, he served as chairman of the trustees of May Memorial Library. In the 1950s he addressed his editorial influence to the need for a lake to vouchsafe Burlington's water supply, thereby supporting the construction of Lake Burlington. Staley Cook died on May 8, 1966, having spent a career advocating for Burlington and Alamance County.

JUNIUS E. "RETT" DAVIS

Junius E. ("Rett") Davis, Jr. was born in 1950 in Greensboro, North Carolina. He is the son of Eleanor Ferris Davis and the late Junius E. Davis, a pharmaceutical representative. As a youngster, Rett became active in scouting. Rett's father died when the boy was fourteen, and he was subsequently influenced by his scoutmaster, Lacy McAllister, a wealthy Greensboro resident whose family helped to found the Jefferson-Pilot Insurance Company. Throughout his teenage years Rett traveled with McAllister to the ancestral McAllister farm in Anson County, where Davis developed an abiding appreciation for the forest and the natural environment.

Davis graduated from Page High School in Greensboro in 1968, and in 1972 he received a bachelor of science

Junius E. "Rett" Davis.

degree in parks administration from the School of Forestry at North Carolina State University. Following graduation he accepted a job as agricultural agent in Montgomery County, a position he held from 1973 until 1985. In 1974 he married Jan Moore, a native of Greensboro, whom he had known throughout high school.

In 1981 Davis received a Master's degree in adult education and crop science from N.C. State University. Four years later, in 1985, he moved to Alamance County, where he accepted a position as County Extension Director, a job he held for 22 years, until his retirement in 2007. During this period Davis became a well-known and highly respected personality in the area.

Public awareness of his personal knowledge and his general visibility within the community increased once he began to write a weekly column centering on horticultural advice for the Burlington *Times-News*, a column which he has continued to write in retirement. A gifted public speaker and a tireless promoter of agriculture, good forestry management, and sound horticultural practices, Davis has come to be universally recognized as the affable and approachable expert to whom citizens could direct their many questions.

In 2007, in recognition for his contributions at the local and state level, Davis was awarded the Order of the Long Leaf Pine, the state's highest civilian honor. Rett and Jan Davis currently reside in Burlington; the couple has two daughters: Jennifer and Emily.

JOHN Q. GANT

John Quinton Anderson Gant was born on July 18, 1847, the third of four children of Colonel Jesse Gant (1803-1888) and Minerva Murray (Anderson) Gant (1812-1879). The elder Gant, who served as colonel of the militia of West Orange, owned one of the first grist mills on Haw River, and also held public office as district constable, justice of the peace,

John Q. Gant and wife, Corinna Morehead Erwin at the time of their marriage in 1879.

deputy sheriff of Orange County, and commissioner for the division and running of the county line. In 1872 he was elected to the state legislature, having also served as president of the Bank of Graham in the antebellum period.

John Q. Gant spent his childhood on the family's 400-acre farm near Big Falls on the Haw River/Stoney Creek watershed in northern Alamance County. As a youngster, he attended the Daugherty School and Hughes Academy, and at the age of 17, on August 28, 1864, he volunteered for service in the Confederate Army, where he was a member of Company C, 40th Regiment of the North Carolina Troops. Gant's company saw action against Sherman's forces at Savannah, Jackson's Mill, and Bentonville. He was paroled in Greensboro on May 10, 1865 and returned to Big Falls to work on his father's farm for the next four years.

In 1869 Colonel Gant secured for his son a job working at the Alamance Cotton Factory of E. M. Holt. Shortly after taking the position in Alamance, Gant became ill with typhoid, and family tradition has it that Gant was nursed back to health by Holt's wife, Emily Farish Holt. After his recovery, Gant remained in the employ of E. M. Holt until 1874, and, during these years, he had his first exposure to the business world, textiles, and cotton

William Allen Erwin, a native of Morganton, N.C. and an Alamance County entrepreneur, eventually operated Erwin Cotton Mills in Durham, N.C.

COLLECTION: ALAMANCE COUNTY HISTORICAL MUSEUM.

manufacturing. The young man worked primarily in the company store at Alamance and served as bookkeeper and paymaster for the mill. The relationship between Gant and the Holts was further solidified when, in 1874, Gant entered into partnership with two of E. M. Holt's sons, Banks and Lawrence, for the purpose of opening a store in Company Shops (now Burlington).

On September 29, 1874, a deed was drawn conveying five lots (.56 acres) in Company Shops from the North Carolina Railroad Company to J. Q. Gant and Co. The firm soon opened a general mercantile business known locally as the "Yellow Store," and William Allen Erwin of Morganton (Lawrence Holt's brother-in-law) was hired as clerk.

Five years later, on April 15, 1879, John Q. Gant married Corinna Morehead Erwin of Bellevue Plantation, Morganton. She was the sister of William Allen Erwin and Margaret (Erwin) Holt (Mrs. Lawrence Holt). Following the wedding, the couple traveled by train to New York City, where they spent a portion of their honeymoon at the St. Nicholas Hotel on Broadway.

On April 16, 1880 Gant sold his interest in the Yellow Store to W. A. Erwin, whereupon the reorganized business came to be known as Holt, Erwin, Holt (with Banks and Lawrence Holt retaining their previous interests). Gant then made a decision to enter into business with Berry Davidson, a

local machinist and millwright. Gant had probably become acquainted with Davidson when the latter rebuilt E. M. Holt's Alamance Cotton Factory following its destruction by fire in 1871. Gant and Davidson expanded a sawmill and grist mill on Davidson's land in Altamahaw, established a general store on the site, and began operation of a cotton spinning mill with 1,000 spindles. Within four years Davidson left the firm, and in December 1884, Banks and Lawrence Holt again entered into business with Gant by purchasing Davidson's interest in the Altamahaw Cotton Mill. Davidson then went on to develop Minneola Mill (1886) in Gibsonville. By 1887 the Altamahaw mill had installed looms and began producing coarse cotton osnaburg fabrics. Records indicate that by 1895 the firm had grown to include 6,500 spindles and 300 looms and employed 275 people.

Sometime around 1890 the Gants established the first telephone line in Alamance County. The line connected the Gant's Burlington residence, called "Bonnie Oaks," with Mill Point (now Elon), and their mill office building in Altamahaw. The mill office, built between 1889 and 1890, was said to be the most modern commercial building in Alamance County, and boasted central heat, hot and cold running water, and carbide lighting.

In order to expand his textile operations, in 1900 John Q. Gant acquired 37.6 acres of land adjacent to the North Carolina Railroad tracks. The site was located on the west side of Burlington in an area then known as "Frog Town." Gant's eldest son, Joe, who had graduated in 1899 from Massachusetts' Lowell Technical Institute, returned home to supervise construction of the new mill. A local builder, Yancey Mitchell, was hired as foreman of the construction crew, and a contract was awarded to James and Joseph Kirkpatrick for brickwork. Much of the lumber for the mill was purchased from Wilson Saw Mills, located in Johnston County. By 1902, the new mill was opera-

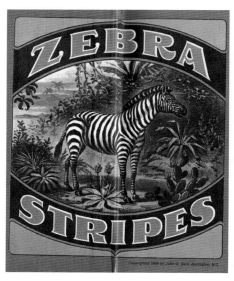

Label from "Zebra Stripes" canvas awning fabric produced by Glen Raven Mills in 1908.

COLLECTION: ALAMANCE COUNTY HISTORICAL MUSEUM.

tional, with 3,000 spindles and 200 looms powered by steam. In spite of some resistance from family members, John Q. Gant named the new mill "Glen Raven Cotton Mills." The mill opened with approximately 30 employees and was formally incorporated in January of 1904 with John Q. Gant and his sons, Joseph E. and Kenneth Gant, as incorporators.

In January 1908, Glen Raven began production of a colored canvas awning fabric with the trademarked name "Zebra Stripes." By 1912, the company began importing vat dyes from Germany and was marketing a line of goods known as "Glen Raven Sunfast Woven Army Awning Stripes." Several other lines were added in 1915, including Corella and Glen Rella Awning Stripes.

In 1928, Glen Raven Cotton Mills began to experiment with the use of the new man-made fabrics. These blended fabrics proved extremely popular with consumers because they had the look of an expensive worsted fabric at a fraction of the price. Soon Glen Raven was producing quality blended fabrics containing other synthetics, such as Orlon and Dacron, which were woven into upholstery, drapery, and luggage fabrics.

By 1930, the effects of the Depression were powerfully felt in Alamance County and throughout the South. As fabric orders dwindled, Glen Raven had to reduce its work force, and throughout much of 1930, the company operated on a two-day work week. The firm suffered a greater blow on October 27, 1930, when John Q. Gant died in his office at the age of 83.

In the 1920's, the Gants terminated their association with the Altamahaw Mill, which members of the Holt family continued to operate for several years. When the mill failed in the 1930s, the Gants purchased the physical plant, modernized the old mill, and reopened it in 1933 as Glen Raven Silk Mills. On October 18, 1933, they began production of a dress weight rayon fabric called "Canton Crepe." In addition to crepe, the mill also produced a rayon gabardine fabric known as "sharkskin," as well as several types of upholstery materials.

In 1936, the Gants began a third venture, known as Glen Raven Knitting Mills. They hired Arthur H. Rogers and James Otha Austin, two experienced hosiery men, to supervise the production of full-fashioned silk hosiery. Production later switched to nylon, and, by the 1950s, such Glen Raven brands as "Cloud Walker," "Chantilly," and "Spectator" were being marketed.

In late 1950, Arthur Rogers, J. O. Austin, Irwin Combs, and Allen Gant began to experiment with the production of a full-fashioned panty and stocking garment which they first referred to as a "panti-tights." Glen Raven patented the name "Pantilegs" for the product, which was eventually produced in a seamless format. For several years thereafter the company became the largest producer of pantyhose in the nation.

Over the years, Glen Raven eventually acquired plants in Kinston, Newland, and Burnsville. During World War II, the firm held lucrative government contracts for the production of parachute and tenting materials, and, in 1962, Glen Raven purchased the only other firm in the United States that made yarn-dyed 100 percent cotton woven awnings. Through this purchase, the firm acquired the

trademarks and production of Otis and Otis Permasol boat duck and gained entry into the manufacture of camping and marine fabrics.

Today Glen Raven remains "the oldest continuous producer of woven awnings," and its trademark "Sunbrella" fabrics are recognized throughout the world. When Walt Disney World was created in Orlando, Florida, Glen Raven was selected to provide awnings and umbrellas for the theme park's "Main Street." In the 1990s, the company continued to expand, and Glen Raven completed an enlarged executive office facility in 1991 and 1992. The firm now employees approximately 2,600 people in six divisions.

CAPTAIN SAMUEL M. HOLT

In late November 1862 Alamance County textile pioneer E. M. Holt anxiously awaited the birth of his eleventh grandchild. As a light snow fell, at about 3 in the afternoon of November 28, E. M. Holt's daughter-in-law, Laura, and her husband, James Holt, became the proud parents of a baby boy. Christened Samuel Moore Holt, the boy was born at "Locust Grove," the Holt family plantation located near the village of Alamance.

Like his cousins before him, Sam Holt would be groomed to take his place in the family's growing textile empire. But as E. M. Holt held his new grandson, he could not have foreseen that Sam Holt's adventuresome spirit would lead the young man to travel far beyond the mills of the Haw River watershed. For Sam Holt would become a sea captain, a world traveler, and a writer whose travel accounts-published under pseudonym "Tropic"-were syndicated in many newspapers in the late nineteenth century.

As a youth, Sam Holt attended the Alexander Wilson Preparatory School and the Hillsborough Military Academy. Apparently a good student, Holt excelled in language arts and mathematics, although his progress reports indicate a

tendency toward "undiscipline" and "independence." Holt's adventurous nature is also revealed in his personal diary, now housed at the Alamance County Historical Museum. In this diary, Sam Holt writes:

> At the age of 21, desiring to extend my knowledge of the outside world and to gratify a life-long desire, I determined to go to sea.

Studio photograph of Samuel M. Holt with pet monkey "Jocko".

COLLECTION: ALAMANCE COUNTY HISTORICAL MUSEUM.

In order to do so, Sam Holt traveled to Richmond, Virginia, where he engaged passage on a barque preparing to sail to South America. But after making these arrangements, Holt says:

> I came home, & made preparations to go, but my parents were so much opposed to my going I had to abandon that voyage, & wait for another opportunity, which soon presented itself. I left home on the 25th of April, 1884, & went to Beaufort, N. C. I told my friends when I left home that I was going to Beaufort, N. C. to spend 2 weeks, but had been there but a few days when I saw a 2 mast Schooner laying out in the harbor. I had determined before leaving home to go to sea, so now was my chance.

Captain Samuel Holt aboard his ship, The Mary Hasbrouck.

Holt booked passage on the schooner *John R. P. Moore* and states:

The next morning I awoke full of expectation. It was a bright, sunshiny day, such as we have along the North Carolina coast in May, and I eagerly looked out in the harbor. There lay the beautiful little Schooner, riding gracefully at anchor, like a thing alive & I gazed with rapture at the scene. It was a very calm day, & there was scarcely a ripple on the water save that made by the heaving motion of the waves. All seemed tranquil & placid, with nothing to disturb the scene, except now and then a porpus (sic) would rise to the surface to blow, and then disappear, to rise again at short intervals or a gull lazily flying across the water uttering his peculiar lonesomecall (sic).

After several days sailing along the Carolina coast, Holt booked a second passage aboard the schooner *Minerva L. Wedmore*, bound for the Caribbean:

I watched the land fade away in the distance until nothing was visible but the upper part of Hatteras light house as it stood in bold relief against the sky, resembling a huge barber pole.

While sailing in the Caribbean, Holt saw pods of whales and scores of flying fish, one of which he captured, dried, and preserved in his diary. He witnessed a volcanic eruption on the island of Montserrat and experienced an earthquake at St. Kitts. Over the next several months Holt made two additional voyages to the West Indies aboard the *Fiery Cross* and *Minerva L. Wedmore*. Along the coast of South America Holt

acquired a parrot and a pet capuchin monkey, which he named "Jocko."

In 1885, Holt traveled to the Arctic as navigator aboard the frigate *Arctic Bird*. In his diaries, Holt describes the perils of icebergs, the beauty of the Northern Lights and encounters with native Inuit people. Writing about what he describes as "the hardest (voyage) of my life at sea," he says:

I would go on deck and lash myself with a rope and look at the boiling sea & mighty waves, & hear the moaning of the wind as it came howling through the rigging & I loved to look upon the scene. There was something so impressive, & grand in the scene that I liked to witness. Nothing could be seen but the angry dark sky above & the rooling (sic) & tossing vessel beneath. And nothing could be seen but our gallant little bark as she rode the waves all alone out on the mighty ocean.

The Mary Hasbrouck, *733-ton barkentine owned by Samuel Holt. Original oil painting by marine artist Antonio Jacobsen.*

Following these early maritime adventures, in July 1886 Sam Holt enrolled as a cadet in the Maryland Military and Naval Academy with the goal of becoming a sea captain. After completing his training, Holt captained a number of vessels, including the schooners *Norman* and *David Carll*, frequently transporting fruit and produce from Baracoa, Cuba to New York City. On at least one of these voyages Holt and his crew encountered a terrific hurricane, after which members of the crew were found to be infected with yellow fever.

Sam Holt's vivid descriptions of

mutiny among the crew of the *David Carll* led his family to prevail upon him to leave the sea in 1893. Holt was immediately placed in business as vice president of Burlington's Lakeside Mill, which was then involved in the production of chambray cloth. Within a year, however, Holt chaffed under the constraints of mill life, and by 1894 he had returned to sea.

In the fall of 1898 Holt purchased from Arnold Cheney and Company of New York a controlling interest in the American barque *Mary Hasbrouck*, a 733-ton vessel capable of voyaging around the world. Holt then commissioned the important marine artist Antonio Jacobsen to paint two views of the ship, one entitled *Bound 'Round the World* and the other, *Off Cape Horn*. On November 30, 1898 Holt departed New York as captain of the *Mary Hasbrouck* on a voyage bound for Auckland, New Zealand. In so doing, he traveled through the islands of French Polynesia and the Pacific Rim, and called on ports in South Africa and Australia.

Upon his return to America in 1900, Holt met Sara Belle Griffis, a native of Alamance County and a granddaughter of English-born William Griffis and his wife,

Trade Card advertising the sailing of The Mary Hasbrouck to Austrailia and New Zealand, 1898.

Sarah Horn. Sara Belle was born on the 1,100-acre Griffis Plantation, located between Haw River and Mebane, where her birth place (an imposing two-story brick house known today as the Griffis-Patton House) still stands along Bason Road. The couple married in The Little Church Around the Corner, located in New York City, in July 1900, and spent their honeymoon traveling in Europe.

Within several years of their marriage, Holt was persuaded by his wife to retire from his seafaring career. By the early 1900s, he moved to the Lamar County, Texas community of Paris, Texas, where his wife's family also had extensive land holdings. There, Sam Holt opened a general mercantile store, although, until his death, he maintained the license which certified him as a "Master of Steam or Sail on any Ocean." He died in 1924, having been perhaps Alamance County's only native-born nineteenth century sea captain and traveler to five continents.

CASWELL HOLT

Caswell Holt was born on Oak Grove Plantation in 1834, one of fifteen children of the slaves Caswell, Sr. (b. 1818) and Rhena (b. 1814). His grandparents were Pattie (b. 1790) and Charles (b. 1770), two of the original slaves belonging to Michael Holt, II (1723-1799).

For almost 30 years Caswell was enslaved by E. M. Holt; in 1840 Holt's diary describes the 16-year old Caswell as a field hand. By the 1850s, however, Caswell was working in the Holts' dye house, and Thomas Holt states that Caswell and his brother Sam (b. 1837) helped to process the indigo from which the first Alamance Plaids were loomed in 1853. Caswell's status as a highly valued and skilled laborer are reflected in his property tax value listed by E. M. Holt in the 1860 census: the brothers Caswell, Sam, and their cousin Washington (an enslaved furniture maker, born in 1837) were each valued at $700.

After emancipation Caswell married Amy (b. 1840), a former slave of E. M.

Caswell Holt.

Holt, who was one of thirteen children of Jude (b. 1797) and Jim (b. 1779). Jude and Jim were two of the original slaves owned by E. M. Holt's grandfather, Michael Holt, II. In 1865 Caswell and Amy left the Oak Grove/Locust Grove plantation complex and set up housekeeping in an abandoned two-room schoolhouse located on the farm of E. M. Holt's cousin, Jeremiah Holt, where they worked as sharecroppers. In the immediate post-bellum period, Edwin Holt maintained a paternalistic relationship with Caswell and Amy Holt, who eventually had nine children: several of Caswell's sons continued helping E. M. Holt with cropping through the 1870s, and on at least one occasion Holt sent Caswell a gift of chickens.

The paternalistic relationship that both Edwin and Jeremiah Holt demanded assumed deferential behavior on the part of recently freed men and women. Caswell Holt, however, was determined to enjoy his newly found rights, including the right to vote for the candidate and party of his choice. The local Klan existed, in part, to curtail these rights and served as an important instrument of coercion against recalcitrant former slaves.

In the fall of 1868 the Klan first targeted

Caswell Holt, ostensibly for "roguish" behavior. In late November sixteen disguised men broke into Caswell's house, tied him with his own bed cording, and dragged him into nearby woods, where they ordered him to confess to the crime of stealing chickens and grain. When he refused, the Klansmen then tied a noose around Caswell's neck and suspended him from a tree so that his toes barely touched the ground. When this tactic failed to elicit a confession, the attackers cut Holt down, "bucked" him by pulling his tied hands over his knees and inserting a broomstick between his knees and arms, after which he was severely beaten with 50 lashes. Caswell Holt was then warned to leave the county.

Court testimony indicates that this initial confrontation was ordered by George Anthony's Klan camp, but was actually carried out by members of the John T. Trollinger camp. Days after the attack, Caswell Holt swore out warrants against several local men, including Daniel Anthony, George Anthony, and Peter Sellars. Holt went so far as to pay a republican lawyer, Henry Badham, to prosecute these men, but the accused managed to prove alibis, and Justice Peter Harden had them released from custody without conviction. When Caswell approached his former master, E. M. Holt, for advice on the matter, he was told "the less (you) say the better...say nothing more about it."

Caswell Holt's beating was doubtless the result of his vote in November 1868 for the Radical Republican ticket. He had done so despite having been warned by Jeremiah Holt to vote for the democratic slate. When Jeremiah Holt learned that Caswell had not done as ordered, he threatened to kick him off his land.

Caswell Holt nearly received a more severe punishment for daring to accuse his attackers in court. At February meetings of the White Brotherhood, a ride through Graham was approved and scheduled, and action against Holt was debated. Plans to whip him were discarded. George Anthony favored hanging him, while Dr. William Tarpley suggested drowning him in the Haw River at Sheriff Albert Murray's millpond. Although this order was passed and sent to Job Faucett's Klan camp for execution, the White Brotherhood Chief of the County, Jacob A. Long, stopped it from being carried out.

In 1869 Caswell Holt joined the Loyal Republican League (Union League) headed by Wyatt Outlaw. Caswell was then deputized and participated in the curfew enforcement in the Graham area. As a result, the White Brotherhood visited him again in December 1869. This time when voices demanded that he open his door, Caswell Holt refused, arming himself with a large knife. The Klan then responded by firing into the cabin, hoping to "blow his brains out." Holt later had 5 bullets and 2 bird shot pellets removed from his body. Klan members then charged into Caswell's house, broke his crockery, spinning wheel, and a looking glass, and slapped his children. When Holt reported the affronts, he was told that there was no such thing as the Klan and that those responsible for the beatings were "resurrected from graves."

Caswell Holt's injuries left him debilitated until April 1870. He spent these four months under the care of Dr. John S. Murphy. One of the gunshots penetrated Caswell Holt's lung, and he contracted pneumonia. In fact, on the night of Wyatt Outlaw's death, Caswell reported that he was "sick and like to die." Once sufficiently recovered Caswell left the county for several months.

In 1870 Caswell traveled to Washington, D.C., where he testified before the U. S. Senate of the Forty-Second Congress about Klan activities in Alamance County. Caswell's reports led again to the arrest of several local men, some of whom were jailed for a short while in the Caswell County Courthouse in Yanceyville. The conclusion of the Kirk-Holden War and the impeachment of Governor William Woods Holden in 1871, effectively led to the release of these offenders, and local Klan violence

abated. Caswell Holt survived Reconstruction and died in 1917 at the age of 83.

DONNELL SHAW HOLT

Donnell S. Holt, president and chairman of the board of Cannon Mills, was born on March 7, 1908 in a small mill house one hundred feet from the gate of Travora Mills in Graham. He was the son of Glenna and Seymour Holt, who was a superintendent of the mill. His grandfather, Isaac Holt, started in textiles as a day laborer, eventually working his way up to head of the carding section of Travora Mills.

Don Holt graduated from Graham High School in 1925 and received his diploma from The University of North Carolina in 1929. Well over six feet tall and weighing over 200 pounds, Holt played end for the Carolina football team, and was named All-State in 1927 and 1928 and All-Southern in 1929.

After graduating from Carolina, Holt took a job with Esther Hosiery Mill. Within months he obtained a new position in the accounting and business section at Travora. He took business courses at night for several years and quickly rose within the organization, becoming vice president of Travora Mills in March 1937. In 1942, at the beginning of World War II, Holt joined the Navy and was commissioned as a lieutenant. For eighteen months he served in the New Hebrides as a ground control officer and was discharged in 1945 with the rank of lieutenant commander.

After the war Don Holt returned to Travora Mill, which was acquired by Cannon Mills as a subsidiary in 1949. Thereafter Holt began a meteoric rise in the company. In 1950 he represented the Cotton Manufacturers Institute during an American textile mission to Japan, and, the following year, 1951, Charles A. Cannon promoted Holt to vice president of Cannon Mills. Holt subsequently orchestrated the establishment of the decorative fabric and bed sheet divisions within the company, and in 1959 he

was elected executive vice president. In 1960 he was named president of Cannon Mills of New York, the sales organization unit of the mill. When Charles Cannon stepped aside in 1962 to fill the newly created position of chairman of the board, he personally chose Don Holt to succeed him as president and chief executive officer. On the death of "Mr. Charlie" Cannon in 1971, Holt was reelected president and named chairman of the board, the first non-Cannon to head the company. Holt remained on the board of directors until 1980, when he stepped down because of ill health. He died on March 20, 1982 of kidney failure, and was survived by his wife, Margaret McConnell, who for many years was superintendent of the music curriculum for the Graham schools. The couple had no children.

Don Holt was instrumental in the development of Alamance County Hospital, and he helped to establish the Alamance Country Club. He served on the board of directors of Wachovia Bank and Trust and the National Bank of Alamance, and in 1973 was named national "Man of the Year in Textiles" by North Carolina State University.

EDWIN MICHAEL HOLT

Edwin Michael Holt, industrial pioneer and planter, was born on February 14, 1807 at Oak Grove plantation, the home of his parents, Michael Holt III and Rachel (Rainey) Holt. He obtained his early education at a local academy operated by a German tutor, Johannes Scherer. At age fourteen Holt began overseeing the wagons his father routinely sent to Fayetteville, North Carolina to supply the family's general store located at the Village of Alamance.

Holt lived with his parents and helped to run the plantation until 1828, when, at the age of 21, he married Emily Farish, the third of thirteen children born to a prosperous planter and his wife from Caswell County. The newly married couple lived in Holt's boyhood home until 1837, when they built a small two-room house across the road from Oak Grove. In 1849 this structure was

Edwin Michael Holt

incorporated into a larger dwelling built from a plan supplied by New York architect, A. J. Davis. The Holts called their new home "Locust Grove," and it became the seat of a 1,690-acre grain plantation where Holt experimented with new farming methods, fertilizers, and crop rotation. By the 1850s the Holt plantation produced about 2,000 bushels of wheat, 2,800 bushels of corn, and 1,200 bushels of oats annually, in addition to substantial quantities of fruits, vegetables, dairy products, beef, and pork. Typically, the Holts salted down some 15,000 pounds of pork each year; in 1860 their gristmill produced 5,000 bushels of meal and 670 barrels of flour. The farm also included a whiskey distillery, vineyard, sawmill, brickyard, and a tannery.

In 1837 Holt joined a small Piedmont proto-bourgeois when, together with his uncle William Carrigan, he founded the Alamance Cotton Factory on the site of Michael Holt III's Alamance Creek grist mill. Initially called the "Holt and Carrigan Cotton Mill," the factory first operated as a spinning mill utilizing 528 spindles. By 1851 Carrigan sold his half-interest in the mill to the Holts and moved to Arkansas.

About 1849 E. M. Holt and his son, Thomas, began converting the spinning mill into a looming operation. By 1853 the firm was producing the now-famous Alamance Plaid, said to be the first

commercially woven colored cotton fabric made south of the Potomac River. Tax records from 1860 show that on the eve of the Civil War the Alamance Cotton Factory employed sixty white women and eight white men, and the business had a tax value of $57,000.

Three years earlier, in 1857, Holt began a process of expansion when he acquired the bankrupt Cane Creek Factory, located in the Quaker area of southern Alamance County, as well as John Trolinger's Granite Factory, located at Haw River. By the time of his death on May 14, 1884, Holt and his extended family owned seventeen cotton mills in the area, and their growing textile enterprise (eventually consisting of twenty-four mills) dominated the industry in central North Carolina and created an industrial legacy that would last for generations. Holt's business acumen also made him a wealthy man; his 1884 estate was said to be the largest probated in North Carolina to that date and confirmed his local reputation as a multimillionaire.

Like his father before him, Edwin M. Holt was concerned with public affairs. In April 1844 he traveled to Raleigh to hear Henry Clay, and he was a consistent organizer of local Whig meetings. Holt frequently attended Orange County court and participated in activities directed by it. He was one of the commissioners for the building of a new courthouse, and he served on the finance committee. When Alamance County was established in 1849, he served on the building committee for the courthouse in Graham, the new county seat. He was also one of the commissioners chosen for the construction of a jail in Alamance County. Both Edwin Holt and his son Thomas served as stockholders and directors of the North Carolina Railroad, which was built between Goldsboro and Charlotte. When surveying began in 1850, E.M. Holt frequently went out with surveying parties.

In many ways E. M. Holt represented the original industrial pioneer: his abilities and industriousness aided in planting the roots of the textile industry in North Carolina, and his efforts fostered a unique social and demographic environment that came to be synonymous with Alamance County. He was survived by all but the eldest of his ten children: Alfred Augustus (1828-56), Thomas Michael (1831-96), James Henry (1833-97), Alexander (1935-92), Fannie H. Williamson (1837-1918), William Edwin (1839-1917), Lynn Banks (1842-1920), Mary Elizabeth H. Williamson (1844-1935), Emma H. White (1847-1904), and Lawrence Shackleford (1851-1937).

JAMES HENRY HOLT

James Henry Holt (1833-1897), textile manufacturer, was born at Oak Grove, the home of his grandparents near the village of Alamance. He was the son of Edwin Michael and Emily Farish Holt, and received his education at the Caldwell Institute, near Hillsborough and the Alexander Wilson Preparatory School. In 1852, at the age of nineteen, Holt joined his brother, Alfred, in the operation of a general store at Graham, where he was also placed in charge of deposits in a private bank owned by his father. Four years later, on January 15, 1856, James Holt married Laura Cameron Moore, of Caswell County, a sister of Louisa Moore who married his brother, Thomas. The couple had twelve children.

Always interested in banking, Holt became the head cashier of a bank in

James Henry Holt

Thomasville in 1862. Two years later he left that post to enlist as a private in Company K, Tenth Regiment of the North Carolina Artillery. While with the Tenth Regiment he was stationed at Fort Fisher from April until December 1864, when he was commissioned as a captain and sent to Fayetteville to serve as commandant of a military school. Shortly thereafter, the war ended, and Holt was paroled.

Upon returning to Alamance County, Holt was made a member of the family firm of Edwin M. Holt's Sons. He also joined his father and brothers in the founding of Commercial National Bank in Charlotte (now Bank of America), and for many years served on its board of directors.

In 1879 Holt and his brother William built Glencoe Mills, the last water-powered mill constructed in Alamance County. About this time he also built a home on Park Avenue in Burlington; the site is now a part of the property of Macedonia Lutheran Church.

In 1890 James Holt helped his sons, James, Jr. and Robert, to build the Windsor Cotton Mills in Burlington. Two years later he assisted his sons Samuel and William in constructing Burlington's Lakeside Mills. The aging industrialist then aided his son Walter in establishing textile plants in Fayetteville and Wilmington.

Holt was a member of the Graham Presbyterian Church until a congregation of that denomination was organized in Burlington. He then became one of the principal contributors to the construction of that town's First Presbyterian Church, where he was an officer until his death. Holt died at home and was buried in Burlington's Pine Hill Cemetery.

LAWRENCE S. HOLT

Lawrence Shackleford Holt (1851-1937), textile manufacturer and capitalist, was born in Alamance County at Locust Grove, the home of his parents near the village of Alamance. He was the youngest of ten children of Edwin Michael and Emily Farish Holt. Holt received his elementary

education at the Reverend Dr. Alexander Wilson's school at Melville, in the southern part of Alamance County, after which he attended Horner Military Academy at Oxford. He then enrolled at Davidson College as a member of the class of 1871, but did not remain to graduate because he was impatient to enter the business world.

To satisfy his son's ambition, the elder Holt placed him in charge of a wholesale grocery business that he owned in Charlotte. After proving himself in this capacity, the young manager persuaded his father and brothers, Thomas, James, William, and Banks, to join him in founding the Commercial National Bank of Charlotte, now Bank of America.

In 1872 Holt married Margaret Locke Erwin of Burke County. They became the parents of seven children: Erwin Allen, Eugene, Emily Farish, Margaret Erwin, Florence E., Lawrence Shackleford, Jr., and Bertha Harper.

The year after his marriage, Holt returned to Alamance County and built a home called "Sunnyside" near Locust Grove. He became a partner in the family firm of Edwin M. Holt's Sons, operator of the cotton mill at Alamance and the Carolina Cotton Mills, which it had built on the Haw River. For the next several years, in cooperation with one or more of his brothers and William A. Erwin, a brother-in-law, Holt helped found the Bellemont Cotton Mills and the E. M. Holt Plaid Mills. He also became one of the owners of a half interest in the Altamahaw Cotton Mills; the other half was owned by J. Q. Gant, his brother-in-law by marriage to Corinna Erwin. The new firm of Holt, Gant, and Holt operated six miles northeast of Mill Point (now Elon, N.C.).

In 1884, Holt attempted to buy the bankrupt Lafayette Mills at Company Shops, but was outbid by R. J. Reynolds. The tobacco magnate soon changed his plans and sold the factory to Holt for $17,000. In this transaction, the industrialist fulfilled his greatest ambition-to become the sole owner of a textile mill. By concentrating all his resources on this ven-

Lawrence S. Holt

ture, he was able to replace the knitting machines used in the defunct plant with 2,160 spindles and 124 looms. In 1885, the Aurora Cotton Mills began production; thereafter its output increased regularly as various additions were made to the plant.

In order to be near his principal business, Holt moved from his country home to "Blythewood," an ornate house he built at Company Shops about the time the town's name was changed to Burlington. Like his father, he firmly believed in a family-owned and operated business, and in 1886 he included his sons in the mill's management by forming the firm of Lawrence S. Holt and Sons. Subsequent expansion followed, and the enterprise eventually included the Gem Cotton Mills in Gibsonville and the Sevier Cotton Mills in Kings Mountain. All of the firms were profitable. Moreover, Holt was credited with being the "first manufacturer in the South" to voluntarily shorten the working day from twelve to eleven hours without reducing pay.

While born into a Lutheran family, Holt married an Episcopalian and became a communicant of that church. In 1879 he played a leading role in the construction of St. Athanasius Protestant Episcopal Church at Company Shops, which still stands. In

1911 he built and endowed the impressive Episcopal Church of the Holy Comforter in Burlington in memory of his daughter, Emily Farish, who died in 1885 at age five.

Grieved by the death of his wife in 1918, Holt closed "Blythewood;" it remained unoccupied for two decades. Leaving his mill operation in the hands of his sons, the industrialist retired to Washington, D.C.

When new materials were introduced into the textile industry, Eugene Holt advised replacing cotton yarn with rayon, but his father would not agree to the change. Shortly after this difference of opinion, Aurora Cotton Mills ceased operation. The plant was first rented, then it was sold to other textile corporations. Eugene moved to Richmond, Virginia, where he pursued his interest in rayon. Lawrence, Jr., became a real estate promoter in Asheville, and Erwin lived a retired life in Burlington. All of the manufacturer's family left Alamance County.

Near the end of his life, Holt moved to western North Carolina in the interest of his health, and he died in a Statesville hospital. His remains were taken to Burlington and interred in the family plot in the cemetery adjacent to St. Athanasius Church.

—*Durward T. Stokes*

Note: A version of this biography appears in Dictionary of North Carolina Biography, *William Stevens Powell, ed., vol. 3, page 186, 1988.*

LYNN BANKS HOLT

Lynn Banks Holt (1842-1920), textile manufacturer, was born at Oak Grove Plantation near the village of Alamance. He was the son of Edwin Michael and Emily Farish Holt and received his secondary education at the Hillsborough Military Academy. When the Civil War began, Banks withdrew from the academy and enlisted as a private with the Orange Guards. For gallantry displayed in the capture of Fort Macon by his company, he was promoted to second lieutenant and assigned to Company I, Eighth North

Burlington's Church of the Holy Comforter.

Carolina Regiment. He later became a first lieutenant, and on September 29, 1864, Banks was severely wounded at the Battle of Fort Harrison and taken prisoner. He was confined as a prisoner of war at Point Lookout and at Fort Delaware until June of 1865.

On October 26, 1865 Holt married Mary Catherine Yancey Mebane, daughter of Giles Mebane and granddaughter of Senator Bartlett Yancey of Caswell County. Holt then joined his father in business at the Alamance Cotton Mill and in 1874 and 1875 he remodeled and expanded his grandfather Michael's nearby Oak Grove home, where he lived until 1885, when he moved to Graham. The Oak Grove house was listed in the National Register of Historic Places in 1977 and now serves as the Alamance County Historical Museum.

Lynn Banks eventually purchased the interests of his brothers in the Alamance Cotton Factory, and in 1879 he and one brother, Lawrence S., built the nearby Bellemont Mill, of which Banks became sole owner in 1887. In 1883 he founded at Burlington the E. M. Holt Plaid Mills, named for his father. Meanwhile he also acquired the Oneida Mill at Graham and the Carolina Mills. In 1909 Holt consolidated the Alamance, Bellemont, Oneida, and Carolina Mills and incorporated the business as the L. Banks Holt Manufacturing Company. He remained president of both the E. M. Holt Plaid Mills and the L. Banks Holt Manufacturing Company until his death in 1920.

In addition to these properties Banks also owned a one-third interest in the

Altamahaw Cotton Mills and was a major stockholder of numerous textile mills located throughout North Carolina. He was also a director of the Merchant and Farmers Bank and the Commercial National Bank, both of Charlotte, and was a director of the North Carolina Railroad.

For many years Lynn Banks Holt was an elder of the Presbyterian Church in Graham, where he eventually built what has been described as "the most ornate textile mansion in Alamance County." The house stood on Banks Street and was considered a local showplace.

Throughout his lifetime Banks Holt's hobby was agriculture, and on his Alamance and Oak Grove farms he raised purebred livestock, including Jersey and Holstein cattle, Belted Gallaways, Shetland ponies, and standard bred pacers. His horse "John Gentry" was a world champion, and set the mark for the highest price ever paid for a racehorse when sold at Madison Square Garden in 1896.

MICHAEL HOLT I, II & III

Michael Holt (Hold or Holtz) I was christened December 30, 1696, the son of Martin Hold (1642-1710) and Anna Maria Brickhmann. He was born in Stetten am Heuchelberg, Bavaria, where his grandfather, Jonas Hold, was burgermeister (mayor).

At the age of twenty Michael Holt, together with his mother and stepfather (Johannes Spath), were among about 140 residents of the Upper Rhine who left Germany in July 1717 seeking opportunities in the American colonies. After a brief stop in England, the colonists were eventually sold into indentureship to Lieutenant Governor Alexander Spotswood of Virginia by their ship's captain. Many, including Michael Holt, were then settled into Spotswood's "New German Town" (second Germanna Colony), where they worked in naval stores and in the governor's iron foundries.

Within a year of his arrival, the twenty-one-year-old Holt married Elizabeth Scheible (Shively), a seventeen-year-old fellow Germanna settler. In 1724 Holt and his father-in-law successfully sued Spotswood and were formally released from their indentureship. Two years later, in 1726, Holt received 400 acres in the foothills of the Virginia Blue Ridge, land granted on the usual "headright" basis of fifty acres per household member. Over the next twenty years the Holts prospered, eventually acquiring about 1,000 acres in the Virginia territory. Not only did Holt prosper, but he seems to have exercised some authority in his community: in 1734 he accompanied Reverend John Casper Stoever to London, Amsterdam, and Germany to collect funds for Hebron Lutheran Church of Virginia.

In 1755, after deeding some of their Virginia lands to four of their seven sons, Michael and Elizabeth Holt sold their remaining Virginia property and immigrated southward to purchase Granville tract land in North Carolina. Holt selected land in the headwaters of Little Alamance Creek, a 739-acre upland tract near the Indian Trading Path in the general area of present-day Webb Avenue in Burlington. By 1759, Michael Holt, I had become one of Orange County's largest and wealthiest landowners. He died in 1767 and is buried at the corner of Williamson Street and Wood Avenue in Burlington, North Carolina.

Michael Holt, II (1723-1799), a son of Michael and Elizabeth Holt, has been described as five feet ten inches tall and weighing approximately 225 pounds, with a complexion so dark he was known locally as "Black Michael." By his first wife, Margaret O'Neill, he had three children: Joseph, Margaret, and Elizabeth. After his first wife's death in 1765 Holt married Jean Lockhart (d. 1813) in 1767, and their union produced the following offspring: Sarah (b. 1769); Joshua (b. 1771); Isaac (b. 1773); Mary (b. 1775); Catherine (b. 1776); Michael, III (b. 1778) and William (b. 1779). The family lived in the area that is today known as Hanford Brick Road, where Michael operated a prosperous blacksmith shop.

In the mid-1700s Michael Holt, II became a magistrate by royal appointment and served as justice of the peace for Orange County. He was also captain in the provincial militia. In 1768, at the beginning of the Regulator disturbance, Holt was ordered to muster out his company and join the militia to suppress the rebellion. Meanwhile Royal Governor William Tryon traveled to Orange County and set up headquarters on Holt's farm. When no fighting occurred, Tryon concluded that the agitation had permanently subsided and returned to New Bern. His assumption was incorrect, however, as the following year the Regulators became violent. Holt was one of several local officials "severely whiped" during the rioting in Hillsborough. The governor returned to Orange, and Captain Holt again led his company to join the militia in ending the insurrection. After subsequent attempts to negotiate a settlement failed, the War of the Regulation ended with the Battle of Alamance, fought May 16, 1717, ironically on Holt's own farmland. After the conflict the sick and wounded were sent to the Holt home for medical attention and nursing. The outcome of the war was retribution for the captain in view of the indignities he had suffered at the hands of the rioters, and he continued to be a loyal subject of the Crown.

When the American Revolution began, Holt was among the militia officers authorized by Tryon's successor, Governor Josiah Martin, to raise companies of fifty men "to resist and oppose" the Patriots. He dutifully recruited his company and led it to join the Scottish Highlander Tories and other Loyalists rallying under General Donald McDonald at Cross Creek (now Fayetteville). En route to the rendezvous, "when he was fully acquainted with the intention of the Tories," he changed his mind and returned home, "inducing a Number of Others to follow his example without a junction with the Scotch Army." Holt then became a Patriot and remained one. Nevertheless, he was arrested as a Tory

Michael Holt, III and Rachel Rainey Holt.

and sent to prison in Philadelphia. From his confinement there, he explained his change of attitude in a petition addressed to the North Carolina Council of Safety. This was supplemented by a similar petition from the Orange County Committee of Safety. As a result, the Council decided "Michael Holt would not in any wise injure the Caus of liberty in this State," and, upon its recommendation, the Continental Congress pardoned the prisoner.

Holt then returned to his farm and lived peaceably for the rest of his life. Shortly after the Revolution, an English author touring the United States was entertained at the Holt home "with great hospitality." The visitor described his host as a magistrate possessed of a considerable property" and "the son of Dutch or German parents, for he himself was born in America." Holt was a sensible man of sound judgment, "but without the least improvement from education, or the embellishment of any kind of polish, even in his exterior."

Michael Holt, II died on June 20, 1799 and was buried in a private cemetery on his farm. This burial ground, still intact, is located on the west side of Hanford Brick Road, a few miles southeast of Burlington. On Holt's tombstone is the epitaph often quoted but seldom actually seen:

> Remember, man as you pass by,
> As you are now, so once was I;
> As I am now so must you be,
> Prepare for death and follow me.

Holt's children inherited his considerable estate and used it with such success that a substantial part of the patrimony remained in the possession of his descendants for three generations.

Michael Holt, III (1778-1842), farmer, magistrate, and legislator was born in Orange County, the son of Michael, II and his second wife, Jean (Lockhart) Holt. He was reared on his father's farm and from him inherited several hundred acres of land along Big Alamance Creek and its tributaries.

During his youth, Holt received only elementary schooling, but from his parents learned the rudiments of husbandry. Building on this foundation, he became one of the most successful farmers in the Piedmont section of the state. In addition to attaining financial affluence, the agriculturist cultivated his mind with "diligent reading, reflection, and conversation" and thereby "possessed the respect and good opinion of his fellow citizens." This was demonstrated in his many years of service as a magistrate and by his election in 1804 as a representative of Orange County in the North Carolina House of Commons. He was elected to the state senate in 1819 and reelected for another term in 1821.

A member and "worth communicant" of the Lutheran church, Holt married Rachel Rainey, daughter of the Reverend Benjamin Rainey, a minister in the Christian church founded by James O'Kelly. The couple became the parents of six children: Nancy Mitcham (Mrs. William A. Carrigan), Jane Lockhart (Mrs. John Holt), Edwin Michael, William Rainey, Alfred Augustus, and Polly (Mary), who never married. Holt lived in a farm house near the present village of Alamance, where his son Edwin eventually built one of the early cotton mills in the state. Known as "Oak Grove" the house is preserved today as the Alamance County Historical Museum.

Holt trained his sons to be master farmers and, though Edwin and William chose other vocations for their lifework, the family cultivated the ancestral acres profitably for two generations, even surviving the economic loss of slave labor. Holt did not share Edwin's enthusiasm for manufacturing, as he failed to envision the potential of the cotton mill at Alamance. He remained skeptical of his son's plans and did not live to see their ultimate success.

When he died, Holt's numerous slaves and tracts of land were divided by his will equally among his children with meticulous precision. He also bequeathed the sum of $200 to enclose "the graves in the garden" with brick or stone. The executors carried out his instructions, and Holt was buried with numerous members of his family at "Oak Grove" in the walled cemetery, now maintained by the county museum.

Note: Portions of the sections on Michael Holt, II and III were written by Durward Stokes and originally published in Dictionary of North Carolina Biography, William Stevens Powell, ed., volume 3, pp. 188-89, 1988.

SAM HOLT

In 1832 the General Assembly of North Carolina passed a law which prohibited "any free negro, slave or person of color" from preaching in public or officiating in any formal worship service. The law did not prohibit informal private worship among slaves, however; and within the slave quarters of several local plantations, a number of slaves were given the unofficial title of "preacher."

Among these was a slave, known as Sam, who was born on the Holt plantation at Alamance on October 5, 1837. One of fifteen children of the slaves Rhena (b. 1814) and Caswell, Sr. (b. 1818), Sam began preaching about 1857. With his elder brother, Caswell, Jr. (b. 1834), Sam worked six days a week in the Holt's dye house, producing the first indigo dyes used in the manufacture of the famous Alamance Plaids. On Sundays, he preached to his fellow slaves, as well as to members of the Holt family, who sometimes attended the informal sermons.

Out of respect for Sam's pious and hardworking nature, E. M. Holt deeded one acre of land to the young black man in the spring of 1863. The deed stipulated that the land be used to develop a church for the black population of southern Alamance County. Until the church was constructed, services were held in a brush arbor near a free-flowing spring located on the small tract. Within a few months, a one-room building was constructed. Initially called "Uncle Sam's Meeting House," the name was later changed to Springdale Church.

Following Emancipation, Sam adopted the Holt surname and continued his ministry at Springdale. Sam Holt came to be known for his riveting sermons, which made use of the so-called "ring-shout," a conversion technique consisting of dancing combined with the singing of Christian hymns accompanied by shouting, stomping, and moaning. Scholars have argued that the ring-shout is a variation on certain West African religious practices adapted to new circumstances. In West Africa, the

Original drawing of preaching at Uncle Jerry's Meeting House from A Fool's Errand, *by Albion W. Tourgee, 1879, p. 93.*

ring-shout enacted the experience of being possessed by spirits. In America, the very physical dance excited participants into an emotional frenzy and prepared them to be filled with the Holy Spirit via the cathartic acceptance of Christ as savior.

The success of Sam Holt's conversion techniques led to the rapid growth of the Springdale congregation, so that by 1867 the church was enlarged to a three-room structure. About this time Sam Holt's success as a preacher seems also to have come to the attention of the Reverend James Walker Hood, an African Methodist Episcopal Zion minister, who came to North Carolina in 1864 and became the most influential African-American clergyman in the state. In the fall of 1867, Hood visited Sam Holt's Springdale Church, where he preached a single service with Sam Holt.

In the Reconstruction fervor that followed North Carolina's Constitutional Convention of 1868, the Reverend James Hood was appointed assistant superintendent of public instruction for the state. In 1871 Hood authorized the development of a school for blacks at Sam Holt's Springdale Church. This school appears to have been one of the first schools for freed blacks in Alamance County and came about largely because of Hood's firsthand knowledge of Springdale Church and his admiration of Sam Holt. Land for the Springdale School, located adjacent to the church, was given by the family of Republican Senator T. M. Shoffner of Alamance, who eventually fled to Indiana during the Kirk-Holden period.

Initially, classes at Springdale were operated for only a few months in the spring and fall of each year. Several early teachers at Springdale were former pupils of Fayetteville's Howard School, which was designated in 1877 as the State Colored Normal School (now Fayetteville State University). Some funds for Springdale Academy seem also to have come from George Peabody, a northern banking entrepreneur and philanthropist, who, in 1867, created the Peabody Education Fund to assist worthy southern

schools, both black and white.

From 1871 until the early 1900s Springdale Academy operated as one of the few schools for blacks in southern Alamance County. The school also trained the area's first generation of African-American teachers, among whom was Eliza Holt, who founded the Patillo School located in northern Alamance County, and Ida Hunter, who founded Woodsdale School and the well-known McCray School (1915).

Sam Holt died in 1912 and is buried in the cemetery at Springdale Church. His grave marker recognizes his contribution as founder of Uncle Sam's Meeting House and Springdale A.M.E. Church. And while his academy closed about 1913, his church survives as an active congregation and a monument to his contributions to Alamance County.

THOMAS MICHAEL HOLT

Thomas Michael Holt (1831-1896), textile manufacturer, legislator, and governor of North Carolina, was born on "Oak Grove" Plantation located near the site of the Battle of Alamance. He was the second son of ten children of Edwin Michael and Emily Farish Holt. Thomas received his early education from a private tutor and subsequently attended the Caldwell Institute in Hillsborough, where he was a pupil of Dr. Alexander Wilson. In June 1849 he enrolled at the University of North Carolina as a sophomore, but left the university in 1850 to gain practical experience in the mercantile trade in Philadelphia, where he became an accomplished salesman and bookkeeper.

In 1851 Holt returned to Alamance County to assist in the operation of the family's spinning mill on Alamance Creek. Over the next two years Holt helped to oversee the mill's transition from spinning to weaving. With the help of the slaves Caswell and Sam, he was instrumental in developing colorfast indigo dyes and is credited with assisting in the production of the first "Alamance Plaid" fabric in 1853. On October 17, 1855 he married

Thomas Michael Holt

Louisa Matilda Moore, by whom he fathered six children.

In 1861 Thomas Holt took over the Granite Mills in Haw River, and with his brother-in-law and partner, Adolphus Moore, he began expansions at the site: by May 1874 some forty houses, a church, and a school were built for the more than 175 employees and their families. During this period (1872-7876) Holt also served as a county commissioner.

In 1876 Holt was elected a state senator on the Democratic ticket. In 1882 he was sent to the North Carolina House of Representatives, where he served three successive terms and was chosen speaker of the house in 1884. Holt's political career capped in 1888, when he was elected lieutenant governor and subsequently became governor of North Carolina upon the death of Governor Daniel Fowle in 1891. Holt then served as governor until 1893, but declined to run for a full term because of ill health.

During his years of public service Thomas Holt helped to secure the establishment of the state Department of Agriculture and the North Carolina College of Agriculture and Mechanical Arts in Raleigh. He urged the expansion of common (public) schools throughout the state and increased appropriations for

Employees at Granite Mills, Circa 1890.

the University of North Carolina. He also sought additional aid for state hospitals located at Morganton, Greensboro, and Raleigh and was a benefactor of the Oxford Children's Home. For many years Holt served as a member of the board of trustees at the University of North Carolina and Davidson College.

Holt was also a director of the North Carolina Railroad Company, president of the North Carolina State Fair, and for thirteen years served as president of the Patrons of Husbandry, also know as the "Grange." From 1859 until 1896 he was a ruling elder of the Graham Presbyterian Church. In 1895 he was awarded an honorary L.L.D. by the University of North Carolina. Thomas Holt died at "Dixondale," his home in Haw River, and was buried in Linwood Cemetery, Graham.

WILLIAM RAINEY HOLT

William Rainey Holt (1798-1868), physician, scientific agriculturalist, and planter, was born at "Oak Grove," the plantation home of his parents, Michael Holt, III and Rachael (Rainey) Holt. He was the oldest of five siblings (Alfred Augustus, Edwin Michael; Jane Lockhart; Polly and Nancy). His mother was the daughter of the Reverend Benjamin and Nancy Rainey, the former a prominent minister of the Christian church. His father was a prosperous planter in the Alamance section who served in the North Carolina House of Commons in 1804 and in the state senate in 1819 and from 1821 to 1822, during which terms he advocated internal improvements in the state.

In 1817 William Rainey Holt graduated from the University of North Carolina; while at the University he formed a lifelong friendship with fellow classmate and future governor, John Motley Morehead. In 1821 Holt received his medical degree from Jefferson Medical College in Philadelphia. Thereupon he moved to Lexington, North Carolina, where he married Mary Gizeal Allen, a descendant of William Allen, who had married Mary Parke, of the Parke-Custis family of Virginia. The couple had five children: Elizabeth Allen, who married Dr. Dillon Lindsay; Elvira Jane, who married Joseph Erwin; Louise, who died young; and Mary Gizeal, who married Colonel Ellis, a brother of Governor John Ellis and John Allen.

In 1834, two years after the death of his first wife, Holt married her cousin,

Louisa Allen Hogan, daughter of Colonel William and Elizabeth (Allen) Hogan. On Main Street in Lexington the couple built an imposing, classically-inspired home, replete with Palladian details; the house remains intact and is called "The Homestead." There the couple had nine children, six of whom died unmarried. Their daughter Claudia married D. C. Pearson; Frances married Charles A. Hunt of Lexington; Amelia, married her first cousin, William E. Holt, son of Edwin Michael Holt.

Holt opened his medical practice in Lexington in 1821. When Davidson County was formed in 1822, Holt became a leader in the community and served on various committees to build the county courthouse, as well as a poor house for indigent widows. He was one of the founding members of St. Peters Episcopal Church, and served as trustee of both the Lexington Academy (1825) and the Lexington Female Academy (1858).

During a term as state senator from 1838 to 1839, Holt supported the passage of the Education Act and was chairman of the Committee on Internal Improvements for the state of North Carolina. In Davidson County he worked for the

Willaim Rainey Holt.

implementation of a tax for common schools, and in 1843 he became a member of the first County Board of School Superintendents. Beginning in 1849 Holt also played a role in the building of the railroad through Davidson County, where one railway station ("Holtsburg") was named in his honor, and a second, called "Linwood," was placed on his plantation of the same name.

Beginning in 1822 Holt began acquiring farmland in the Jersey Settlement near the Yadkin River, where he eventually amassed a 2,500 acre plantation which he called "Linwood." There he practiced the latest techniques of scientific agriculture, including crop rotation, improved drainage and ditching, and the use of cover crops, green manure, and commercial fertilizers.

The 1860 census graphically illustrates the success of Dr. Holt's agricultural experiments:

"He owned 1,600 improved acres, and 901 unimproved. His real estate was valued at $87,000 and his personal estate at $90,000. His livestock was valued at $13,200 and his farming implements at $2,000. His livestock alone was worth more than a few of Davidson County's other farms. He owned 220 swine, 160 sheep, 10 horses, 25 mules, 50 milk cows, 6 oxen and 60 "other cattle." His farm grew 4,000 bushels of wheat, 3,000 bushels of corn, 3,000 bushels of oats, and lesser amounts of peas, beans and Irish potatoes. He was the county's largest cotton farmer with a production of sixty-three 400 pound bales. He grew 100 tons of hay. His farm had orchard products and honey producing bees. He even produced 10 gallons of wine. Holt owned 99 slaves, which he housed in 15 slave houses."

Dr. Holt's interest in promoting scientific agricultural methods extended beyond his Davidson County plantation to his home county of Alamance and elsewhere in the state. He was a charter member of the North Carolina Agricultural Society, which was organized in 1852, and he served as the organization's president from 1860 until 1868. In 1865, he purchased, outside the state, a purebred Shorthorn bull that is believed to have been "the first registered animal of all breeds of cattle in North Carolina" (Sink and Matthews 1972: 162). This animal improved the herds at Linwood and, in 1867, the bull was shipped by rail to E. M. Holt's "Oak Grove" and "Locust Grove" farms at Alamance, where the animal helped to replenish livestock herds devastated by the Civil War.

Throughout his life Holt was frequent contributor to *The Arator*, one of the most significant agricultural journals of the day, and he corresponded regularly with fellow proponents of the scientific agricultural method such as Judge Thomas Ruffin of Alamance, Edmund Ruffin of Virginia, and Professor Ebenezer Emmons.

During the last years of the Civil War, Holt's health began a drastic decline, and by the war's end he was also suffering under the burden of heavy debt. In 1866 E. M. Holt purchased Dr. William Rainey Holt's Lexington properties, where the doctor continued to live until his death on October 3, 1868 at the age of 70.

EARL BAYNES HORNER

Earl Baynes Horner was born April 15, 1882, the son of Thomas J. and Annie (Terry) Horner of Person County, N. C. His paternal ancestors came to America in 1770 from Chestershire, England. Horner's father owned a small farm in Person County, where he also worked as a millwright.

At the age of 22 Earl Horner left the family farm, and, on May 6, 1904 he arrived in Burlington in search of job opportunities. With little work available in the Burlington area he traveled by train from Burlington to Greensboro where he found temporary employment at White Oak Mill as a carpenter's assistant. Within six months he returned to Burlington and was hired by Virginia Bridge and Iron Company, initially working as a member

Ralph Scott and Earl Baynes Horner.

of the "bull gang," doing heavy carrying labor at the plant.

About 1906 Horner began taking a series of correspondence courses in civil engineering, focusing on bridge construction. By 1910, through diligent evening study, Horner received his diploma and began working as a draftsman and field engineer for Virginia Bridge and Iron Co. at their offices in Burlington and Roanoke, Virginia; he also later worked for the Joliet Bridge and Iron Company in Burlington.

On June 15, 1919 Horner was elected mayor of Burlington on the Democratic ticket. Immediately he began to study Burlington's municipal problems. He saw an increased need for improvements to Burlington's water supply system, and through his advocacy the 500-million gallon Stoney Creek impoundment was created; these improved water resources were fundamental to the growth of Burlington's hosiery industry in the mid-1900s when the town became known as the "Hosiery Center of the South."

In April 1921, two years after Horner took office, the streets of downtown Burlington were brightened when electric street lamps were installed on Main, Davis, and Front Streets. Working in conjunction with the chamber of commerce and local business leaders like W. E. Sharpe, M. B. Smith, H. F. Mitchell, and Colonel Robert Holt, Horner pushed for the creation of a new city hotel, and in 1925 the Alamance Hotel opened in the heart of downtown Burlington. During his administration more than 40 miles of sewer lines were added, street and sidewalk paving programs were carried out, the Burlington fire department was modernized, the police and library systems were improved, and meat and milk inspection standards were instituted. Main Street was extended north of the railroad when a "mysterious" explosion opened a pathway for the extension.

In addition to his service to Burlington, Horner held several state appointments: in 1931 Governor Max Gardner named Horner to the board of the State Tobacco Commission. In 1933 he was also named a member of the North Carolina Local Government Commission by Governor J.C.B. Ehringhaus.

Horner married Dallie McPherson on December 20, 1920. The couple had two children: Earl Baynes, Jr. (b. 1926) and Rebekah Ann (b. 1931). Horner was mayor of Burlington from 1919 until his death on October 8, 1944. Mrs. Horner died March 18, 1976. They are buried at Pine Hill Cemetery in Burlington.

HERMAN HUSBAND

Herman (Harmon) Husband(s) was born October 3, 1724 in Maryland into the Anglican faith. As a youth he embraced Quakerism. Variously described as a patriot and a zealot, Husband played a major role in two key events that helped shape the evolution of democracy in the United States—the War of Regulation in North Carolina (1771-72) and the Whiskey Rebellion of 1794.

As a young man Husband's fervent beliefs drew him to immigrate to the North Carolina frontier, where he sought opportunities to fashion a "New Jerusalem" based on utopian ideals. In November 1755 Husband came to Orange County, where he first settled in Corbinton (now Hillsborough, N.C.). In 1765 he married Amy Allen (b. 1743), a native of Chester County, Pennsylvania, then living in the Alamance section of Orange County. Soon thereafter Husband obtained from Earl Granville a grant of 640 acres in what is now Randolph County, where his Deep River holdings eventually grew to include almost 3,000 acres.

In the mid 1760s North Carolinians on the western frontier became increasingly disturbed by what they saw as tyrannical rule by the colony's eastern elite, whose loose methods of levying, collecting, and accounting for taxes were viewed as unjust. Husband emerged as unofficial leader of this opposition movement, whose members came to be known as the Regulators. A skilled pamphleteer and poet, whose poem *Impartial Relations* (1770) was widely read, Husband advocated winning over public sentiment to the Regulator cause through constructive engagement with the government.

On the night of May 1, 1768 Husband was arrested and imprisoned in Hillsborough to await trial in New Bern for his association with the Regulators and his perceived support of the Hillsborough riot of the preceding April. Released on bail until the fall court session, Husband was eventually acquitted of charges in September of 1768 by the Superior Court on the grounds that there was "no evidence that he was a member of the Regulator organization or that he aided or abetted the riot."

In 1769 and 1770 Husband was elected to the North Carolina Assembly, whereupon he was placed on the Committee of Public Accounts. In December 1770, however, he was discharged from the Assembly, again on grounds that he was a leader of the Regulators.

Overt combat soon broke out between the Regulators and North Carolina militia, led by the Royal Governor, Lord William Tryon. The War of the Regulation, as it came to be known, was settled at the Battle of Alamance on May 16, 1771, in which government militia crushed the Regulator rebellion outright. Husband tried to the end to dissuade his fellow Regulators from fighting, but in the aftermath of the rebellion he was named an outlaw and forced to flee North Carolina, resettling on the western Pennsylvania frontier in Somerset County in June 1771. The ensuing years of difficult pioneer life did nothing to dim Husband's vision of a utopian frontier democracy, however.

The revolution that ultimately freed the American colonies from English rule left the newly created United States of America saddled with heavy foreign debt. To raise funds in 1791 Congress passed an excise tax on distilled spirits. Western Pennsylvania farmers were outraged; there was little cash on the frontier to begin with, and given the difficulties of travel common to the region, farmers had no practical means of getting their crops to market other than converting them into portable distilled spirits. To add insult to injury, the tax was regressive—smaller producers of distilled spirits, most of whom were farmers, were taxed at a higher rate than larger commercial producers. Western farmers began a campaign of harassment against the federal tax collectors that by 1794 bordered on outright rebellion.

The parallels with the Regulator movement were obvious. To Herman Husband it must have seemed all too familiar; once again he found himself a leading figure of frontier protest against an unresponsive government perceived to be in the service of an eastern elite. A delegate to the Parkinson's Ferry and Redstone meetings in the summer of 1794, Husband advocated moderation, eschewing violence in favor of a campaign petitioning for the repeal of the tax. Events moved quickly beyond Husband's control, however. An army of 13,000 militia under the personal command of President George Washington crushed the so-called "Whiskey Rebellion," and Husband was one of the first figures taken into custody. He was sent to Philadelphia, where he spent seven months languishing in prison before the charges against him were dropped. He was eventually freed, but the ordeal had broken his health. Herman Husband died in 1796, shortly after his release. After Husband's death his widow, Amy, went to Henderson, Kentucky in 1797 where she died while living with a daughter, Amy (Husband) Bennett.

Portions of this article are based on research by David Husband published in Annals of the Early Settlement of Somerset County, *Somerset County Historical and Genealogical Society, 2004, Ronald Bruner, Rockwood, Pennsylvania.*

N. JANE ISELEY

Nancy Jane Iseley (born July 6, 1944) is the daughter of Edward Frank Iseley (1907-1987) and Nancy Jane (Vincent) Iseley (1910-1968). Her father, a 1930 graduate of Elon College, was a teacher and coach at Pleasant Grove School for eleven years before being named principal of the school, a position he held until 1971. Jane's mother, also a teacher, graduated from Queens College in 1931, and received her master's degree and Ph.D. from the University of North Carolina in Romance Languages and Literature. In 1952 she edited and published the thirteenth century epic poem *La Chancun de Williame.*

Jane Iseley, architectural photographer, publisher, and farmer, graduated from Walter Williams High School, attended Coker College, and graduated from Radford College and the New York Institute of Photography. Following school she worked for nine years as staff photographer for the Colonial Williamsburg Foundation, and for a number of years she also freelanced for the real estate division of Sotheby's photographing international luxury properties. In 1989 she founded Legacy Publications in Greensboro, North Carolina to provide photo documentation of the architectural heritage of places like Charleston, S.C., Savannah, Georgia, Williamsburg, Virginia and New Orleans. Today she is known as one of the most respected and productive

architectural photographers in the southeast. She is the photographic author of more than 30 books, many of which, have won state and national awards.

In 1981 Jane returned to the Burlington area to assist her father with farming operations at the family farm, which has been owned by the Iseley family members since about 1790. Currently she divides her time between her two passions: "From about the middle of March I farm. By Thanksgiving I change caps-from the farm cap to publisher/ photographer."

In 2008 Iseley's "Home Farm" has been in continuous production by the Iseley family for 218 years. Through this period the farm has produced timber, tobacco, fruits, and vegetables, as well as grazing pastures and feed for cows and horses. Today the farm is recognized as a Conservation Farm, is a member of the Forestry Stewardship Program, and is a NCDA Certified Roadside Farm Market. All produce sold at the farm's Vegetable Barn is organic, or is grown with limited pesticide use, and vegetables grown by the farm are labeled "Jane's Pride." Produce includes early spring cabbage, lettuce, onions, squash, cucumbers, tomatoes, corn, beans and peas, peppers, strawberries, and blueberries. Fall crops include pumpkins, heirloom apples, and mums. The farm also produces organically grown tobacco.

Iseley has served on the Alamance County Historic Properties Commission and the board of directors of the Alamance County Historical Museum. In 2002 she was named Alamance County Entrepreneur of the Year.

JOHN WILLIAM JEFFRIES

John William Jeffries was born on January 15, 1897, the oldest of eight children of Charles Edward and Arnieda (Jones) Jeffries. He was reared in the Little Texas community of northern Alamance County, where he attended the Martin School and helped on his father's tobacco farm. At the age of 16 he was admitted to A&T State College, but within a year he was called home to assist his ailing father

John William Jeffries.

with the family farming operation. On October 29, 1917 he married Mamie Jeffries (1895-1976), daughter of Levi and Dixie (Parker) Jeffries of Pleasant Grove.

Wishing to resume his education in 1922 Jeffries returned to high school (at the age of 25) and began taking a series of locally-offered college credit extension courses. These credits allowed him in 1943 to return to A&T State College as a senior. In June 1944 Jeffries completed his college education, some 31 years after he had entered college as a freshman.

During the 1920s Jeffries came to be recognized as one of the area's premier farmers. As a result, in 1922 he was appointed the first minority County Agricultural Agent and, in this position, he successfully organized a number of 4-H Calf Clubs throughout the county. Through his efforts more than 1,100 registered dairy animals were eventually placed on black and minority farms in 40 counties throughout North Carolina.

In 1940 John W. Jeffries was appointed District Agricultural Agent and was later promoted to Assistant State Agent. In May 1951 the United States Department of Agriculture honored Jeffries with its Superior Service Award for outstanding contributions to the Agricultural Extension Program in North Carolina.

During the 1950s Jeffries became active in the nascent civil rights movement, primarily through his organization and sponsorship of local voter registration drives. Shortly after retiring from his position as Assistant

State Agricultural Agent in 1960, in an effort to promote racial harmony and dialogue in the community, he organized the Alamance County Committee on Civic Affairs. He remained an active member of this organization until illness forced him to reduce his activities in the early 1970s. In 1970 Jeffries was named Alamance County Father of the Year. He died in 1974 and is buried at Martin's Chapel near his ancestral farm.

B. EVERETT JORDAN

Benjamin Everett Jordan was born on September 8, 1896 in Ramseur, North Carolina. He was the son of Annie Elizabeth (Sellars) Jordan and the Reverend Henry Harrison Jordan, a circuit riding Methodist minister. At the age of 18, in 1914, B. E. Jordan entered Trinity College (now Duke University), but within a year he dropped out, and, at the invitation of his uncle, Fred Sellers, Everett moved to Wellington, Kansas, a country town in the flatlands of the Wheat Belt. There he worked selling watches and fitting glasses at his uncle's jewelry store.

In 1918, near the close of World War I, Jordan was drafted and assigned to Casual Company A, Tank Corps, of the American Expeditionary Forces. He was later reassigned to the 819th Motor Transport Company and spent most of his military career as a private with the occupation forces in Germany.

Following his brief military service, Jordan returned to his former employment in Kansas, but within a short time he was persuaded to return to North Carolina, where he took a position as floor sweeper at Myrtle Textile Mill in Gastonia. From this humble beginning during the next seven years Jordan received a series of promotions and by 1927 he was superintendent of Gastonia's Myrtle Mill and Gray Manufacturing Company. During these years Jordan had ample opportunity to observe and study the dynamics of a cotton mill and its employees. Working with both labor and management, he became acquainted with

B. Everett Jordan

all factors involved in running a mill.

While working in Gastonia he met Katherine Augusta McLean (1898-1987), whom he married on November 29, 1924. Their partnership was such that it was said that "Mrs. Jordan contributed more to her husband's total success than anyone…. Always she stood at his side and was his constant companion." Within less than two years of marriage the couple's first son, B. F. Jordan, Jr. was born on July 18, 1926. The couple was later blessed with two additional children: Rose Ann and John McLean.

In 1927 Jordan's uncle, Charles V. Sellers, a Burlington merchant, and other members of the Sellers family purchased the bankrupt White-Williamson Company and its associated mill property and village located at Saxapahaw. Charlie Sellers then hired B. F. Jordan as secretary-treasurer and general manager of the mill, which was reorganized as Sellers Manufacturing Company. Within months several of Jordan's former employees at the Gastonia mills moved to Saxapahaw to work with their former boss. Once in Saxapahaw they continued a milling tradition that had begun there as early as 1844 when John Newlin and his sons

James and Jonathan established the first textile mill on the site. By 1930 Sellers Manufacturing began production of mercerized cotton. The company later expanded into the manufacture of synthetic fibers including blended yarns. These yarns were incorporated into products sold nationally by such chains as Sears and JC Penney.

By 1938 B. Everett Jordan became the major stockholder in the Saxapahaw mill, controlling 52.3 percent of shares. As principal heir of Charles Sellers, who died in 1941, Jordan's absolute control of the Saxapahaw mills was consolidated. The company also grew exponentially: what had begun in 1927 as a single operation in Saxapahaw with less than 10,000 spindles grew by the 1960s to a business with plants in Cedar Falls and Wake Forest with a combined 75,000 spindles operated by nearly 1,000 employees.

As the mill prospered, Jordan became active in local politics, bolstered in part by his friendships with local business leaders Clyde Gordon, Reid Maynard, M. B. Smith, and others. In April 1958 Jordan was appointed by Governor Luther Hodges to fill the unexpired term of the late United States Senator Kerr Scott. Jordan then successfully ran for re-election in 1958, 1960 and 1966. During these years he chaired the Senate Committee on Rules and Administration, as well as the Joint Committee on the Library of Congress, the Joint Committee on Printing and the Joint Committee on Inaugural Ceremonies. He also served on the Agricultural and Forestry Committee and the Public Works Committee and gained a reputation as a good "behind the scenes worker", an effective and shrewd deal-maker, and a good politician and pragmatic statesman—a "peoples' senator."

Throughout his extraordinary life Jordan moved easily from the halls of power in Washington to his roots in his home community. From 1927 until his death he remained an active member of the Saxapahaw United Methodist Church. He was chairman of the Board of Trustees of the Alamance County Hospital and was a member of the Burlington Rotary and Shriners Clubs. He organized Boy Scout Troop 65, served as its first chairman, and remained on the troop's committee until his death. In addition to underwriting a scholarship program for Troop 65's Eagle Scouts, he built the scouts a cabin on Saxapahaw Lake and personally financed the new dining hall at the Cherokee Scout Reservation. In 1966 he was the recipient of the Silver Beaver Award, the highest honor given to a volunteer for outstanding service to scouting. From 1943 to 1971 Jordan was an active member of the Board of Trustees of Duke University, from which he received an honorary LL.D. degree on March 1, 1974.

Days later, on March 15, 1974 Senator B. Everett Jordan died at his home in Saxapahaw. In tribute to the man from Saxapahaw, the largest congregation ever assembled at the Saxapahaw Methodist Church included leaders of local and national prominence, mill workers and friends from the community—the "ordinary folks" who counted Jordan as neighbor and friend.

THE KERNOLDE FAMILY

Ancestors of the Kernodle family of Alamance County arrived in the colonies from Germany in 1750 aboard a ship called *Two Brothers*. Through more than 250 years the family has been associated with the political and historical life of the community and is intimately connected to the development of medical services in the region.

In the nineteenth century Josiah and Jane (Cummings) Kernodle became parents of eight sons, three of whom were local physicians: Dr. Franklin Kernodle (1853-1934); Dr. George Washington Kernodle (1857-1937); and Dr. James Loftin Kernodle (1869-1933). Another son, Robert Thomas Kernodle (1855-1938), served as sheriff of Alamance County from 1894 until 1906, and sat two terms (1916, 1917) in the North Carolina House of Representatives.

In 1896, a cousin, George Albert Kernodle, married Lillian Belle Long, daughter of Reverend Albert Long, a minister, scholar, and teacher, who was president of Graham Normal School (later Graham Institute and the forerunner of present Elon University). Together with George Colclough and Staley Cook, Mrs. Lillian (Long) Kernodle was instrumental in obtaining recognition (in 1952) of Alamance Battleground as a state historic site. She was an active member of the Daughters of the American Revolution at the local and state levels and eventually served as Vice President General of the national DAR.

John Robert Kernodle, the youngest child of G. A. and Lillian Kernodle, graduated from Elon College and Duke Medical School with a specialty in obstetrics and gynecology. In 1949, Dr. John Robert Kernodle and his cousins, Dr. Harold B. Kernodle, Sr., and Dr. Charles E. Kernodle, Jr., founded Kernodle Clinic, which came to be known as one of the most modern and best-equipped facilities of its kind in the south.

In 1995 Kernodle Clinic moved to a state-of-the-art 75,000 square foot medical facility located on the campus of Alamance Regional Medial Center. Today, Kernodle Clinic is a multi-specialty group practice with more than fifty associated physicians working in fifteen areas of specialty medical practice, including echocardiography, nuclear imaging, ultra- sound, and peripheral vascular imaging. The clinic also maintains three satellite facilities located in east Burlington, Mebane and Elon.

THE KIVETTE SISTERS

For more than fifty years Florence Olga Kivette Childress and Camille Kivette were fixtures on the Alamance County social scene in which they attended nearly every social, athletic, or cultural event held in the county. With their fur coats and matching muffs the Kivette sisters attended virtually every Elon College football and basketball game, theatre production and museum event, always arriving in their vintage 1965 baby blue Cadillac.

The daughters of Mr. and Mrs. P. L. Childress of Gibsonville, the "girls" were also well-known in their hometown, where they led the annual Christmas and Independence Day parades. They attended all sorts of community events, whether they were invited or not. "They were legends back when I came to Elon in 1945," says friend Jo Watts Williams. Florence Olga, who majored in English, graduated from Elon in 1937, followed by sister Camille in 1947.

For at least forty years the Kivette Sisters hosted one of the area's largest annual Christmas parties. They spent weeks decorating the family's Southern Colonial home. Several hundred guests would gather at "the big house," as the sisters liked to call it, and their guests included business leaders, local politicians, governors and congressmen, as well as NASCAR driver Richard Petty and the merely curious. The party was so popular the sisters never bothered sending invitations to the standing room only event where locks of their "papa's hair" were prominently displayed in a silver epergne.

Some sense of the Kivette phenomenon may be gathered from the following society page article concerning the wedding of Florence Olga quoted from a June 16, 1965 edition of the *Greensboro Record*:

Gibsonville Gala-According to Camille Kivette while describing the wedding of sister Florence Olga to Clifton Childress on June 6: "It was the biggest thing that has happened to Gibsonville since the train wreck 20 years ago!"

The fairy tale romance has not only left the local community in a happy state, but the Kivette family as well, and a recent inspection of the family home revealed that even though the wedding is over Lohengrin lingers on. Still on display are the wedding gifts bestowed upon the couple by a multitude of well-wishers, among which are complete sets of breakfast china, dinner china, silver, crystal, and a ton of finely embroidered linen

The Kivette sisters.

that represents hours of patience and love in the making.

"We might leave these out all summer," beamed the happy bride. But the bridegroom acceded (with a note of warm authority) "Well, dear, you may leave yours on display, but I think I might start to use mine pretty soon."

It would seem that a new house to hold the wedding gifts might be next on the agenda, but with only Camille and their mother, Mrs. P. L. Kivette, left at the home place they rather need the newlyweds about, and, as everyone knows, there is plenty of room for all.

Clifton himself said, "I married all three of them and now I have a real family of my own....." We've never seen a more radiant bride than Florence Olga, and she's the ONLY bride we've ever known who liked her bridesmaids gowns so well that she bought an identical one for herself. She also has one of the silver charm bracelets which she presented to the bridesmaids. Attached to it is a polished silver heart with appropriate initials and the wedding date inscribed. Mama Kivette has one too, and all three "Kivette girls" were wearing their wedding charms when we saw them earlier in the week.

"We'll just have to throw these flowers out," explained Florence Olga, as she pointed to the dried, but still exquisitely arranged flower appointments that were used, as well as the bouquets of the bride and maid of honor. But she's going to keep them as long as she can so that friends who didn't make it to the wedding can still visualize the big day.

Camille caught the wedding bouquet, and she's next in line for a wedding. She thought she wanted an Air Force man but thinks a Navy man might do as well—she'd better wait awhile, however, because Gibsonville just can't take another speck of excitement anytime soon."

The inseparable sisters remained active in the Alamance County social scene until their health declined in the late 1990s when Florence Olga died. Camille currently resides at Blakely Hall in Elon.

JOHN LAWSON

John Lawson (1674-1711), eighteenth century explorer, surveyor and naturalist, was author of *A New Voyage to Carolina* (1709), the only book to come out of proprietary North Carolina. Lawson's book has been described as "the best travel diary of the early eighteenth century colonies and the most inclusive account of the manners and customs of the Indian tribes of that day." The book also includes detailed descriptions of the flora and fauna of the Carolinas, as well as discussions of the natural geography of the region.

Little is known of Lawson's early life, although he appears to have been a native of London and the only son of Dr. John Lawson (b. 1632) and Isabella (Love) Lawson. As a young man Lawson may have attended lectures at London's Gresham College, where he became an associate of James Petiver, the famed English botanist and apothecary; the Sloan Collection of the British Museum currently includes about thirty specimens collected by Lawson for Petiver.

Self-described as an "educated gentleman" Lawson tells us that in 1700, while making preparations to travel to Rome for the Pope's Jubilee, he met a man "who had been abroad" and fueled his imagination with the possibilities of adventure in the New World. On May 1, 1700 he sailed from Cowes, England, and, after a stormy voyage lasting about three months, he arrived off Sandy Hook (New York) and then traveled by sea to Charleston, South Carolina. Nothing is known of Lawson's sojourn in Charleston until December 1700, when he was appointed by the Lords Proprietors to make a reconnaissance survey of the Carolina interior.

On December 28, 1700 Lawson and five other Englishmen, three Indian men, and the wife of the Indian guide left Charleston in a large canoe. They entered the mouth of the Santee River on January 3, 1701. Traveling northwest, the party eventually reached the area known as Health Springs near present-day Great Falls, South Carolina, and on January 20 crossed into what is now North Carolina, where they soon encountered Catawba and Saponi Indians. Near the present-day city of Charlotte the group connected with the famous Indian trading path, and on February seventh, Lawson crossed the Haw River at a ford near what is now the Alamance County town of Swepsonville. On Sunday, February 8 at about 3:00 p.m. Lawson reached "Achonechy Town" on the Eno River, where the party was fed venison and bear meat and given lodging in the "King's cabin." Here they acquired a new Indian guide, called "Enoe-Will", who was said to be a Shakori Indian and "chief man of all the land extending east to the Hau River." Lawson describes Enoe-Will as "of the best and most agreeable Temper that I ever met within an Indian."

Enoe-Will then guided Lawson's party east along the Neuse River to the Tar River; ultimately, on February 23, he delivered the explorers to the English settlers on "Pampicough River" (Pamlico River) near present Washington, N.C. In 59 days Lawson had covered almost 600 miles following a horseshoe-shaped course from the South Carolina coast, through the North Carolina Piedmont, and eastward to the North Carolina coast with only the aid of Indian guides. During this period he managed to keep an extensive journal, making daily notes on the topography, flora, and fauna, and he began a vocabulary of Indian words.

Following this remarkable journey in the spring of 1701 Lawson constructed a dwelling for himself on a tributary of the Neuse River; to this day the tributary is known as Lawson's Creek. In 1705 he was hired to survey the town of Bath, the oldest incorporated town in North Carolina; there Lawson acquired two building lots and eventually constructed a second home where he seems to have set up housekeeping with a woman by the name of Hannah Smith. In 1707 the couple had a daughter, who was named Isabella, after Lawson's mother. During this period Lawson also served as Clerk of Court of Pamlico Precinct.

On April 28, 1708 John Lawson was appointed Surveyor General of the province of Carolina by the Lords Proprietors. One year later he returned to England in order to oversee the publication of his book; during this period he also published a map of Carolina. In 1710 he returned to North Carolina accompanied by a group of three hundred Palatine immigrants to be settled along the North Carolina coast. Their settlement—surveyed and planned by Lawson—came to be the town of New Bern. One year later, in 1711, while traveling on the Neuse River, Lawson was captured by a party of Tuscarora Indians, by whom he was tortured and killed somewhere along Contentnea Creek near the present town of Grifton, (Pitt County, N.C.).

J. SPENCER LOVE

In March 1999, from a list of the 20 most influential business figures in the history of North Carolina, the publication *Business North Carolina* named J. Spencer Love (1896-1962) as the state's premiere leader. In so doing *Business North Carolina* stated that "Love was responsible for an unparalleled textile corporation in the creation of Burlington Industries...he did so as a fierce competitor, taking awesome risks, diversifying, and investing heavily in new technology."

James Spencer Love, son of James Lee Love and Julia (Spencer) Love was born July 6, 1896 in Cambridge, Massachusetts. He graduated with an A.B. degree from Harvard in 1917 and served in France on the headquarters staff of the 78th Division, U. S. Infantry during World War I. Following his

J. Spencer Love.

army service, at the age of twenty-seven, Love came to Gaston County, North Carolina, where his father's Scots-Irish Presbyterian relatives had deep roots and were early textile mill owners.

In 1919 Love joined his paternal relatives in the Gastonia Cotton Manufacturing Company (1887), where he initially served as paymaster. Within months Love and his father purchased full ownership of the struggling mill, and the younger Love was named secretary/treasurer. In 1922 he married Sara Elizabeth Love, by whom he would father four children: James Spencer, Jr.; Robert Lee; Richard; and Julian.

The Depression-era collapse of the Holt textile empire in Alamance County proved fortuitous for Love. In 1923 the town fathers of Burlington offered Love a $250,000 loan, underwritten by the chamber of commerce, to revitalize the area's flagging mill industry. After liquidating the Gastonia Cotton Mill, Spencer Love moved much of his equipment to Burlington, consolidating several of the old Holt mills, and began production of rayon bedspreads in the county's old cotton mills. Within a year the business expanded, and by 1929 Burlington Mills boasted a New York sales office in anticipation of domestic and international demand for his products. By 1937 Spencer Love had incorporated 22 textile plants into the Burlington Mills Corporation. On September 26, 1941 Love married Dorothy Ann Beattie, by whom he had no children.

At the outbreak of World War II Love

Period drawing depicting the death by torture of John Lawson following his capture by Tuscarora Indians in 1711.

NORTH CAROLINA COLLECTION: UNIVERSITY OF NORTH CAROLINA AT CHAPEL HILL.

was appointed director of the National Bureau of Textiles, Clothing and Leather Goods of the War Production board. One year later, in July 1944, he married Martha Eskridge of Shelby, N.C., by whom he had four children: Charles E., Martha E., Cornelia Spencer, and Lela Porter Love.

By the early 1950s Burlington Mills entered into a phase of major diversification. In addition to their signature rayon bedspreads the company produced parachutes, ribbons, hosiery, carpeting, and an astounding variety of fabrics for use in clothing and home decor products. In 1955 Love changed the Burlington Mills imprimatur to "Burlington Industries," reflecting the widening scope of his company's activities.

Spencer Love died on January 20, 1962 while vacationing in Palm Beach, Florida. By that time Burlington Industries was the largest textile company in the world and the forty-eighth largest United States corporation. The company had become an international conglomerate with plants in eighteen states and seven foreign countries. Today, the Love School of Business at Elon University is named in honor of Martha and J. Spencer Love.

B. V. AND W. H. MAY

Benjamin Victor May was born on January 30, 1880, on Beaver Creek in southern Alamance County. He was the third of four sons of Henry P. and Barbara Catherine (Clapp) May. As a youth he attended Shoffner Schoolhouse and the Whitsett Academy. Following schooling May worked for a time at the Van Lindley Plant Nursery of Greensboro as a traveling fruit tree and nursery stock salesman. From this early work experience he saved nearly $5,000, which he then used to invest in the textile business.

At the age of 20, and using his saved earnings, in 1900 Ben May purchased the bankrupt stock of the late W. C. Thurston, whose failing Daisey Hosiery (1896) was located on Church Street in Burlington. There May became partner with his brother, W. H. May (b. 1875), in the develop-

ment of May Hosiery Mills. The mill's physical plant was eventually located on South Main Street, Burlington, where it subsequently became the main plant of the May-McEwen-Kaiser Corporation. For a number of years the company produced men's hosiery under the "B. V. May" trademark. These quality socks came to be recognized around the world for their comfort and durability. In 1948 the corporation became a division of Burlington Industries.

Throughout their textile careers, the May brothers enjoyed an enviable reputation as businessmen of the highest caliber. Their capabilities, their integrity, and their ever-active interests in progressive new ideas were outstanding. During World War II, when the government requisitioned the nation's supply of silk for use in the manufacture of parachutes, the May brothers were some of the first textile manufacturers in the south to promote and use new synthetics, such as nylon and orlon.

Will and Ben May were also said to be the perfect pair to be in business together. Will was president of the company and Ben served as treasurer and salesman/promoter of their products. In fact, it was said that Ben May was "one of the best salesmen in North Carolina," because of his charm and outgoing personality.

On August 23, 1927, B. V. May married Louise O'Neal Simpson (b. 1901) of Chester County, South Carolina. The couple had four children: Barbara (b. 1929); Louise (b. 1930); Ann Elizabeth (b.

The May Brothers with their mother, Barbara Catherine (Clapp) May. B.V. May is seated on the left side of the photo; W.H. May is seated to the right.

COLLECTION: ALAMANCE COUNTY HISTORICAL MUSEUM.

1937); and Benjamin Victor, Jr. (b. 1937). Ben May died on February 27, 1945, of a pulmonary embolism; he was survived by his brother, W. H. May, who died in 1954.

JOHN ALOYSIUS "JACK" MCKEON

Jack McKeon, baseball player and major league manager, was born November 23, 1930 in South Amboy, New Jersey. His father, Aloysius Joseph ("Bill") McKeon, operated a taxi livery and towing service, and at age 20, the elder McKeon became the youngest Ford automobile dealer in the country.

A standout baseball player during his high school years, Jack McKeon received an athletic scholarship to attend Holy Cross, but before graduating he signed with the Pirates baseball team at $215 a month. During summers he continued taking college courses at Seton Hall. In 1949 he entered spring training in New Orleans, and was eventually assigned to a Class D team in Greensville, Alabama. By 1953 he was playing Class B baseball in Burlington, North Carolina, where he met and married his wife, Carol Jean Isley. During this period McKeon attended Elon College, where he also helped to coach the baseball and basketball teams.

By 1959 McKeon's playing career was effectively ended and he began to contemplate a career in baseball management. His first managerial contract was with the Missoula Montana Timberjacks. Three years later, in 1961, he was named manager of the Triple-A Vancouver Mounties, and, during off-season winter months, he also managed several clubs in Puerto Rico. During the late 1960s and early 1970s McKeon managed several major league teams, including the Kansas City Royals and the Oakland A's.

In 1979 McKeon was named assistant general manager of the San Diego Padres, where he developed a lasting friendship with Ray and Joan Kroc, founders of McDonald's and owners of the Padres. Initially McKeon's primary responsibilities were for scouting

John Aloysius "Jack" McKeon.

and trading (hence his nickname, "Trader Jack"), but by 1984 he served as Padres general manager and took the team to win the National League pennant. McKeon's managerial career was capped in 2003 when he came out of retirement to lead the Florida Marlins to a World Series victory. McKeon was named National League Manager of the Year in 1994 and 2003.

When Jack McKeon retired after the 2005 season at age 74, he was the third oldest manager in major league history, behind only Connie Mack and Casey Stengel. Jack and Carol McKeon currently reside in Elon. The couple has four children: Kristi, Kori, Kelly and Kasey.

BENJAMIN FRANKLIN MEBANE

Benjamin Franklin Mebane (1823-1884), physician and manufacturer of a widely used patent medicine, was born at Mason Hall near the town of Mebane. He was the son of George A. and Otelia (Yancey) Mebane. As a boy he attended the famed Caldwell Institute, and in 1847 he graduated from the University of North Carolina, where his senior honors paper discussed the effects of climate on health. In 1850 he received a medical degree from the University of Pennsylvania.

Mebane then established a successful medical practice at Mason Hall, where he treated wounded soldiers during the Civil War. Shortly after the war he patented a medicine that was produced in nearby Mebanesville: the Taraxcum Company sold its "Taraxcum Compound" throughout the United States. The medicine was described as a vegetable tonic and was prepared from dried dandelion roots. Mebane advertised that it "cures and prevents indigestion and dyspepsia."

A Democrat, Mebane represented Alamance County in the General Assembly from 1879 to 1880, and in 1881 he was elected to one term in the state senate. In 1857 Mebane married Frances Lavinia Kerr of Caswell County, by whom he had five children.

The oldest of these children, Benjamin Franklin Mebane, Jr. (1865-1926), married in 1893 Lily Connally Morehead, the granddaughter of Governor John Motley Morehead. B. Frank Mebane became a successful textile industrialist and served as president of the Leaksville Cotton and Woolen Mill and the Spray Water Power and Land Company, and came to own six additional textile mills by 1911. In 1912 these mills were purchased by the Marshall Field Corporation of Chicago and later, in 1953, they became a part of Fieldcrest, Incorporated.

At his death in 1926 B. Frank Mebane, Jr. was described as a "multimillionaire and one of the largest landowners in North Carolina." He died suddenly in New York City while awaiting the sailing of the *Aquitania* for England.

GILES MEBANE

Giles Mebane was born on January 25, 1809 near the Mill Creek community in eastern Alamance County. The scion of an illustrious political family, Giles was the third generation of Mebanes to become a North Carolina statesman. His grandfather, Alexander Mebane, Jr. (1744-1795) served as a local justice of the peace and sheriff of Orange County, and was a member of the Provincial Council that met at Halifax in 1776 to form a constitution for the state. From 1787 to 1792 Alexander was a member of the House of Commons and the N. C. General Assembly. During this period he also assisted in laying out the village of Chapel Hill, and helped to found the University of North Carolina, which opened in 1795. In 1793, during George Washington's first term as President, Alexander Mebane was elected a member of the U. S. Congress, where he served two sessions. He died July 5, 1795.

James Mebane (b. 1774), Alexander's son and the father of Giles, graduated from the University of North Carolina, where he distinguished himself as first president of the Dialectic Society. James was a member of the General Assembly of North Carolina for four terms (1798; 1808; 1821; 1828), and served as Speaker of the House from 1821 to 1823. He died in 1857 at the age of 83.

Family tradition states that Giles Mebane received his earliest instruction from his father, James. As a teenager Giles attended Mt. Repose Classical School, located less than two miles from his boyhood home, where he was prepared for university by the Reverend William Bingham. Giles graduated from the University of North Carolina in 1832, and, for several years thereafter, he read law in Hillsborough under Chief Justice Thomas Ruffin. Five years after graduating, on March 8, 1837, Giles married Mary Catherine Yancey, a daughter of Senator Bartlett Yancey of Caswell County.

Early in life Giles became interested in promoting industrial progress in North Carolina. As a young man of nineteen, in August of 1828, Giles traveled to the home of William Albright, where he attended the first public meeting in the state to promote the building of a railway. Some years later, in 1835, Mebane joined the Whig Party (because, he said, "Whig means progress"), and, as a Whig candidate he was elected to the North Carolina House of Commons in 1844, 1846, and 1848. During this period he worked tirelessly in the legislature for authorization of a state railroad system. In 1849 Mebane

Giles Mebane

was appointed a director of the North Carolina Railroad, a position he held until 1871. When the rail lines finally reached the Piedmont in the early 1850s Giles Mebane took a contract for grading that part of the road running from what is today the Orange County line to the town of Haw River. This area came to be known as Mebanesville, in honor of Alexander, James, and Giles Mebane, a name it retained until 1881 when the town of Mebane was formally incorporated and the "ville" suffix was dropped.

During his years in the House of Commons representing Orange County, Giles Mebane served with Colonel John Stockard, a local Democrat. During the 1848 and 1850 sessions, these two political rivals began to discuss the possibilities of dividing Orange County into two smaller counties. And while Giles Mebane was initially not very enthusiastic about the proposed division, he eventually acceded to the Stockard plan, and it was actually Giles Mebane who introduced the division bill in the House. The bill, captioned "An Act to Lay Off and Establish a New County by the Name of Alamance" was ratified on Thursday, April 19, 1849. The name "Alamance" for the newly separated portion of Orange County was suggested by Giles Mebane's wife, Mary Catherine Yancey Mebane.

Prior to formation of the new county, John Stockard headed a committee to select a site for the proposed county seat

that would be as close to the geographical center of the county as possible. The actual name of the new county seat was suggested by Giles Mebane, in honor of his close friend and political ally, William A. Graham, then governor of North Carolina.

In March 1861 more than 1,000 citizens of Alamance County overflowed the new Graham courthouse to address the question of succession. Arguments from states righters and federalists were heard—pro and con—and a vote was finally taken: 1,116 to secede versus 284 against. Giles Mebane was chosen to take the secession vote to the State Secession Convention held on May 20, 1861.

In the fall of 1865, a few months after surrender, Giles and Mary Catherine Mebane moved to her family land in Caswell County. For a number of years while living in Caswell Giles served as chairman of the county court system, and, in 1879, when the Twentieth Senatorial District was composed of Alamance, Orange and Caswell, Giles was elected state senator and speaker of the senate. He was then the oldest man in the General Assembly. Giles lived another twenty years. He died at the age of 90 on June 3, 1899 at the home of his daughter, Mary Catherine (Mebane) Holt (Mrs. Banks Holt) in Graham, North Carolina.

WASHINGTON IRVING AND VIOLA (COVINGTON) MORRIS

Washington Irving Morris was born in Reidsville, North Carolina on April 9, 1912. As a boy he lived in the home of his paternal grandparents, Bragg and Annie (Mitchell) Morris, and worked in the tobacco fields of Rockingham County.

After graduating from Reidsville's Booker T. Washington High School, Morris enrolled at the Agricultural and Technical State College, where he served as president of the student body during his senior year. On June 8, 1937 he married Viola Covington (1913-1993) of Southern Pines, and on August 8, 1940

the couple moved to Alamance County, where W. I. Morris became principal of Pleasant Grove Negro High School. While serving as principal he took summer courses at Harvard University and later earned his master's degree in High School Administration from New York University. After many years as a public school administrator in Alamance County, Morris was eventually named Director of Placement and Associate Professor in Elementary and High School Administration at his alma mater, A&T State University; he held this position for twenty years.

Noted for his interest in social activism, Morris was a founder of the Alamance County Committee on Civic Affairs and served as chairman of the Alamance County Human Relations Council. He organized and chartered the Alamance County Senior Democrats, and, over the years he held numerous offices within the Baptist Church Association.

In 1956 Morris helped to organize the Gentleman's Club, a social organization comprised of prominent black professionals and community leaders, many of whom worked in the community to remove racial barriers and improve the lives of minority citizens. Today, more than fifty years after its founding, the club remains strong, and its current membership includes such community leaders as Orlanda C. Blount, Charles C. Maye, Dr. Kary Dodd, Barry L. Alston, Dow M. Spaulding, Blairton S. Hampton, Johnny A. Freeman, Christopher Watkins, Early Kenan, Gary B. Bailey, Dr. Earnest Eason, Anthony Foriest and John A. Peterson, Jr.

In November 1966 Morris was honored by the National Association of African-American Baptists as their "Man of the Year." The award recognized Morris' service to the Baptist Church and his longstanding contributions to the civic, educational, and political life of North Carolina. The award was presented to W. I. Morris by Dr. Martin Luther King, Jr., who also served as keynote speaker for the occasion.

Viola, Gladys-Marie, and W. I. Morris.

Over the years many service awards also came to Mrs. Viola Morris, who taught in the Alamance County School System for 31 years. This public recognition culminated on May 4, 1984, when Mrs. Morris received the National Volunteer of the Year Award presented by the American Association of Negro Business and Professional Women's Clubs. The award enabled Mrs. Morris to travel to Senegal, Africa in August 1984, capping a life-long dream to visit that continent. Following several years of declining health, she died in 1993.

W. I. Morris survived his wife by seven years and died in 2000. He and Mrs. Morris are buried in the new Jeffries Cross Cemetery located on Highway 62 in northern Alamance County.

ARCHIBALD DEBOW MURPHEY

Born in 1777, Archibald DeBow Murphey was one of seven children of Archibald and Jane (DeBow) Murphey of Caswell County. His childhood years were spent at the family's five hundred acre plantation on Hyco Creek, located about two miles from Red House Presbyterian Church in Caswell. Murphey received his early education at Dr. David Caldwell's famous classical school in Guilford County, and he enrolled in 1796 in the second class of the newly created University of North Carolina, whereupon he graduated with distinction in July 1799. One year later he was named

Professor of Ancient Languages at the University; records indicate that he taught Latin and Greek languages and literature, English grammar, and 'Belles-Lettres.'

On November 5, 1801, Murphey married Jane Armistead Scott of Hawfields, having previously purchased the former Scott plantation, known as "The Hermitage"; the plantation was located on the bend of Alamance Creek, just north of its juncture with the Haw River. The newly married couple took residency at "The Hermitage" on Tuesday, November 5, 1801. That same year Murphey also began to read law in Hillsborough, N. C. under the tutelage of William Duffy, one of the state's leading judicial scholars. By May 1802 Murphey made his first court appearances as a lawyer.

As his law practice expanded, over the next twelve years Murphey set about building up The Hermitage, which became a showplace of the region. By 1812 the plantation consisted of more than 2,000 acres and included a grist mill, saw mill, distillery, a general store, and Murphey's law office, which was furnished with a personal library of more than 2,000 volumes. In 1807 Murphey also purchased the 1,650-acre Lenox Castle estate located near Caswell; the estate consisted of a tavern and a well-known nineteenth century spa known as 'Rockingham Mineral Springs,' said to be "the most popular summer resort in the state."

As one of the state's most esteemed lawyers, Murphey also came to be responsible for training many young men in the legal profession. Among these were Saunders Donoho and Bartlett Yancey of Caswell, John R. Donnell (later Judge of Superior Court), James T. Morehead, William Bingham, Jonathan Worth (later governor of the state) and Thomas Ruffin (Justice of the Supreme Court of North Carolina). Murphey's expertise in the law also led to an interest in politics. In 1812, at the age of 35, Murphey was elected state senator, a position he held until 1818, when, at the age of 42, he became Judge of the Superior Court.

While state senator in 1815 Murphey

set in motion a program of internal state improvements that he believed would contribute to the economic development of North Carolina. As a member of the Board of Internal Improvement in the summer of 1819 Murphey drafted a pamphlet entitled "Memoir on the Internal Improvement Contemplated by the Legislature of North Carolina and on the Resources and Finances of the State." The report proposed improvements to the navigability of six principal rivers in the state and called for the creation of a series of interconnecting roadways that would foreshadow the vast network of modern highways which now cover North Carolina.

Although Murphey's program for internal improvements to the state's riverine system was only modestly realized, his greatest contribution to the development of North Carolina lay in the field of public education. On November 29, 1817 Murphey submitted to the legislature a detailed plan which called for the funding of public instruction, the creation of a state school board, and the organization of a state-wide system of primary schools and academies. The plan also established a standardized curriculum and a method of instruction based on the "Lancaster System" utilized in England. Murphey's proposal also included provisions for the education of poor children at public expense and the development of a state-run asylum for the "deaf and dumb."

While Murphey's plan was not immediately adopted by the legislature, it made education a matter of continuing concern within the Assembly for years to come. It led to the eventual passage of the Free School Act of 1839, as well as the ratification of the so-called Cherry Bill, which effectively divided counties into free public school districts. Not until January 8, 1848 was an act passed providing for education of the state's visually handicapped and hearing-impaired children.

Following a brilliant career as Judge of the Superior Court Murphey resigned from the bench on July 22, 1820. Murphey's resignation was due, in part, to his growing indebtedness, disagreements with creditors, and to the general Financial Panic of 1819. His financial difficulties also led to the sale in 1821 of "The Hermitage" to Thomas Ruffin, his former law student and the husband of his wife's niece. "The sale of The Hermitage marked a turning point in Murphey's career. After that the popularity which he had enjoyed throughout the state faded, and his influence in State affairs declined never to be regained" (Turner, 1971:142).

Murphey's personal distress over the loss of his estate was publically compounded in 1829 when he was sent to debtor's prison in Guilford County for a period of twenty days. Upon his release Murphey was virtually penniless, suffering from rheumatoid arthritis, and his personal property was reduced to a single slave, "Bridget," portraits of various family members, and a small portion of his once vast library. Murphey died on February 1, 1832 in a rented house in Hillsborough. At the time he was engaged in writing a history of North Carolina, which was never completed.

On his deathbed Murphey expressed a wish to be buried at his old estate, "The Hermitage", beside his wife Jane who was buried there in 1829. Due to winter weather conditions and bad roads, Murphey's body was interred in a cemetery of the Presbyterian Church in Hillsborough.

The monument which marks Murphey's resting place in Hillsborough was not erected until 1895. His granddaughter, Mary Elizabeth Carter Worth, was concerned that no suitable marker had been erected to his memory; and on her golden wedding anniversary, June 26, 1895, she let it be known that she wanted gold pieces. Forty-five members of her family, including children and grandchildren, were present, and they presented her with more than three hundred dollars in gold. It was with this money that the monument was erected. It is now shaded by a large magnolia tree and has a square

base which supports a granite shaft ten feet tall. The engravings on the sides of the base tell briefly of the contributions which he made; to the University; as State Senator and Judge; as advocate of Public Schools and Internal Improvement; and as explorer of North Carolina History. (Ibid.: 217)

DONNA HILL OLIVER

Donna Oliver (b. 1950), educator, is the daughter of Clarence J. and Annie P. Hill and a native of Burlington, North Carolina, where she graduated from Walter Williams High School in 1968. In 1972 she received an A.B. degree in biology from Elon University, followed by a master's degree in education from the University of North Carolina at Greensboro in 1978; she received a Ph.D. in curriculum and teaching from UNC-G in 1995. Oliver also holds an M.S. degree in education administration from North Carolina A&T State University (1987) and completed the Institute for Educational Management Program at Harvard University in the summer of 2004. She is a member of the Kappa Delta Pi Education Honor Society.

In 1986, while teaching biology for the Burlington City School System, Oliver was named North Carolina Teacher of the Year. One year later, in 1987, having been selected from America's 2.5 million K-12 teachers, Oliver was recognized as the National Teacher of the Year. The award was presented at an Oval Office ceremony hosted by President Ronald Reagan. That same year Oliver was honored as the first recipient of Elon University's "African American Young Alumnus of the Year" award, and was also recognized by Howard University as an "Outstanding African American Woman of Achievement."

From 1989 to 1991 Oliver served as Associate Professor of Education at Elon University. In 1991 she was named Director of Teacher Education at Bennett College in Greensboro, N.C., where she later served as Chair of the Department of Curriculum and Instruction (1966-97). In 2001 she was

named Vice President for Academic Affairs at Bennett College, a position she held until June 2007 when she was named Provost of Edward Waters College in Jacksonville, Florida. Edward Waters College is Florida's oldest independent institution of higher learning and the first institution established for the higher education of African Americans in the state of Florida. Oliver was named the sixth president of Mississippi Valley State University in October 2008.

In 2004 Oliver was listed in the "Who's Who in American Education" section of the 6th edition of The Chronicles of Human Achievement. She has also been profiled in the Chronicles of Higher Education (1995). Oliver has conducted numerous workshops on diversity training and pedagogy, and is the author of "Multiculturalizing Teacher Education," published in *Teaching About Diversity* by the North Carolina Council for Social Studies.

She is married to James Oliver. The couple has one daughter, Rachel Oliver, who, in 1986, was named "Miss Black America."

WYATT OUTLAW

The murder of Wyatt Outlaw in 1870 has been viewed by historians as "second only to the Battle of Alamance as the most widely recognized event in the county's history." While the violence and tragedy of the man's death and its repercussions at the local and state level have been widely discussed; the circumstances of Outlaw's private life are more obscure.

Recent research by Carole Troxler (1999) and others (Scott Nelson, 2001) suggests that Wyatt Outlaw was born in the Jordan Creek area, Faucette Township, of northern Alamance County. Census records from 1870 indicate that Outlaw was born in 1820. Nineteenth century public opinion held that Outlaw was the illegitimate son of wealthy merchant and plantation owner Chesley Faucett(e) (born 1792) who, at the age of 28, sired the boy by a slave woman named Jemimah (Phillips). Little is known of Wyatt Outlaw's early life although it appears that he may have been raised in the household of Nancy Outlaw, a white landowner whose 100-acre farm on Jordan Creek was sometimes referred to as the "Faucett place."

In December of 1863 the 43-year old Outlaw appears to have traveled to eastern Virginia, where he joined the Second Regiment, United States Colored Cavalry. Records indicate that Outlaw fought in the Battles of Swift Creek and Fort Darling and was involved in fighting at Petersburg and Richmond. The 2nd Regiment also saw action in Texas.

Upon returning to Alamance County at the close of the Civil War Outlaw rented a building in Graham, N.C. from Will Albright, a former pro-Union member of the so-called "Red Strings", a secret organization formed in central North Carolina to help local men evade conscription and assist Union prisoners in escaping across battle lines. Outlaw lived in the rented structure, together with his mother, and he operated a portion of the building as a cabinet-making and wagon repair shop. A portion of the building also seems to have been used as a barroom.

It was in this shop in Graham that Outlaw also organized the Alamance County chapter of the Loyal Republican League (sometimes referred to as the Union League). The League functioned to encourage Republican voter registration and was also actively involved in efforts to create a school and church for former slaves. These activities seem to have come to the attention of Governor William Holden who, in an effort to establish a stable Reconstruction Republican political constituency, appointed Outlaw as a commissioner of the town of Graham. Such appointments were also expected to dampen the activities of local conservative Democrats, many of whom were involved in secret organizations such as the White Brotherhood and were implicated in local activities targeting former slaves, carpetbaggers, and "scallywags."

Outlaw and other local Republican officials quickly responded to local Klan violence by establishing patrols and a curfew and by giving authority to former slaves such as Caswell Holt to enforce curfew regulations. By the latter part of 1869 armed Republicans, black and white, guarded the streets of Graham and stopped people traveling at night. To support the patrol, Governor Holden sent militiamen and detectives into Graham, an uncomfortable reminder for many local residents of the activities of the North Carolina Home Guard during the conscription years of the war.

By 1870 Klansmen escalated their attacks on Republican leaders, both black and white. These events culminated on the evening of Saturday, February 26, 1870 when a group of armed men broke into the shop of Wyatt Outlaw, dragged him to the nearby courthouse, where he was hanged from a large elm tree located on the courthouse square. The body was intentionally left hanging in the square until the next morning so that Sunday churchgoers would see the evidence of Klan violence; in fact, local Klansmen threatened to kill anyone who removed the body and they openly discussed additional lynchings of Republican sympathizers.

On March 7, 1870 these provocations led Governor Holden to declare Alamance County in a state of insurrection and to institute martial law in the immediate vicinity. These actions resulted in the so-called "Kirk-Holden War," during which time many Klan perpetrators were arrested and imprisoned in the nearby Caswell County seat of Yanceyville. Through these actions Governor Holden himself came to be labeled as a radical by the old conservative power structure, and, on December 14, 1870 impeachment charges were brought against him. Holden was formally removed from office on March 22, 1871.

Interestingly the story of Wyatt Outlaw became the primary plot of a fictionalized but thinly veiled account incorporated in the novel *Bricks Without Straw* (1880) by Albion Tourgee. Tourgee, who settled in Greensboro after the Civil War, was the judge who recorded most of the depositions concerning Outlaw's death.

CHARLIE POOLE

Charles Cleveland Poole was born on March 22, 1892 in Randolph County. The lives of Charlie Poole and his parents, John Philip Poole and Bettie Ellen Johnson Poole, were interwoven with the growth of the Piedmont North Carolina textile industry. During the 1920s and '30s Poole would become a leader and style-setter for one of the richest pockets of country music centering in the textile communities of Leaksville-Draper-Spray (now Eden, Randolph County) and the Haw River area of Alamance County. Of the hundreds of string band musicians who recorded in this 'Golden Age' of country music, Charlie Poole stands out as a larger-than-life figure. Known as 'The North Carolina Rambler,' Poole's country tunes were later recorded by such luminaries as Roy Acuff, Bill Monroe and Ralph Stanley, and his unique three-finger banjo style contributed to the development of modern bluegrass.

From 1900 until 1919 Charlie Poole lived in Haw River, N. C., where, as a child, he worked as a doffer in the Granite Mill. The Poole family lived in a flea and bed-bug infested company owned house. ("The fleas held me down while the chinches crept around", *Hungry Hash House*). By an early age Poole and his brothers gained a reputation for rough and rowdy behavior. In 1913, for example, the Poole brothers hijacked a streetcar which ran between Haw River and Burlington, and, over the years, the boys were jailed numerous times in Burlington, Gibsonville and Haw River for fighting and public disturbances. As a result of this unruly behavior Poole could convincingly sing such lines as:

"Gonna buy me a razor, gonna scrape the blade, Gonna lay some son-of-a-gun in the shade," (*Coon from Tennessee*).

Charlie Poole

On February 24, 1912, at the age of 19, Charlie Poole married 17-year old Maude Gibson. The couple moved in with Maude's parents, and Charlie continued working as a doffer in the spinning room of the Granite Cotton Mill. Although Poole enjoyed a good reputation as a spinner, he was increasingly drawn from work by the lure of music and a good time. His constant ramblings and his penchant for liquor caused his wife to seek a divorce, which was granted just 10 months after the couple's marriage. During this period Poole's only child, James Clay Poole, was born on December 2, 1912.

Sometime during the winter of 1918, while traveling in West Virginia, Poole met a crippled young fiddle player named Posey Rorer. On December 11, 1920 Poole married Posey's sister, Lou Emma Rorer, and shortly thereafter he began to work in the textile mills of Spray. Charlie Poole and Posey Rorer were soon joined by guitar players Will and Norman Woodlieff and Clarence Foust, and the group began calling themselves 'The North Carolina Ramblers.' Poole's unique banjo style, coupled with his treble-toned singing, served as the perfect complement to these talented instrumentalists, and by 1924 The Ramblers were making show trips throughout the southeast.

In 1925 Poole, Rorer and Norman Woodlieff traveled to New York to audition for Columbia Records. On July 27, 1925 The Ramblers recorded four songs including the famous tunes *Don't Let our Deal Go Down Blues* and *Can I Sleep in Your Barn Tonight, Mister?* Their first two-sided release proved to be a smash hit and sold over 100,000 copies at a time when record sales of 5,000 were considered a success. Additional recordings released in 1926 included the now-famous *Hungry Hash House* and *Budded Rose* and solidified the group's reputation. With such superb musicians as Lonnie Austin, Odell Smith, and Ray Harvey, the North Carolina Ramblers became one of the best-loved and most eagerly followed of all the old-time string bands. Their recordings of *There'll Come a Time*, *If the River Was Whiskey*, and *White House Blues* are the stuff of legend and have now become staples of the bluegrass songbook.

On the night of May 21, 1931 Charlie Poole suffered a fatal heart attack in Spray. Earlier he had summed up his life and career by saying he had lived "high, wide and handsome" for thirty-nine years.

THOMAS EDWARD POWELL, JR.

Thomas Edward Powell, Jr., was born in Warrenton, North Carolina, on July 6, 1899. He was the only son, along with four sisters, of Thomas Edward Powell, Sr., and Clara Morton (Bobbitt) Powell. The country house in which he was born had been built around 1740 and had passed into the Powell family through John B. Powell, his grandfather, who had inherited a sizeable plantation from Dick Davis in 1832. Thomas Edward Powell, Sr., received one-ninth of the farm, about 140 acres, but this was the poorest portion on which to raise crops. The Powells had a difficult time growing cotton, tobacco, and other crops, and the only son quickly learned to work hard plowing the fields, milking cows, chopping wood, and doing other chores.

By the time the young Powell was in high school, he knew he wanted to leave the farm and pursue an education. His principal at Macon High School had been one of the first graduates from Elon College and encouraged him to attend there. Starting at Elon College in 1915, Dr. Powell studied geology under Professor Randolph and received his A.B. degree in 1919.

Along with several other Elon students, he interrupted his studies to serve his country during World War I. He traveled to Plattsburgh, New York, and became a member of Company F, where he was commissioned as a Second Lieutenant and served on active duty from September 17 to December 17, 1918. He served in the Army Reserve, beginning in 1923, and was promoted to first lieutenant and then captain of infantry with the 81st Division of the 321st Regiment. He resigned his commission in 1935.

When he returned to Elon College after the army, Dr. Powell discovered that Professor Randolph had resigned and moved to Texas, leaving no one to teach the geology laboratory courses. During his senior year he took over the laboratory classes in geology, and he later accepted a full-time faculty position beginning in the fall of 1919.

One of his exceptionally bright students, Sophia Maude Sharpe, caught the young teacher's eye and they were married in 1922. This was a very busy time, for in addition to starting a family, helping to lay out many of the roads in Alamance County, and teaching biology and geology at Elon, Dr. Powell decided he must continue his education if he wanted to succeed. Subsequently, he received his A.M. degree from the University of North Carolina in 1923 and completed the Ph.D. in Biology at Duke University in 1930. Dr. Powell was ranked as a full Professor when he left Elon College in 1936.

Dr. Powell's marriage with Sophia Maude Sharpe, who died in 1944, was blessed with four children: Sophia Maude (Powell) Wolfe (Mrs. A. E. Wolfe); Dr. Thomas Edward Powell, III; John Sharpe Powell; and Dr. James Bobbitt Powell.

In 1945, Dr. Powell married Annabelle Council, a school teacher in Elon. They also were blessed with four children: William Council Powell; Joseph Eugene Powell; Dr. Samuel Christopher Powell; and Dr. Annabelle Council Powell.

While teaching at Elon, Dr. Powell frequently made trips to nearby fields and ponds to gather specimens for his biology classes. Often he would collect more than he needed and supply the extra materials to his colleagues. Gradually he realized that other teachers were devoting a large part of their time to gathering specimens—time that would be better spent in the classroom. From this realization sprang the birth of a company whose goal was "not to get rich quick but to build a company that provided services to the biologists throughout the country."

Dr. Powell started Carolina Biological Supply Company on a part-time basis in 1927 while teaching. His first laboratory was a small shed beside a pond in Elon College. From this humble beginning, and under Dr. Powell's full-time guidance after 1936, Carolina Biological Supply Company has grown to become the largest biological supply house in the world. The Burlington plant includes approximately 140 acres and 12 main buildings. Powell Laboratories in Gladstone, Oregon, collection stations in Maine, Texas, and Louisiana, and the Warren County farm are all part of the supply network that reaches out to customers throughout the United States and around the world.

Although there is no doubt that Dr. Powell was the inspiration behind the company, he was always quick to give credit to others. When his first wife died in 1944 and the company was still struggling, his sister, Miss Caroline E. Powell, gave up her career as a biology teacher in Raleigh to move to Elon and care for the Powell children. "Miss Caroline," as she was affectionately called, worked by her brother's side and became a partner in the company in 1944. When the organization was incorporated in 1947, she became secretary.

Dr. Powell was a member of the Elon College Community Church. He served on the Alamance County Board of Education from 1934 to 1961 and was President of the North Carolina School Board Association from 1943 to 1945. He received many prestigious honors and degrees, but his most satisfying reward was perhaps the growth of Carolina Biological and the contribution that he, his family, and the company have made to educational institutions. Dr. Powell died in December 1987.

Powell's success and his contributions to the community have been mirrored by the accomplishments of his offspring. Over the years a number Powell's children and grandchildren have become involved in various company subsidiaries. Granite Diagnostics, with a lab in Burlington and a 1,500-acre animal facility in Mecklenburg County, Virginia, produce sterile blood media for medical and educational laboratories. Bobbitt Laboratories manufactures plastic teaching models and electronics, and Wolfe Sales imports microscopes and related supplies for classroom use. Omni Resources imports maps from around the world and produces geologic teaching supplies. Warren Laboratories in Warrentown, North Carolina, includes 2,500 acres of land devoted to production of genetic corn.

In 1969 three of Dr. Thomas E. Powell Jr's sons—James, Edward and John—together with Ernest A. Knesel, Jr. formed Biomedical Laboratories (later Biomedical Reference Laboratories), a medical diagnostic testing firm. The firm was initially located in the former Rainey Hospital building on Rainey Street. In 1982, the company was one of the three testing labs the Hoffman-LaRoche

Company united to form Roche Biomedical Laboratories, which by 1989 was one of the four largest medical testing labs in the nation. During the early 1980s, the corporate headquarters was located on a 60-acre tract on York Road between Burlington and Elon College.

In 1984 the company acquired the former Kayser-Roth office building on Maple Avenue in downtown Burlington, which was used as the company's financial and billing facility. Subsequently, Roche Biomedical Laboratories also acquired the former Federal Building and extended operations into other downtown structures including the old JC Penney building, the former First Federal Savings and Loan building, and Rose's. The company's major acquisition was the 1929 Atlantic Bank and Trust tower, which had previously been occupied by Security National Bank and NCNB. The multistoried building became the company's headquarters and the centerpiece of a major corporate campus in downtown Burlington.

In 1996 Roche-Biomedical Laboratories substantially completed an operational consolidation it undertook on April 28, 1995, when the company merged with National Health Laboratories Holding, Inc. The newly merged company, known as Laboratory Corporation of America (LabCorp), resulted in the formation of the nation's largest reference laboratory for molecular diagnostic testing. LabCorp currently offers more than 1,700 different clinical trials, from routine blood analysis to more sophisticated technologies. The $1.6 billion company performs diagnostic tests nationwide for physicians, managed care organizations, hospitals, and industrial companies. On August 5, 1997, the company announced that it was to become the first commercial reference laboratory to offer HIV genotyping using GeneChip DNA probe assays and trials based on polymerase chain reaction. AutoCyte, a laboratory founded by Dr. James Powell, M.D., concentrates on PAP smear diagnostics and their standardization.

Note: Portions of this article previously appeared in Alamance County: The Legacy of Its People and Places (1984): pp. 344-35, and Shuttle and Plow: A History of Alamance County, North Carolina (1999): pp. 392-93.

SARAH RHYNE

Sarah Barbara (Hambright) Rhyne was born November 2, 1912 in King's Mountain, N. C. A graduate of Brenau College in Gainesville, Georgia, with degrees in speech and dramatic arts, she was the wife of Myron A. Rhyne, a textile executive and former mayor of the city of Graham. In 1946 she and her husband moved to Graham where Sarah came to be known as the "First Lady of Graham" and "Mother of the Arts in Alamance County."

In the 1950s and 60s Sarah devoted her time and talent to the local branches of the United Way, the Parent Teacher Association, and the Girl Scouts of America. She served as President of the Alamance County Girl Scout Council from 1959 to 1961. During this period she also served on the Board of Directors of the Alamance County Health Department and was President of the Community Council from 1966 to 1968. She founded the Candy Striper Volunteer Program at Memorial Hospital of Alamance, and was director of that program for over four years, giving 6,000 volunteer hours in service to the hospital and its patients.

In the 1970s Mrs. Rhyne served on the Governor's Beautification Commission and began a campaign in March 1970 to clean up Alamance County. Her personal efforts to beautify Graham resulted in the organization of the Graham Appearance Commission, of which she served as Chairman for well over a decade. She also served as Chairman of the Graham Tree Board founded in 1980, and, through her diligence, Graham was named a Tree City USA. In 1977, due to the efforts of Sarah Rhyne, the Alamance County Historic Properties Commission was formed. She also sat on the original governing boards of the Alamance County Historical

Sarah Rhyne in an original portrait by local artist David Nance.

COLLECTION: ALAMANCE COUNTY ARTS COUNCIL.

Museum and the Graham Historic Properties Commission.

Mrs. Rhyne was instrumental in saving some of the most important architectural and historical landmarks in Alamance County and in preserving Alamance County's rich history of mills and houses related to textile magnate E. M. Holt and his descendants. In 1992, Mrs. Rhyne almost single-handedly convinced NationsBank (now Bank of America) executives not to demolish "Elmhurst," a significant 1898 Second Empire house belonging to the daughter of E. M. Holt. The house was adapted for re-use, and, in 1994, NationsBank won the L. Vincent Lowe Award from Preservation North Carolina for this project.

Sarah Rhyne had the vision forty years ago that the Glencoe Mill and Village, developed from 1880 to 1882 by two sons of E. M. Holt, was an extraordinary place which should be preserved. Over the years half ownership of the mill and village had come to Sarah and Myron Rhyne, and, under their influence, the mill and the houses were kept intact until 1995 when their portion of the property was donated to Preservation North Carolina. Today Mrs. Rhyne's preservation vision for the county—a restored mill village museum site—is a reality.

Partnering with many others in the community, Mrs. Rhyne was also able to

help save the Captain James White House, built in 1873. The Captain James and Emma Holt White House is now the home of the Alamance County Arts Council. Mrs. Rhyne and her sister Mary Helen Hambright Patrick gave generously to the restoration of the Captain White House, and the main exhibition galleries are named the "Sister Galleries" in their honor.

Over the years, Sarah won numerous awards for her good works. The awards include the Friends of the Arts award sponsored by the North Carolina Association of Arts Educations; Alamance County's Woman of the Year; The Order of the Long Leaf Pine presented by Governor Robert Scott; the first C. Fletcher Moore Leadership in the Arts Award by Elon University and the Alamance County Arts Council; Outstanding Volunteer Service Award by United Way; the Brenau College Community Service Award and the Gertrude S. Carraway Award of Merit presented in 1997 by Preservation North Carolina. She was honored by the citizens of Graham in October 1971 when the city celebrated Sarah Rhyne Day and by the citizens of Alamance County when the county's "Living Christmas Tree" was dedicated in her honor. Two scholarships are presented each year in Alamance County in honor of Sarah Rhyne: the Alamance County Arts Council's Sarah H. Rhyne Scholarship in the Performing Arts and Alamance Community College's Sarah Rhyne Art Endowment.

Rhyne died on July 10, 2007 having served her adopted community for over fifty years. She is survived by her daughter, Janet (Rhyne) Andrews.

JEANNE SWANNER ROBERTSON

Jeanne (Swanner) Robertson (b. September 21, 1943), nationally known professional speaker and humorist, is a native of Graham, North Carolina. In 1963, while representing her hometown she achieved the title "Miss North Carolina" in the state beauty pageant, and later that year she was named "Miss Congeniality" in the Miss America Pageant held in Atlantic City, New Jersey. At 6'2" she was the tallest contestant to ever compete in the Miss America Pageant, a distinction she holds over forty years later.

Using reality-based and regionally-flavored humor, Robertson has built a career and reached the top of her profession as a humorist and public speaker. In 1989 she received the Cavett Award, the highest honor presented by the National Speakers Association. In 1998 she became the first female professional speaker to receive "The Golden Gavel," the top award presented by Toastmasters International. She has been featured on the CBS television program *60 Minutes*, and is heard regularly on the XM Satellite Radio program Laugh USA and Radio Channel 151, the Family Comedy Channel.

In 2001 the North Carolina Press Association named Jeanne Robertson its "North Carolinian of the Year" for "her popularity on the speaking circuit, her award-winning ways, and her representation of North Carolina." The Miss North Carolina Organization named Jeanne its 2003 Woman of Achievement. Two years later *Southern Lady* magazine named Jeanne "Southern Lady of the Year 2005."

Jeanne is the author of several books and since 1998 has marketed her humor through CDs, videos, DVDs and audio tapes. On May 21, 2005 she was asked to deliver the Commencement address at Elon University's 115th Commencement Exercise, where she substituted for the Crown Prince of Jordan.

As might be expected, Robertson was elated at the prospect of speaking before more than 950 graduates of the institution where she also serves as a member of the Board of Trustees. As Don Bolden relates in a *Times-News* story of May 29, 2005:

She (Jeanne) was excited. So much so that she went on the Internet and did a search, typing in her name, Elon and

graduation. Much to her surprise there appeared a blog written by an Elon senior. She said the headline was "What were they thinking!" "Is this the best we can do?" Comments compared the choice to going from the president of the United States to the mayor of Burlington. The writer was just not happy with the choice. Jeanne didn't react until graduation day. It's tradition that President Leo Lambert and the speaker meet the graduates in the gym before the ceremony. After Dr. Lambert made his remarks, Jeanne had her turn. She made the writer of the blog stand up. Travis Lusk was reluctant at first, putting up his hand. Other students made him stand. Jeanne said she did this because "I wanted the people around Travis in line to remind him right after he went on stage that he should walk around the edge. I'm not above sticking my foot out and tripping a graduate."

Then she gave the mike back to Dr. Lambert and walked in front of the group looking for Travis. The place erupted. Travis stood again and climbed over an entire row and he and Jeanne met in the aisle-with a big hug. In the middle of Jeanne's speech at graduation, a train came by. She had to stop. So she pulled out a camera and shot pictures of the crowd. She said, "Maybe we can put these pictures on Travis Lusk's Web site." That might have been her biggest laugh. When Travis came by to get his diploma, she did not trip him. Instead he pointed to her and said "I love you, Jeanne," as he passed. Later, there was a new message on his Web site, which by the way, is a very good one, and the headline read "I stand corrected...I love you Jeanne." He told about his blog remarks and being called out by Jeanne in front of 1,000 people. Was he upset by that? No way. "It was all in good fun." And then he added, "Jeanne, I STAND CORRECTED. You were way more entertaining than the prince ever would have been. You were definitely everything you were slated to be. By far you were definitely cooler than the Prince. We really did get the Queen!""

Jeanne Swanner Robertson.

Recently, in 2008, as part of National Volunteer Week, Jeanne Robertson delivered the keynote address to White House Volunteers at a ceremony in the Executive Office Building adjacent to the White House.

Jeanne is married to Jerry Robertson. The couple lives in Burlington and they have one son.

THOMAS RUFFIN

Thomas Ruffin (1787-1870) was the son of Alice (Roane) Ruffin and Sterling Ruffin, a planter from Essex County, Virginia. He was born at "Newington," the plantation residence of his maternal grandfather, Thomas Roane, located in King and Queen County, Virginia.

As a youth Ruffin attended the classical academy operated by Marcus George in Warrenton, North Carolina, and in 1805 he graduated from the college of New Jersey (now Princeton University). In 1807 he completed law studies under Archibald Murphey and was admitted to the North Carolina Bar in 1808. On December 9, 1809, Ruffin married Anne Kirkland, a daughter of William Kirkland. The wedding took place at "Ayr Mount," the Kirkland mansion near Hillsborough, North Carolina.

Thomas Ruffin.

From 1813 until 1816 Thomas Ruffin served three terms in the North Carolina House of Commons. In 1816 he was elected by the legislature as superior court judge, and served as reporter of the state supreme court in 1820 and 1821. For one year, in 1828, Ruffin also served as president of the State Bank of North Carolina. In 1833 he became chief justice of the Supreme Court, a position he held until 1852.

Throughout his lifetime Thomas Ruffin maintained an extensive correspondence with his Virginia kinsman, Edmund Ruffin, on the development of scientific agricultural practices. Many of these practices were implemented at Ruffin's Alamance County plantation, known as the "Hermitage," which he acquired in 1821 from Archibald Murphey in payment for debt. The "Hermitage" has been described as one of the region's premiere plantations, and was located on the confluence of the Alamance Creek and Haw River in southern Alamance County. Ruffin's interest in agriculture led to his appointment as president of the State Agriculture Society, a position he held for almost fifteen years.

In February 1861, Ruffin served as North Carolina delegate to the Washington Peace Conference, which was called in an attempt to avert the Civil War. Although initially an ardent Unionist, Ruffin became a supporter of the Confederate cause once secession proved inevitable; on May 20, 1861 he was elected to the Secession Convention in Raleigh, where he spoke publically in favor of the war.

Throughout his career Ruffin maintained a law office and a second home in the town of Hillsborough. In 1825 he gave land in Hillsborough for the construction of St. Matthew's Episcopal Church, which was built on the exact site where Anne Kirkland accepted Ruffin's proposal for marriage in 1809.

Following the Civil War Thomas Ruffin lived primarily at his Hillsborough home, which now serves as municipal offices for the town. When Ruffin died in 1870, he was buried in the church yard of St. Matthew's. He was survived by his wife and thirteen of his fourteen children.

Thomas Ruffin is generally recognized as a pioneer in adapting English common law to the circumstances of America. One dean of the Harvard Law School has rated Ruffin as "one of the ten foremost jurists in the United States." Ruffin's opinions are characterized by clarity; they are wide-reaching and embrace almost every topic of civil and criminal law.

JAMES EDWIN SCOTT

James Edwin Scott (1859-1888), merchant and tobacco manufacturer, was born in Alamance County, the son of Robert W. Scott. He attended the Bingham School when it was under the direction of Major Robert Bingham and studied at the University of North Carolina during the period from 1877 to 1878. He was close to his brother, Robert W., and the two joined in several business ventures.

Scott briefly attended a business college in Poughkeepsie, N.Y., before opening a general store in Mebanesville (after 1883, Mebane). Because of the number of merchants already there, however, he became a salesman of fertilizer to farmers living along the Haw River. After several unwise business investments, Scott left Mebanesville for Philadelphia in 1880 and established a tobacco business. On June 8, 1881 he returned to North Carolina and founded a new tobacco firm that proved to be successful. His brother Robert, owner of the Alamance Stock Farm, at Melville, where he bred cows, horses and sheep, and his friend, Joseph A. Tate, a dealer in leaf tobacco in Hickory, became minor partners in the business. They formed Scott Brothers Merchants and Scott and Company, Manufacturers of Tobacco, with primary operations centered in Mebanesville.

To establish agents and buyers for his product, James E. Scott traveled to Chicago, Indianapolis, St. Louis, Cincinnati, Louisville, Memphis, Nashville, Vicksburg, Birmingham, New Orleans, Mobile, Montgomery, Atlanta, Buffalo, Toledo, Cleveland, Grand Rapids, Milwaukee, La Salle, Davenport, Burlington, Bloomington, and Springfield. He developed a strong market in those cities.

Scott was innovative in packaging his product. He sold tobacco in pouches that advertised his firm's name. With the purchase of a pound of "processed" tobacco, his customers received a free handmade pouch. Scott's wife and her friends in Mebanesville made the pouches, so the cost of production was countered by the savings on the paper pouches.

The business grew slowly but steadily and produced such chewing tobacco brands as *Alamance, Beauty Bright, Carolina, Della, Honest Sam, Josie, Mattie May, Melville Chief, Robina,* and *Rob Roy.* Smoking tobacco brands were *Old Bill* and *Tried and True.*

On September 15, 1885 Scott married Mary Belle, daughter of Dr. Benjamin Franklin and Frances Lavina Mebane of Mebane. They were the parents of a daughter, Margaret Graham, who married John Rumple Ross. After suffering poor health and an extended illness, Scott died at the age of twenty-nine.

—*F. Craig Willis*
Note: Originally published in Dictionary of North Carolina Biography, *William Stevens Powell, Ed., vol. 5, pp. 303-04, 1994.*

RALPH HENDERSON SCOTT

Ralph Henderson Scott (1903-1989), dairyman, political leader, and legislator, was born near Haw River in Alamance County, the son of Robert Walter and Elizabeth Jessie Hughes Scott. His brother, William Kerr Scott, and his nephew, Robert S. Scott, were governors of North Carolina during the years 1949 to 1953 and 1969 to 1973, respectively. A 1924 graduate of North Carolina State College, he owned and was president of Melville Dairy, Inc., a milk distributor in Burlington.

A Democrat, Scott served consecutive terms in the North Carolina House of Representatives between 1951 and 1956 and between 1961 and 1980; serving one term in the Senate, he was president pro tem in 1963. He was a member of such committees as Agriculture, Propositions and Grievances, Rules, Higher Education, Finance, Education, and Appropriations. At various times he held a seat on the Advisory Budget Commission and on the North Carolina Department of Human Resources' Council on Developmental Disabilities. In the General Assembly in 1953, Scott introduced the bill that created the State Milk Commission, and he was vocal in his opposition in the Speaker Ban bill. He was a member of or served in advisory and official capacities in numerous organizations, among which were those concerned with education, retarded citizens, agriculture, senior citizens, and health care.

As a relative of two governors, Scott worked effectively between the legislative and executive branches during their incumbency. He played significant behind-the-scenes roles in the resolution of a strike by food workers at the University of North

Hazeleene and Ralph Henderson Scott.

Carolina in Chapel Hill and in questions concerning the creation of a medical school at East Carolina University in Greenville. He was awarded an honorary doctorate by Elon College and received the North Carolina Award in 1981.

Scott married Hazeleene Tate of Alamance County in 1925, and they were the parents of a daughter, Mariam, and two sons, Ralph H., Jr., and William Clevenger. Scott was a Presbyterian and an active member of the Hawfields Church.

Note: Originally published in Dictionary of North Carolina Biography, *William Stevens Powell, ed., vol. 5, p. 304, 1994.*

ROBERT "BOB" W. SCOTT

Robert Walter Scott was born June 13, 1919, the son of Mary Elizabeth (White) and W. Kerr Scott, who served as governor of North Carolina from 1949 to 1953. He grew up in the Hawfields area of Alamance County, where he attended the local public schools. From 1947 to 1949 he was enrolled as a pre-medical student at Duke University, after which he transferred to North Carolina State College, where he earned a B.S. degree in animal husbandry in 1952.

On September 1, 1951 Scott married Jessie Rae Osborne (b. 1929) of Swepsonville, who had been his classmate at Alexander Wilson High School. A graduate of Woman's College of the University of North Carolina, she entered the teaching profession. Her later activities in Scott's gubernatorial campaign won the praise of the national Democratic party.

From 1953 to 1955 Bob Scott served as Special Agent, Counterintelligence Corps of the United States Army. Following military service Scott returned to Alamance County, where he became manager, and eventually the owner, of the 2,400-acre Melville Farms.

The veteran's interests were not confined to his own farm. He became a member of the Veterans of Foreign Wars, the Burlington-Alamance County Chamber of Commerce, the American Society of Farm Managers and Rural Appraisers, the Soil Conservation Society of America, the North Carolina Farm Bureau Federation and the North Carolina Literary and Historical Association. He served as Chairman of the United Forces for Education in North Carolina and, in 1957, he was chosen Alamance County "Young Farmer of the Year." In the same year, he also served as president of the North Carolina Society of Farm Managers and Rural Appraisers. In 1959, the Scotts were named the National Grange "Couple of the Year," and at the same time, "Farmer Bob" was named Master of the North Carolina State Grange, a post he held for two years. In 1964, he received the Haw River Junior Chamber of Commerce Distinguished Service Award.

Continuing to follow his ancestral footsteps, Scott became actively involved in political life. He served as Democratic Precinct Chairman, County Vice-Chairman and State Solicitorial District Executive Committee member, 1961-1964; member of the State Board of Conservation and Development, 1961-1964; member of the Kerr Reservoir Development Commission, 1962-1964; and member of the North Carolina Seashore Commission, from 1962 to 1964. His contribution in all these fields was recognized in 1964, when he was elected Lieutenant-governor of North Carolina on the Democratic Party ticket. His promotion of the functions of this office to an unprecedented degree led to it eventually becoming a full-time salaried position in the state government. His success in the

Robert "Bob" W. Scott and Jessie Rae Scott.

office also paved the way for him to be elected governor of the state in 1968, the youngest North Carolinian elected to that office in the twentieth century.

During his four-year term in office, Governor Scott's administration expanded and improved every phase of the state's governmental program. New industry was attracted, education was developed to a higher degree while student unrest was subdued, prison reforms begun, highway improvements increased, and the state's bureaucracy completely reorganized. Home rule for local government was promoted to such an extent that Scott was made a lifetime member of the North Carolina League of Municipalities, the first chief executive of the state to receive that distinction. In addition, planning for the future was greatly facilitated by the creation of the North Carolina Council on State Goals and Policy in 1971 by the General Assembly at the request of the governor. Recognition of his accomplishments included honorary degrees conferred upon the governor by the University of North Carolina, and by both Elon and Davidson Colleges.

After his gubernatorial term was concluded, Scott served from 1973 to 1975 as executive vice president of the Agribusiness Council of North Carolina. This was followed by serving, from 1977 to 1979, as federal co-chairman of the Appalachian Regional Commission, to which office he was appointed by President Jimmy Carter. In 1980, he unsuccessfully ran again for governor of

the state. On March 7, 1983, Scott became President of the Department of Community Colleges in North Carolina, by appointment of the State Board of Community Colleges.

Like all his family, Robert Walter Scott became a member of the Hawfields Presbyterian Church during his youth. In 1959, he was made one of its deacons, and in 1963, elected to the office of elder. He served from 1976 to 1977 as president of the North Carolina Presbyterian Historical Society, and in 1983, was elected Moderator of Orange Presbytery.

The Scotts have five children: twins Mary Ella and Margaret Rose (b. 1956); Susan Rae (b. 1957); William Kerr (b. 1958-2007); and Janet Louise (b. 1963).

Editor's note: Following several months of failing health, Governor Scott died on January 23, 2009.

Note: Portions of this entry were previously published by Durward Stokes in Alamance County: The Legacy of its People and Places, *Elinor Euliss, ed.,* Alamance County Historical Museum, 1984.

ROBERT WALTER SCOTT

Robert Walter Scott was born on July 24, 1861. He was one of nine children of Henderson and Margaret Graham Kerr Glass Scott, and received his education at the Hughes Academy in Cedar Grove, the Bingham School, and the University of North Carolina. On June 17, 1883 he married Elizabeth Hughes (1865-1914), with whom he had fourteen children.

While rearing this large family, Scott was associated briefly with the Henderson Scott Tobacco Factory, then devoted his energy successfully to becoming a master farmer, specializing in the raising of cows, sheep and hogs. Keenly aware of agricultural problems in the state, he championed the Farmers' Alliance, and in 1888 entered political life as a member of the Democratic Party on behalf of the Alliance program. As a result, he served in the State House of Representatives in both of its 1889 and 1891 sessions, representing Alamance County, and in the 1903 session, represented District 18 in the State Senate. While engaged in legislative affairs, Scott enthusiastically supported the North Carolina Agricultural and Mechanical College, which later became State College and is now a part of the State University, and served as a trustee of the institution from 1910 until 1915, and again from 1915 to 1927. The senator also played a significant role in the passage of Aycock's Education Bill through the General Assembly, and in founding and financing the Hawfields Public School.

In 1901, Governor Aycock appointed Scott to membership on the State Board of Agriculture, and he was reappointed to the position by each of the six succeeding governors. His special interest in the position was the chairmanship of the Board's Test Farm Committee, and he devoted his time generously to its function. By this time, he had become generally known throughout the state as "Farmer Bob Scott," and he was presented with a "Certificate of Merit" by State College as a tribute to his contribution to agriculture. He was also a leader in persuading his native Alamance County in 1911 to establish Farm Demonstration Work, which proved a continuing advantage to the county's economy. In 1927, State College and The Progressive Farmer joined in presenting him with the prestigious "Master Farmer Award." An additional tribute was

Robert Walter Scott

paid posthumously in 1952 to his meritorious promotion of agriculture and education when Scott Hall, a new building of the State College campus, was named for and dedicated to the memory of the Master Farmer.

Following family tradition, on May 8, 1888, Robert W. Scott formally joined the Hawfields Presbyterian Church. Four years later he was elected to the office of deacon, and in 1897 he was made a Ruling Elder. He served his church and denomination both locally and state-wide in numerous capacities, including membership on the Board of Trustees of Flora MacDonald College. In 1913, he led in the founding of the Hawfields Memorial Association, an organization to care for the growing cemetery, and in the purchase of the site of the original Hawfields church and cemetery, located at some distance from the present church, and to have the tract marked for historical purposes. On March 19, of the following year, Mrs. Scott died and was buried in the new church cemetery.

On December 29, 1915, Scott married Miss Ella Anderson, a member of one of the pioneer families in the area. She was affectionately known as "Miss Ella" before and after moving to her husband's Hawfields home. She died December 23, 1956, after outliving her husband twenty-seven years.

In 1918, "Farmer Bob" was again elected to the State Senate. He resigned his membership on the State Board of Agriculture in order to serve in only one public office at a time but was immediately appointed to the office again by Governor O. Max Gardner after the General Assembly adjourned. He held this office when he died a few weeks later, on May 16, 1929, and was buried in his beloved Hawfields Cemetery. Six of his sons served as active pall bearers at the funeral.

The occasion was noted in the local newspaper by the publication of a detailed obituary, which included the comment, "In the passing of Mr. Scott the career of one of the most useful and best citizens ever produced in Alamance County came to a close."

—*Durward T. Stokes.*
This article originally appeared in Alamance County: The Legacy of Its People and Places, *1984, pp.377-78.*

SAMUEL FLOYD SCOTT

Samuel Floyd Scott was born June 9, 1894, the seventh of fourteen children of Robert Walter and Elizabeth (Hughes) Scott. He grew up on his father's farm in the Hawfields community south of Mebane, N.C. and graduated from the University of North Carolina in 1915. He received an M.D. degree from the University of Pennsylvania in 1918 and returned to Alamance County on April 20, 1919. One of his brothers, Kerr Scott, served the state as governor (1949-1953) and was a U.S. Senator (1954-1958), while a second brother, Ralph Scott, served in the North Carolina Senate. Floyd's nephew, Robert, the son of Kerr Scott, served as lieutenant governor and governor of the state from 1969 to 1973.

In October 1921 Dr. Scott married Frances Somers of Caswell County, by whom he had five children. In many ways Dr. Scott was a typical country doctor, serving his patients for over half a century. During that time it is said that he delivered over 6,000 babies. In the early years his office was in his home in Union Ridge. Because communication with the people of the rural area was difficult, Dr. Scott installed a telephone system extending about five miles from his home office to the homes of various community residents. About 1954 he also installed a two-way radio in his car so that patients could reach him when he made house calls.

By 1949 Dr. Scott decided that he and his patients needed a clinic to better serve Union Ridge; his idea became a community project, and more than 200 residents of northern Alamance County helped with the construction of the new Scott

Samuel Floyd Scott

Clinic. Eventually, Dr. Floyd was joined at the clinic by two physician sons, Dr. Peter Somers Scott (b. 1924) and Dr. Samuel Edwin Scott (b. 1937), and, for a while, by a third son, Dr. Ludwig Gaston Scott, who received a D.D.S. degree from the University of North Carolina in 1954.

In 1954 Dr. Floyd Scott was named "Doctor of the Year" by the Alamance-Caswell Medical Society, and on April 20, 1969, he was honored for fifty years in the medical profession by the citizens of Union Ridge. He continued to practice until his death on June 5, 1972.

WILLIAM KERR SCOTT

William Kerr Scott (1896-1958), U.S. senator, North Carolina governor, and agricultural leader, was born at Haw River in Alamance County. He was the sixth of eleven children of Robert Walter and Elizabeth Josephine Hughes Scott. A farmer by profession, his father served in the North Carolina General Assembly and was a member of the State Board of Agriculture and a trustee of North Carolina State College. His mother died when Kerr (pronounced kar) was eighteen.

Scott attended Alamance County public schools, graduating from Hawfields High School in 1913. Four years later he received a B.S. degree in agriculture from North Carolina State College, where he excelled in track and debating.

William Kerr Scott

Following a brief stint as emergency food production agent for the U.S. Department of Agriculture, he enlisted as a private in the U.S. Army Field Artillery. Shortly after receiving his army discharge, Scott purchased 224 acres of land near his birthplace and began a lifelong career as a farmer. In 1920 he was elected master of the North Carolina State Grange. As master, he supported rural electrification during the early days of the Great Depression. From 1934 to 1936 he served as regional director for the Farm Debt Adjustment Program, Resettlement Administration.

Scott first ran for public office in 1936, when he waged a successful campaign for the post of North Carolina commissioner of agriculture, defeating incumbent William A. Graham. Serving for three terms, he led a successful effort to rid the state of Bang's disease, an ailment afflicting cattle. In 1938 the *Progressive Farmer*, a leading farm journal, named Scott "Man of the Year," citing his attempts to revitalize the State Department of Agriculture.

By 1948, when Scott resigned as commissioner of agriculture to seek the state's highest office, he had established a broad base of support among Tar Heel farmers. Placing second in a field of six candidates in the May Democratic primary, he requested a runoff against state treasurer Charles M. Johnson. Scott's advocacy of improved roads and his plea for ending the state's "deficit in services" resulted in his victory over Johnson in the 26 June runoff primary. In the November general election he easily defeated Republican candidate George M. Pritchard of Asheville, thus becoming the first farmer to be elected governor in the twentieth century.

In his January 6, 1949 inaugural address, Scott assigned top priority to road construction and improvement and public school construction. His effective leadership was a major factor in voter approval of a $200 million bond issue for construction of a secondary road system and a $25 million bond issue for expansion of public schools in a June 4, 1949 referendum. Both bond issues were major projects in Scott's "Go Forward" program, much of which was enacted into law by the 1949 General Assembly.

Scott's energetic leadership was directly responsible for expansion of electric and telephone service in the state's rural areas. During his term as governor, 21,000 miles of power lines were strung to homes occupied by almost 150,000 people.

At a time when racial segregation was firmly embedded in the state's social fabric, Governor Scott appointed the first black to serve on the State Board of Education and ordered elimination of salary discrimination against staff members at the mental hospital for blacks in Goldsboro. Moreover, recognizing the need to utilize the latent talents of North Carolina women, he appointed more women to state boards and commissions than any of his predecessors. Particularly significant was his selection of Miss Susie Sharp of Rockingham County as the first female superior court judge in the state's history.

Progressive measures proposed by Scott during his term included lowering the minimum voting age to eighteen, stricter enforcement of existing liquor laws and a statewide referendum on the question of liquor sales, stream pollution control, minimum wage legislation, and reinstatement of the 1947 motor vehicle inspection law repealed by the 1949 General Assembly.

When Senator J. Melville Broughton died in 1949, Scott appointed Consolidated University of North Carolina president Frank P. Graham to complete his unexpired term. Graham's defeat in his bid for a full Senate term in the 1950 Democratic primary diminished Scott's prestige and strengthened anti-Scott forces in the 1951 General Assembly.

When his gubernatorial term ended in January 1953, Scott returned to his Alamance farm; however, his retirement from public life lasted only a few months. A triumph over Wilmington attorney Alton Lennon in the May 29, 1954 Democratic primary assured Scott a seat in the U.S. Senate the following January. As a freshman senator, Scott spent the majority of his time listening and learning. On those few occasions when he did speak on the Senate floor, his remarks were invariably succinct. He served as a member of three Senate committees: Agriculture, Interior and Insular Affairs, and Public Works. On the latter committee he played a major role in the framing and enactment of legislation providing financing for the interstate highway network, then in its formative stage. Development of water resources and a more prosperous farm economy were goals he strove to achieve during his senatorial career.

His rural background, coupled with his daily custom of wearing a rose in his coat lapel, led one observer to describe Scott as "a jet-propelled plowboy with a rose in his lapel." During his entire public career "the Squire of Haw River," as he was affectionately called, played the political game to the hilt to accomplish goals he considered worthwhile. He knew how to trade a vote, honor a pledge, do a favor, and demand one in return, always with the public well-being as his ultimate objective.

Throughout his life Scott was a champion of the average man or, in his phrase, "the branchhead boys." Both as a governor and as a senator, his philosophy and programs reflected his years on country back roads with rural people. He felt equally at home making a college commencement address or milking a cow.

On July 2, 1919 Scott married Mary Elizabeth White, a childhood friend whom he called "Miss Mary" throughout his life. They had two sons, Robert and Osborne, and a daughter, Mary Kerr. Scott suffered a heart attack in April 1958 and was admitted to Alamance General Hospital, in Burlington, where he died. He was buried in the cemetery of the Hawfields Presbyterian Church near the graves of his parents and grandparents.

—F. Craig Willis

Note: Originally published in Dictionary of North Carolina Biography, *William Stevens Powell, ed., vol. 5, pp. 303-04, 1994.*

BENJAMIN ABEL SELLARS

Benjamin Abel Sellars (1816-1896) was the son of Thomas Sellars, Jr. (1782-1865) and Nancy (Rainey) Sellars (1795-1881), a sister of Rachel Rainey, who married Michael Holt, III. B. A. Sellars was born at the family home place located between Burlington and Hopedale. On March 4, 1844 he received a medical degree from Philadelphia's Jefferson Medical College of the University of Pennsylvania. Following medical school he returned to North Carolina and began a medical practice in Randolph County.

In 1850 Sellars married Frusannah Kime (1833-1922), who was not quite seventeen at the time of their marriage. For the next 22 years Dr. and Mrs. Sellars remained in Randolph County where Dr. Sellars continued his medical practice, serving patients in both Randolph and Guilford Counties. During this period the couple had ten children; an eleventh child was born after the couple moved to Alamance County.

In 1872 Dr. and Mrs. Sellars moved to Company Shops (Burlington) in Alamance County, where they built a home at the corner of Church and Front Streets. About the same time Dr. Sellars also built a 2,500 square foot wooden store on Front Street; initially, the store served as an apothecary and pharmacy, but over time the business expanded into selling seeds, piece goods, and hardware. By the 1880s the store was operated by the Sellars' eldest son, Benjamin Rainey Sellars (1855-1916), who eventually moved the business to Main Street, opposite Neese Jewelers. Over time the grocery and hardware supply business was dropped and the firm became a department store. The store is believed to have been the first business in Alamance County to employ women as clerks. In 1900 Miss Amelia Burch was hired as the first female clerk; later Miss Nerta Holt was hired as officer manager.

Over the years the business expanded and came to be known as B. A. Sellars and Sons. The size of the store's physical plant also increased, and it eventually came to have entrances fronting on three downtown Burlington streets, and for many years was the leading department store in the area. Later the business was moved to a strip shopping center near Holly Hill Mall. In 1998 the business closed after more than 126 years in business.

WILLIAM LUTHER SPOON

William Luther Spoon was born in southern Alamance County on March 18, 1862. He was the son of Nancy (Stafford) and George Mason Spoon, who died in the Civil War. The younger Spoon was raised by his widowed mother and attended Oakdale and Friendship Academies, and in 1882 he received his teacher's certification after passing the state teachers' examination. For the next four years he taught at Fairfield, a small community school located in southern Alamance County.

In 1886 Spoon entered Graham Institute (now Elon University) where it is said he traded a cow for his tuition. In 1891 he graduated at the age of twenty-nine with a degree in civil engineering. On July 7, 1897 he married Susan Addeline Vernon (1868-1936), by whom he had two children, Nancy Miriam and William Mozart.

After graduating college Spoon briefly taught school in Texas, but in 1890 he returned to North Carolina to become Supervisor of Roads for Alamance County. In 1893 he finalized and published the first of his well-known maps of the county; this map was later updated and reprinted in 1928. Spoon also prepared the North Carolina Mineral Exhibit for the Chicago World's Fair of 1893.

For much of his later life, W. L. Spoon worked for the United States Bureau of Public Roads, then a branch of the Department of Agriculture. He became an authority on the construction of sand-clay roads and supervised road building throughout much of the southern United States. He wrote numerous government publications on the subject and spoke frequently to explain the construction program to the public.

In the 1920s Spoon purchased Pilot Mountain, a noted Piedmont landmark. He then engineered the first road to the top of the pinnacle, a roadbed that is still in use today. During this period W. L. and Addie Spoon also adopted four children, John M., Annie, Mildred and Margaret Rush, the orphaned children of Mrs. Spoon's first cousin. In 1925 Spoon founded the engineering firm of Spoon and Lewis, based in Greensboro, North Carolina.

William Luther Spoon.

W.L. Spoon supervising highway construction in northern Alamance County.

COLLECTION: ALAMANCE COUNTY HISTORICAL MUSEUM.

Throughout Spoon's professional career he maintained close ties to Alamance County, where his farm, known as "Meadowlawn," became an area showplace. Locally he operated a grist and saw mill, as well as a wooden parts manufacturing shop, in partnership with a cousin, J. Everette Stafford. Spoon was a charter member of the E. M. Holt School Board and also served on the Alamance County Welfare Board.

Following the death of his first wife, Spoon married Ruth Baldwin on August 26, 1940. They were the parents of one daughter, Willie Ruth, born April 14, 1943. Mr. Spoon did not survive to see his last child. He died August 28, 1942 and is buried a few miles from "Meadowlawn Farm" at Mount Pleasant United Methodist Church.

SALLIE W. STOCKARD

Sallie Walker Stockard was born October 4, 1869 in the Cane Creek community of southern Alamance County. She was the eldest of six children of John Williamson Stockard and Margaret Ann Albright Stockard. At the age of 8 Stockard began her formal schooling at a one-room schoolhouse located near Spring Friends Meeting, but in 1881 she moved to the home of her maternal grandparents in Graham. There she excelled in the expanded curriculum offered by the Graham Graded School.

While living in Graham in the 1880s Stockard earned money as a seamstress making dresses for mill workers who were employed at Travora, Sydney, and Oneida textile mills. These earnings allowed her, at the age of 23 in 1892, to enter Guilford College. She graduated from Guilford in the spring of 1897.

In the fall of that year Sallie Stockard became the first of five women admitted to the University of North Carolina at Chapel Hill. Although already in possession of an A. B. degree from Guilford, she was entered at the university as a "senior." Stockard thus became, in 1897, the first female graduate of the university. Stockard continued post-graduate work at the University and, in 1900 she received an M.A. Her master's thesis dealt with Alamance County history. This thesis served as a basis for the publication of Stockard's first book, *The History of Alamance* (1900), which was also the first published volume wholly devoted to Alamance County's past.

During the 1902-1903 school year, Stockard continued her graduate studies at Clark University in Worcester, Massachusetts. While attending Clark she completed *The History of Guilford County* (1902), and in 1903 she published her first book of poetry entitled *The Lily of the Valley*. Following a move to Arkansas, in 1904, Stockard published her fourth book, *The History of Lawrence, Jackson, Independence and Stone Counties of the Third Judicial District of Arkansas*.

While living in Batesville, Arkansas Stockard married and gave birth to two children: Scott Albright Magness (November 26, 1906) and Ione Mona Lisa Magness (September 20, 1904). But in late 1909 Stockard separated from her husband, and within several years she resumed using her maiden name. She also moved with her two children, first to New Mexico and later to Texas, where she operated a series of small one-room schoolhouses. Her students were Native Americans, Hispanics, and the children of Texas pioneers. In 1919 she was employed as state normal examiner for the Texas Department of Education in Austin. About this period she stated, "I have fought ignorance and filth of all sorts on the western frontier."

In 1923 Stockard moved her family to New York City where she enrolled at

Sally W. Stockard.

Columbia University. Within a year she received a second master's degree and resumed teaching. She eventually established a permanent home in the Long Island community of West Hempstead, where she published a monthly newsletter and society page called *Golden-Fleece News Gleaner*. She died on Long Island on August 6, 1963 at the age of 93 and is buried in Greenfield Cemetery, Hempstead.

GEORGE WASHINGTON SWINNEY

George Washington Swinney was born in 1897 in the Blue Ridge Mountains of Floyd County, Virginia. When George was ten years old his father, Samuel Swinney, died, and George left the farmstead together with his widowed mother and five siblings when they sought work in the textile industry. In 1907, with only a third-grade education, George Swinney began working as a doffer, first in the textile mills of Schoolfield, Virginia, and later in Draper, North Carolina. In 1920 the Swinneys moved to Greensboro, where George worked in the Pomona Cotton Mill. One year later he married Etta Gay Dalton, an orphan who was also a native of Floyd County, Virginia and fellow Pomona Mill employee.

In May 1923 the couple attended a local tent revival where Swinney was converted in a dramatic fashion. Within weeks the couple was baptized in Rock Creek, and they began attending Pomona Baptist Church where George served as a janitor, usher and Sunday school teacher. By 1927 Swinney felt a call to the ministry, and, on September 13, 1927 he and a group of Pomona Church congregants visited the Piedmont Heights section of Burlington adjacent to Spencer Love's Pioneer Plant. While there Swinney delivered a fiery extemporaneous sermon entitled, "Prepare to Meet Thy God." The result was electric, and almost immediately Swinney was called to the pastorship of the newly formed Glen Hope Baptist congregation.

Because Glen Hope was initially unable to provide a salary or a parsonage, Swinney

and his wife continued to live in Greensboro for the first three years of his pastorship, and he continued working weekdays at Pomona Mill. Each Sunday Swinney took a bus from Greensboro to downtown Burlington and the couple walked five miles to the village in time for the services. Finally, in February 1930, Burlington Mills donated the use of a mill house for the family, and the Swinneys moved to Piedmont Heights. The congregation began paying the preacher twenty-five dollars a week. In 1931 the first brick building housing Glen Hope Church was built on a lot donated by Burlington Mills.

From the onset Preacher Swinney established a special rapport with his congregation and the mill community from which it was drawn. He understood firsthand the working conditions of his congregants, their family life, and the pleasures and perils of their amusements, and he exhorted his church members to wrestle with sin and subdue it. To Preacher Swinney the rough life of the mill village was a challenge to his call, and he took as his primary task the redemption of the Piedmont Heights community, which was sometimes called "Little Chicago" because of its rough and tough reputation.

The impact of Swinney's presence in the village was palpable, and by the mid-1930s Piedmont Heights was a changed place. Mill owner Spencer Love soon took notice and began to support Swinney's work. Burlington Mills paid the church's electric bill for many years, the company donated an enlarged parsonage, and in 1949, when fire destroyed the church, Spencer Love helped Glen Hope to rebuild. Love's support of the church and Swinney's ministry was such that it was said that church members "put more faith in Spencer Love than God's love."

Swinney exhorted not only from his own pulpit but also from tents, tabernacles, and pulpits throughout the state. He was one of the first ministers to take to the airwaves, and he broadcast a weekly radio sermon heard throughout the Southeast. His popularity as a radio minister led to invitations to preach at revivals throughout North

George Washington Swinney.

Carolina, as well as in Virginia, Tennessee, Georgia, and South Carolina; for several years he spent as much as 40 weeks on the road traveling with his own musicians and choir. He preached a fiery theology in which the soul lay in mortal danger through the ever-present nature of temptation and sin.

Swinney continued to preach at Glen Hope until a heart attack at the age of 76 forced him to retire from the pulpit. He died on January 14, 1977. His forty-year pastorate was remarkable for he was able "to combine both the stability of a traditional denomination and the fervor of the sects. Together he and the villagers of Piedmont Heights built an institution that fulfilled their spiritual desires and became the polestar of the community" (Hall, et. al., 1987: 288).

SPENCER THOMAS

Spencer Thomas, minister and master tinsmith, was born about 1840 in Wake County. He was a slave of Romulus Mitchell Saunders (1791-1867), a nineteenth century judge and member of the House of Representatives who was also a director of the N.C. Railroad and served as U.S. Ambassador to Spain (1846-1850). Spencer Thomas' early life was spent at Elmwood Plantation in Raleigh and at Saunders' Caswell County home located near Milton, N.C.

The Reverend Spencer Thomas.
COLLECTION: JULIE JORDAN.

Around 1856, when Spencer Thomas was about sixteen, he was hired out by Saunders to work at Company Shops. Thomas performed various tasks for the North Carolina Railroad and over time came to be recognized as a master tinsmith and foundry man. Shortly after Emancipation Thomas opened his own foundry and tin shop, which became the first black-owned business in Company Shops (now Burlington).

In 1864, Thomas began an association with the Reverend Jesse Sumner and Elder Walter Hayden, two black ministers from Greensboro, N.C. Shortly thereafter Thomas was baptized and the three men founded the First Baptist Church (1864/1865) of Company Shops. Originally located in a log building on what is now Church Street, the congregation later moved to Fonville Street, and finally, to its present location on Apple Street. Spencer Thomas served as pastor of this congregation from 1870 to 1896. Over the years Reverend Thomas also founded five additional Baptist churches: one in Graham, N.C.; two in Guilford County; and two in Rockingham County.

In the 1880s Thomas became an active member of the Democratic party, and in 1885 he was selected as a local delegate, together with Jesse Sumner and Walter Hayden, to attend the inauguration of President Grover Cleveland. The three black ministers traveled to Washington with three white local representatives: Captain George A. Mebane, Dr. G. W. Horn, and T. P. Moore. Commenting on the group, the *Gleaner* newspaper of March 5, 1885 stated: "If three preachers, one doctor, and a captain can't represent us all right we will be 'left'."

Throughout his life Reverend Thomas promoted the value of education within the black community. He is credited with helping a number of early black teachers trained at the local Springdale Academy to achieve partial wage parity with their white counterparts.

Reverend Thomas was married twice. By his first wife, Mary, who was born a slave in Virginia, he had eleven children. There was no issue from his second marriage to Millie Thomas. Reverend Thomas died on November 21, 1912, and was buried in the African-American cemetery located near present South Church Street. When the town of Burlington grew to the west, the cemetery was removed, and Reverend Thomas' body was exhumed; his remains now rest at Rest Haven Cemetery on Glencoe Road.

JOE THOMPSON

Born December 9, 1918, in Orange County, North Carolina, Joe Thompson grew up in a family where fiddle and banjo music was heard on nights and weekends after farm work was completed. Joe's father and uncle played fiddle and banjo and were sought after by neighbors, both African-American and white, to provide music for local square dances. As soon as Joe took up the fiddle, he was included in the music-making along with his brother, Nate, and cousin, Odell. On many a Saturday night during his youth, Joe would find himself positioned with his fiddle in a doorway between two rooms that had been cleared of furniture to accommodate couples dancing four- and eight-hand sets.

Thompson modeled his music on his father's playing, which came from a fiddle and banjo ensemble tradition in North Carolina. The African roots of the banjo in America are well established and some evidence supports a theory that African fiddling traditions existed side-by-side with traditions from the British Isles. However fiddle and banjo ensemble playing originated, a common repertory was created in African-American and mixed-race communities in the South during the nineteenth century. Some of the tunes, such as *Georgia Buck* and *Hook and Line* have become standards among Southern fiddlers and banjo players. Joe Thompson plays these pieces as well as tunes that are not heard widely today, such as *Pumpkin Pie*, *Riro's House*, and *Dona Got a Rambling Mind*.

Thompson has received many honors since the 1970s, when he began performing his music outside of his home community. He and Odell Thompson were the recipients of the North Carolina Folk Heritage Award in 1991. Joe and Odell performed at Carnegie Hall, at the Festival of American Fiddle Tunes, the National Folk Festival, the Tennessee Banjo Institute, and the International Music Festival in Brisbane, Australia. Joe, Odell, and Nate are documented in Alan Lomax's American Patchwork film series. In 1989 Joe and Odell recorded *Old-Time Music from the North Carolina Piedmont* for Global Village Music and Joe was featured on *Family Tradition*, released by Rounder Records in 2000. His music is also included on *Black Banjo Songsters of North Carolina and Virginia* and *Backroads to Cold Mountain*, anthologies issued by Smithsonian Folkways. In 2007 Joe Thompson was recipient of the National Folk Heritage Award given by the National Endowment for the Arts. He currently resides in Mebane, N.C.

Note: Portions of this article originally appeared in Kennedy Center's "Millennium State Artist Details."

EFFIE MURRAY WHITE

Effie (Murray) White was born September 30, 1880 on the former Andrew Murray Plantation located in the Cross Roads Community of northern Alamance County. Her parents, Josah and Sallie (Holt) Murray, were two of the thirty-nine slaves owned jointly by the brothers Andrew and Eli Murray in 1860. Sallie was a servant in the household of Andrew Murray; Josah was a blacksmith and wheelwright. His skills were utilized in the manufacture of the large interstate transport wagons which were made on the Murray farm and purchased by many area planters: records show that such wagons were bought in 1842 by Duncan Cameron and Thomas Bennehan of Stagville Plantation. In 1844 Duncan Cameron's son, Paul, also purchased wagons from the Murrays for transporting goods to the Cameron's newly acquired plantation lands in Alabama (Anderson, 1985: 74;97).

When Effie Murray was ten, her mother Sallie died of typhoid, and that same year, in 1890, Effie and her younger brother Jerry were sent to live with their maternal aunt, Francis (Holt) Fonville. Effie remained in the Fonville household until her late teenage years when she met and married her first husband, George Foust. Together they had one child, whom they named Mattie (1900-1963).

When Mattie was only six weeks old, her father, George, was killed at a local corn shucking party. After George's death the widowed Effie and her infant daughter moved back to the Andrew Murray farm in the Cross Roads Community, where Effie met her second husband, Charles White (d. 1970). The couple married in 1903 and had six children: Ernest (b. 1903); Octavis (b. 1906); Willie (b. 1908); Minebell (b. 1910); Murray (b. 1912); and Irene (b. 1914).

Charles and Effie White worked as tenants on the Murray farm, and for many years Charles also served as sextant at Cross Roads Presbyterian Church. Although he and Effie were members of the nearby Kimes' Chapel, they frequently

Undated photograph of Charles and Effie (Murray) White (standing, second and third from left) with their six children.

COLLECTION: ALAMANCE COUNTY HISTORICAL MUSEUM.

Effie (Murray) White house located in the Cross Roads Community, northern Alamance County.

PHOTO: PAT BAILEY, ALAMANCE COUNTY HISTORICAL MUSEUM.

attended services at Cross Roads Church, particularly on holidays and at homecoming events. Charles was also well-known in the community as a string band musician; he played the banjo and the fiddle and frequently performed at area barn raisings and harvest festivals. Effie never attended these gatherings, however, out of respect for the fact that she lost her first husband at just such an event.

As Effie grew older it became apparent to everyone who knew her that there was one thing she loved to do—talk! It seemed she never tired of reminiscing; she had an excellent memory, and could retain and recall facts. As matriarch of her family she became a kind of 'griot'— a keeper of family stories and genealogy.

In 1974, while researching the book *Roots*, the author Alex Haley came to Alamance County in search of his ancestry. Haley believed that his great-great grandfather, Tom (Murray), had been sold to the Murray Plantation in 1858. Oral traditions in the Haley family described Tom as a skilled ironworker and blacksmith, just as Effie's own father, Josah, had been a metalworker.

While pursuing his local research, Alex Haley was led to the home of Effie Murray White. Sitting on the porch of her small home on Highway 119 North, Haley experienced an epiphany and a revelatory moment, for Effie Murray's memories of

her parents, grandparents, and stories of Haley's slave ancestors provided the tangible link to completion of Haley's Pulitzer Prize-winning book.

Effie Murray White died on July 22, 1978, four years after this pivotal event. At 97 she was the oldest member of her church congregation. She was survived by twenty-six grandchildren, forty great-grandchildren, and twenty-two great-great grandchildren. In the eulogy delivered at her funeral, Alex Haley said that Effie Murray White "should be thought of now as an ancestor and as a woman who lived to share her history with the world."

WILLIAM E. WHITE

William Edgar White (1861-1935), furniture manufacturer, was born in Mebane, the son of Mary Jane (Woods) White and Stephen Alexander White, III, who was postmaster of Mebane from 1855 to 1908. "Will" received his education at the Bingham Military Academy before working as a telegraph operator for Southern Railway until 1881. In that year, with his brother David A. White and a capital investment of $420, he founded White Furniture Company, of which he remained president until his death. "Dave" worked as general manager of the plant until he was killed in an automobile accident in 1916.

Eventually, two other brothers joined the firm. When J. "Sam" White finished

Train loaded with White furniture destined for the Panama Canal, Mebane, 1906.

college in 1896 he came to work in the company as a day laborer making five cents an hour; later he assumed the position of secretary/treasurer of the corporation. A fourth brother, Steven A. White, joined the company as a salesman.

Initially, White's made wagon wheels and round oak dining tables; by the late 1880s the company specialized in the production of solid oak bedroom suites that sold for nine dollars. By the 1890s the company began to solidify a reputation for making quality furniture that was well-advertised in the North and South: White's is credited with being the first furniture company in America to advertise a "line of furnishings" as a way of consolidating its reputation. At the annual International Furniture Exhibition of 1897 the company advertised a "center table of unique design, built of the famous Mai-Pado wood from Siam." Articles about this table soon appeared in newspapers all over the United States, and the White Furniture Company became synonymous with quality.

In 1906, when the U.S. government needed furniture for American officers in Panama, the contract went to White's. A total of 58 boxcars full of White furniture was shipped from Mebane in a handsomely placarded train bearing the words "From the White Furniture Company, Mebane, NC for U. S. Government, Panama Canal: The White Line Guarantees Satisfaction." One year later, in 1907, the company solidified its reputation by winning an award as the "Best Manufactured American Furniture" at the Jamestown World Trade Exposition. In 1912 the company also supplied millwork and furnishings for the newly constructed Grove Park Inn in Asheville, N.C.

On December 21, 1923 tragedy struck when the large factory, located on a five-acre site at the corner of Fifth and Center Streets, burned to the ground. Through the efforts of Will White the DuPont Corporation provided emergency funds for rebuilding the plant and helped to keep the business solvent during the Depression years.

White Furniture Company fire, 1923.

Will White died in 1935, having never married. In addition to his lengthy tenure as president of White's, he served as director of the North Carolina State Fair, he was a member of the Mebane School Board and was a booster of the Mebane tobacco market. Upon Will White's death, J. Sam White (called "Mr. Sam") became president; he expanded the company, purchasing a second plant in Hillsborough, N.C., and, by the end of World War II, the firm employed over five hundred people. In 1966 Mr. Sam received a 70-year service pin from the firm. Three years later, in 1969, he assumed the largely honorary title of chairman of the board, and made his son, Stephen A. White (d. 1995), president. A nephew, Steven Millendar, became vice president and director of sales.

In 1985 White Furniture Company was sold to Hickory Manufacturing Corporation, and the Mebane plant was closed in 1993. The closing of White's and its dramatic impact on its employees and the community at large has been the subject of a compelling and award-winning photo essay entitled *Closing: The Life and Death of An American Factory* (1998) by Bill Bamberger and Cathy N. Davidson.

ALEXANDER WILSON

Alexander Wilson (1799-1867), educator and Presbyterian clergyman, was born in the town of Newforge, near Belfast, Ireland. He was a descendant of Alexander Wilson, Sr., a Scotsman whose family had settled in Northern Ireland in the seventeenth century. Little is known of Wilson, Jr's. early life, although some evidence suggests that he may have been awarded a medical diploma before leaving Ireland to come to America.

Wilson immigrated to the United States and arrived in Baltimore on July 4, 1818. In October 1818 he traveled from Boston to Raleigh, North Carolina, where he found employment as a teacher in the Raleigh Academy, headed by the Reverend Dr. William McPheelers. Wilson remained in Raleigh until 1821, when he moved to Granville County, where he became principal of Williamsborough Academy. He remained there for sixteen years.

In the spring of 1837 Wilson moved to Greensboro when he was named principal of the classics department of the famous Caldwell Institute. When the school moved to Hillsborough in 1845, Wilson also moved to Hillsborough and continued to teach at Caldwell, where he remained until the school's closing in 1850.

Wilson then purchased a tract of land in Alamance County known as "Burnt Shop," located near the present community of Swepsonville and the town of Mebane. Between 1850 and 1851 Wilson constructed three structures on the property, including a home, a three-room academy, and a small dormitory. He changed the name of the area to "Melville," and in July 1851 the Melville Academy opened for students. Wilson remained principal of the school for the last sixteen years of his life.

In 1826 at a meeting of Orange Presbytery in Milton, Caswell County, Alexander Wilson was accepted as a candidate for the ministry, and in 1830 he was licensed and ordained at a meeting at Hawfields Presbyterian Church. As far as is known, Wilson's only pastoral charge was the Spring Garden Church, located in Granville County, where he preached for four years while also serving as principal of the Williamsborough Academy.

Wilson died on July 22, 1867 at the age of sixty-eight. His funeral service was conducted at Hawfields Presbyterian Church with interment in the adjacent cemetery. He was survived by his wife, Mary (Willis) Wilson, a native of Ireland whom he married in Boston on July 9, 1821. The couple had five children, two of whom, Alexander and Robert, continued the operation of their father's school until the late 1870s.

Eva Wiseman (second from right) and Burlington Boys Choir in concert at the Nixon White House, December, 1971. To the right are N.C. Senator B. Everett Jordan and wife, Katherine, and President and Mrs. Nixon.

COLLECTION: ALAMANCE COUNTY HISTORICAL MUSEUM.

EVA WISEMAN

Miss Eva Wiseman (1908-2005), a native of Salisbury, N. C., received her bachelor of fine arts in music education from Converse College. In 1937 she was hired by Dr. L. E. Spikes to become the first director of music for the Burlington City School system, a position whose title was later changed to superintendent of music instruction. While working with the public schools Wiseman earned a master's degree from Columbia University in 1943, and for a number of years she taught music education at Elon College as a member of the evening faculty. During the 1940s and '50s she directed six local church choirs. Wiseman is also credited with introducing, in 1963, the now-famous Kadaly Music Instruction Method into the Burlington City Schools.

In the fall of 1958 Miss Wiseman auditioned 325 boys, ranging in age from nine to thirteen, for inclusion in a citywide Boy's Choir. Of this number, fifty boys were selected (of whom 41 accepted) and on April 29, 1959 the Burlington Boys Choir gave its first performance at the local Elk's Club. One year later, in 1960, the

Burlington Rotary Club decided to sponsor the choir, a relationship which would continue for more than twenty years, during which time the choir was known as the Burlington Rotary Boys Choir.

For the next thirty-five years, until 1994, Wiseman served as director of the choir, during which time she had direct contact with over 500 members. The Boys Choir became internationally known, was featured in numerous magazines, and performed over 400 concerts throughout the United States and Europe for an estimated half-million people. Under Wiseman's direction the choir sang on numerous occasions for state functions at the North Carolina Executive Mansion, and in 1971 the group gave a Christmas performance at the White House for President and Mrs. Richard Nixon. For this performance, as director of the choir, Wiseman received the presidential service medal. The Boys Choir gave a similar presidential concert in 1984 for President and Mrs. Ronald Reagan.

In 1965 Wiseman developed a friendship with Maria Augusta von Trapp (the real-life heroine of *The Sound of Music* story). From Maria van Trapp Miss Wiseman received numerous orchestrations and sheet music later utilized by the Boys Choir. Mrs. von Trapp also assisted Eva Wiseman in organizing European concert venues for the choir during the 1960s and 1970s.

September 20, 1988 was proclaimed "Eva Wiseman Day" by Mayor James Gerow of the City of Burlington. In doing so Gerow honored Wiseman for her efforts in bringing the musical arts to the area and touching the lives of so many young boys.

Due to declining health, Mrs. Wiseman formally retired as director of the Burlington Boys Choir in 1994, and Bill Allred assumed directorship of the group. Wiseman died on January 18, 2005 at the age of 97.

J. FRED YOUNG

James Fred Young, seventh president of Elon College (now Elon University) was born in Burnsville, N.C. in 1935. He attended Mars Hill College prior to graduating from Wake Forest University in 1956 with a Bachelor of Science degree. The following year he earned a Master's degree from UNC-Chapel Hill and seven years later received his Ph. D. in education from Columbia University. Between the two periods of graduate study, he served six months in the U. S. Army. Later, he pursued additional postdoctoral studies at Appalachian State University, East Carolina University, and the University of Virginia.

While completing his advanced degrees, Dr. Young was employed with the public school system in North Carolina, where he served as assistant

J. Fred Young.

superintendent of the Burlington City Schools from 1964 until 1968. During his service in this office he wrote "Collective Negotiations for North Carolina Teachers?," which was published in *Popular Government* by the Institute of Government at Chapel Hill.

In 1968 Young moved to Virginia, where he became associated with public schools in Lynchburg. In 1971 he was named Deputy Superintendent of Public Instruction for the Commonwealth of Virginia, a post he held until the late spring of 1973, when he was named president of Elon College. At that time he became the first president of Elon without a previous connection to the institution nor membership in the school's affiliated religious denomination (United Church of Christ). Young assumed presidential duties on August 1, 1973 and was formally installed in October of that year. By early 1974 steps began under his administration to expand the college program and its basic operations.

To assist in the development of these expansions, Dr. Young proposed establishment of the Elon College Presidential Board of Advisors "to assist the President in defining and interpretation of Elon College aims, objectives, and programs."

Twenty-nine members were appointed to the new board. Alumni members included: Ray C. Euliss, Maurice Jennings, Ernest Koury, C. Almon McIver, Dr. Phillip R. Mann, and Max Ward, all of Burlington; Dr. M. Cade Covington, of Sanford; James F. Darden, of Suffolk, Virginia; the Reverend Beverly M. Currin, of Pensacola, Florida; G. T. Holmes, of Badin, North Carolina; Miss Marjorie Hunter, of Washington, D.C.; Robert B. Smithwick, of New York City; A. G. Thompson of Lincolnton, North Carolina; and Dr. Daniel T. Watts, of Richmond, Virginia.

The other members were Laurence A. Alley, of Elon College; Mrs. Alyse S. Cooper; Ralph M. Holt, Jr.; James W. Maynard; the Reverend James W. Morrison; Mrs. Maxine O'Kelley; Dr. Brank Profitt; and Mrs. June Strader, (all of Burlington); Dr. James D. Glasse, of Lancaster, Pennsylvania; the Reverend Rober M. Mitchell, of Pawtucket, Rhode Island; Mrs. Sarah Rhyne, of Graham; Renold Schilke, of Chicago, Illinois; Irwin Smallwood, of Greensboro; and Dr. Edwin G. Wilson of Winston-Salem.

Another component of the administration's platform was an expansion of the school curriculum. In 1975 the Department of Community Services and Allied Health (Department of Human Services) was established under the direction of Dr. Frances Marlette to "prepare students for work in mental health, vocational rehabilitation... and government services." About the same time the Department of Military Science was created. Innovative courses for a short winter term were devised, chapters of national honor societies were organized, a student biweekly newspaper, *The Pendulum*, was established, and in 1977 an educational radio station, WSOE, opened on campus. In 1974 Elon also established the Black Cultural Society, and the college received as a gift the 48,315-volume library of the defunct Stratford College of Danville, Virginia.

In 1976 President Young unveiled a Master Plan to meet the long-range needs of the college. Trustees voted to authorize

the President to plan and conduct a capital fund campaign for $5.5 million, and appointed Wallace Chandler as general fundraising chairman. Referred to by the acronym PRIDE (for "Providing Resources for Institutional Development at Elon"), the campaign raised almost $3 million in two years, with 64% of these funds coming from citizens of Alamance County.

Support of college academic programs climaxed in 1978 when Dr. Thomas E. Powell, Jr. created with a major gift an endowed chair in biology. At that time the Powell gift (from an alumnus, former faculty member, and founder of Carolina Biological Supply Company) represented the largest single monetary gift to the college. Following this contribution, five sons of the donor, Thomas E., III; Samuel C.; James B.; Joseph E. and John S. Powell gave a major portion of the funding necessary to pay for the Classroom-Office Building. The gift honored their aunt, Miss Caroline E. Powell, for whom the building came to be named.

In 1977 Wilburne Newsome, a former athletic standout, donated funds to build the Webb Newsome Athletic Field on the north side of the campus. Two years later, in 1979, local industrialists Maurice and Ernest Koury provided funds to build the John A. Koury Field House adjacent to Newsome Field. Another boon to the Physical Education Department was received in 1978 when the Belk-Beck department store group gave money to build an olympic-sized indoor swimming pool in honor of Allen Vance Belk, one of their executives.

In June 1977 the college received the largest financial boost in its history with a $2 million grant from the government's Advanced Institutional Development Program, under provisions of Title III of the Higher Education Act. The grant provided funding for development of a learning resources center, academic and student life enrichment, and a career placement office. Dr. Jo Watts Williams, from the faculty of the Education Department, was appointed director of the Learning

Resources Center. During the late 1970s major funding for various college programs was also received from the Z. Smith Reynolds Foundation and low-interest, long-term government loans.

As Elon began to move into the decade of the eighties, the Young administration provided mature and solidified leadership. Fred Young's visionary planning set the mark for the transformation of Elon into a vital university under the leadership of his successor and Elon's eighth and current president, Leo Lambert.

TOM ZACHARY

Tom Zachary was born in Graham, NC in 1896, but spent much of his early life on a farm just west of NC 87 near the community of Eli Whitney. The son of devout Quakers he attended Guilford College where he became a college baseball standout.

In 1918, while still a college student, Zachary traveled to Philadelphia, where he tried out as a pitcher for Connie Mack, the legendary manager of the Philadelphia Athletics. Using the alias 'Zach Walton' to protect his college eligibility, Zachary was immediately hired by Mack but played only two games for the Athletics before joining a pacifist Quaker Red Cross Unit to serve in Europe during the closing months of World War I.

Tom Zachary.

Upon his return to the states in 1919, Zachary was hired by Washington Senators owner Clark Griffith, and he remained with that team through several seasons. In 1924 he pitched two winning games over the New York Giants, thereby propelling the Senators to their only World Series triumph.

Pitching for the Senators, Zachary is also remembered as the man who gave up Babe Ruth's sixtieth home run. With a score tied at 2-2 and a man on third, Zachary threw a high curve ball to the Yankee's Babe Ruth, who hit the ball straight down the right field and over the wall for a home run. The play resulted in a win for the Yankees.

Speaking about the game Zachary later recalled: "That ball Babe hit for his sixtieth home run was the kind of ball no other batter would have tried for. It was a curve ball, high, straight at him. You might call it a bean ball. I wanted to get Babe away from the plate. But instead of stepping back he lunged for it before it ever got near the plate and pulled it around into the stands. I don't see yet how he did it." (Boyer, *Times-News* 09/08/07:A2)

Ruth's sixtieth home run was a Major League baseball season record, which stood until 1961, when the record was broken by Roger Maris. Ironically, Zachary would later be traded to the Yankees, when he then became both teammate and roommate of the great Babe Ruth. In 1929, still playing for the Yankees, Zachary became the first pitcher in Major League history to have a 12-0 record for the season.

Over the ensuing years Zachary also played for the Boston Braves and the Brooklyn Dodgers. He finished his professional baseball career in 1936 as a pitcher for the Philadelphia Phillies. Soon thereafter he turned to Graham. Zachary died on January 24, 1969 and is buried at Alamance Memorial Park.

BIBLIOGRAPHY

Anderson, Jean B. *Piedmont Plantation.* Durham, North Carolina: The Historic Preservation Society of Durham, 1985.

Ashe, Samuel., ed. *Biographical History of North Carolina*, Vols. I-VIII. Greensboro, North Carolina: Charles L. Van Noppen, 1905

Beatty, Bess. *Alamance: the Holt Family and Industrialization in a North Carolina County, 1837-1900.* Baton Rouge, Louisiana: Louisiana State University Press, 1999.

Beaudry, Mary. "Colonizing the Virginia Frontier: Fort Christianna and Governor Spotswood's Indian Policy." Ms. Submitted for publication in *The Comparative Archaeology of European Colonization*, Stephen Dyson (ed.), 1981.

Bolden, Don. *Alamance: A County At War.* Burlington, North Carolina: Times-News Publishing Company, 1995.

Bolden, Don. *Remembering Alamance County: Tales of Railroads, Textiles, and Baseball.* Charleston, South Carolina: the History Press, 2006.

Bulla, Ben F. *Textiles and Politics: The Life of B. Everett Jordan.* Durham, North Carolina: Carolina Academic Press, 1992.

Dickens, Roy S., et. al. *The Sioaun Project: Seasons I and II.* Chapel Hill, North Carolina: Research Laboratories of Anthropology, University of North Carolina, Monograph Series No. 1, 1987.

Euliss, Elinor S., ed. *Alamance County: The Legacy of Its People and Places.* Greensboro, North Carolina: Legacy Publications, 1984.

Haley, Alex. *Roots.* Garden City, New York: Doubleday and Co., 1976.

Hall, Jacquelin, et. al. *Like A Family: The Making of a Southern Cotton Mill World.* Chapel Hill, North Carolina: University of North Carolina Press, 1987.

Hazel, Forest. "Occaneechi-Saponi Descendants in the North Carolina Piedmont: The Texas Community." Southern Indian Studies, 40: 3-30, 1991.

Lawson, John. *A New Voyage to Carolina.* Hugh T. Lefler, ed., Chapel Hill, North Carolina: University of North Carolina Press, 1967.

Lederer, John. *The Discoveries of John Lederer in Three Several Marches from Virginia, to the West of Carolina.* London: Samuel Heyrick, 1672.

Powell, William S. *Dictionary of North Carolina Biography.* Chapel Hill, North Carolina: University of North Carolina Press, 1979.

Stockard, Sallie W. *The History of Alamance.* Burlington, North Carolina: Alamance County Historical Museum, Inc., 1986.

Stokes, Durward T. *Company Shops: The Town Built By a Railroad.* Winston-Salem, North Carolina: John F. Blair, 1981.

Stokes, Durward T. *Elon College: Its History and Traditions.* Elon College, North Carolina: Elon College Alumni Association, 1982.

Troxler, Carole W. and William M. Vincent. *Shuttle and Plow: A History of Alamance County, North Carolina.* Burlington, North Carolina: Alamance County Historical Association, Inc., 1999.

Turner, Herbert S. *The Dreamer: Archibald DeBow Murphey, 1777-1832.* Verona, Virginia: McClure Printing Company, 1971.

Turner, Herbert S. *The Scott Family of Hawfields.* Unknown printer, 1971.

Whitaker, Walter, et. al. *Centennial History of Alamance County: 1849-1949.* Burlington, N.C.: Burlington Chamber of Commerce, 1949.

An original oil painting by Mort Künstler entitled, Alamance Plaids: First Commercially Dyed Cottons in the South. *The painting depicts Thomas Holt in the dye house of the original Alamance Cotton Factory. He is holding a cut of the first Alamance Plaid fabric produced in 1853. Also included in the painting are Holt's wife, Louisa Moore Holt, and her friends, Ann and Mary Louise Moorehead, daughters of North Carolina Governor John Motley Moorehead. The Holt slaves "Sam" and "Caswell," who helped develop the colorfast indigo dyes used in the production of Alamance Plaid, are also depicted.*

PAINTING: COLLECTION OF THE ALAMANCE COUNTY HISTORICAL MUSEUM.

SHARING THE HERITAGE

historic profiles of businesses,

organizations, and families that have

contributed to the development

and economic base of Alamance County

CAROLINA BIOLOGICAL SUPPLY COMPANY

Thomas E. Powell, III, M.D., chairman.

Unlocking the world of science for students across the globe is what Carolina Biological Supply Company is all about, and has been since the day its founder, Dr. Thomas E. Powell, Jr., began collecting plant and animal specimens for his students at Elon College in the late 1920s.

You see, in those days, if teachers wanted their students to dissect bullfrogs or look at algae through the microscope, they had to get out and hunt for the samples themselves. And that is exactly what this biology and geology professor did.

In fact, it was not uncommon for the good professor to pitch a tent near the coast and spend several nights on specimen-finding expeditions, coming home with enough brain-enriching natural treasures for his classes as well as the classes of other teachers. When he found out that many of these teachers were willing to pay for his surplus collections, he decided to go into business, and, in 1927, he founded the company that today serves teachers and students around the world.

But, the desire to be the owner of his own company was not born due to market demand alone. In fact, Dr. Powell once told *Discover Science Magazine* that he felt the academic world was too routine and scheduled and it bothered him to see colleagues forced to retire.

"I knew if I started a company of my own," he told the magazine in a 1982 interview, "I wouldn't have to retire."

And, retire he did not. Powell, who was eighty-eight when he died, headed the company until his death in 1987, first as president and then as chairman. He also kept the business in the family, with his sister Caroline, his children and grandchildren happy to do their part, whether it was on the management team, in the boardroom, or in the fields collecting specimens like he himself had so often done.

As for heading up the company, he actually passed that torch on to his eldest son and namesake, Dr. Thomas E. "Ed" Powell, III—a medical doctor and former administrator at the National Institutes of Health—who succeeded his brother John as president in 1980, and who, today, as chairman, still runs the company along with Jim Parrish.

Together, he and Parrish, who joined the company as president in 2004, steer and guide a bank of approximately 400 employees, many of whom have worked for the company for decades, and including three third-generation Powell family members—Frances Powell Barnes, Thomas E. Powell, IV, and Caroline Powell Rogers.

A worldwide supplier of scientific products with customers in eighty-three countries, Carolina Biological is located on forty-five rolling acres in Burlington. The campus includes fifteen buildings as well as ponds and other natural habitats where the company actually raises much of its own specimen inventory. Additional specimens are purchased from collectors in other states.

All told, the company's catalog features more than twenty thousand products and is a virtual superstore of science whose shelves are stacked high with plastic containers filled with live tarantulas, vials full of still-buzzing fruit flies, and the skulls and various other bones of humans and animals sorted neatly by kind. There are frogs kept in an area with automatic watering systems and a house of beautiful butterflies. There are rooms filled with massive fish tanks and thousands of small fish waiting to be shipped to destinations around the globe where they will be studied and bred. There is everything from the complex human brain made of plastic to the most primitive one-celled organism. There are nearly one hundred different types of fungi, and even more strains of algae and bacteria. There is every manner of creepy, crawly creature and their neatly dissected innards vacuum-packed, freeze-dried, framed, pickled in alcohol or embedded in plastic for posterity.

At Carolina Biological, you can even buy a perfect specimen of the common squid, a creature often studied for its neurological features and the inspiration for the company's own logo.

In addition to their traditional specimen fare, the company has recently branched out to offer whatever is "hot in science education," such as crime scene microscopic forensic kits geared to the elementary and middle school set. They have also delved into the world of mathematics and have partnered with leading providers of inquiry-based curriculum to offer a new product category—"Carolina Curriculum"—designed to help kindergarten through eighth grade teachers reach students in a unique and proven way.

Examples of exclusive "Carolina Curriculum" programs include: Science and Technology for Children® or STC®, a complete science program for children in grades kindergarten through eighth developed by the National Science Resources Center and filled with innovative hands-on activities designed to motivate young students; Great Explorations in Math and Science® or GEMS®, a leading resource for innovative

CAROLINA BIOLOGICAL SUPPLY COMPANY
2ND ANNUAL
NATIONAL SALES MEETING
AUGUST 28, 1990
BURLINGTON, NORTH CAROLINA

The second annual sales meeting,
August 28, 1990.

science and mathematics education developed at the University of California at Berkeley and successfully tested in thousands of preschool through eighth grade classrooms nationwide; and Math Out of the Box®, a complete kindergarten through fifth inquiry-based math curriculum developed by Clemson University's College of Engineering and Science and based on the latest research about how children learn.

"Our goal is to give products to teachers that help them teach better and that help students learn and achieve better," company President Parrish said in a recent newspaper article. "So we'll continue to invest and grow in new endeavors such as our 'Carolina Curriculum,' but at the same time we will continue the things that got us here—specimens for dissecting and studying."

The combination of old and new has proven fruitful, Dr. Powell, III, agrees, as the company is still growing. Evidence of this healthy growth can be seen in the company's product offerings as well as at the company's three warehouses in Rock Creek Center, almost a quarter of a million square feet of additional storage purchased in 2001 and now overflowing.

Indeed, Carolina Biological and the Powells have made a profound impact on the world and the state of North Carolina.

And, at various times over the years, institutions and people have showed their appreciation by honoring them, such as in 1981

when founder Dr. Powell, Jr., was honored during the dedication ceremonies for *Cape Hatteras*, North Carolina's largest oceanographic research vessel located at the Duke Marine Research Laboratory in Beaufort. While working towards his doctorate degree from Duke University and teaching at Elon College, Dr. Powell had spent much time studying the richness of the plant and animal life along the North Carolina coast and collecting the many samples that gave birth to his company. He shared his enthusiasm for the area with colleagues at Duke and encouraged them to establish a marine research laboratory there. They took his advice and, in 1938, established the lab which eventually evolved into one of the foremost marine research centers in the world.

Most recently, in November 2007, Alamance Community College named its newest building—home of the school's biotechnology and allied health departments—for the Powell family.

As for the future, the company is looking forward to creating additional new and exciting products and plenty more growth. With a new Fed Ex hub coming to the Greensboro airport and plans to continue expansion of its teaching materials and biotechnology resources, the possibilities seem limitless.

For more information on Carolina Biological Supply Company, please visit www.carolina.com. For more information about Carolina Curriculum, visit www.carolinacurriculum.com.

❖

The 2008 Carolina Curriculum and Carolina Biological Supply Company catalogs.

GLEN RAVEN,

Though today global in reach, Glen Raven Inc.'s past, present and future remain tightly woven in the very fabric of Alamance County.

After all, it was Alamance that helped nurture Altamahaw Mills, a small family-owned cotton mill which began operation more than 125 years ago, giving birth to the Glen Raven of today. Glen Raven is a collection of companies of global magnitude with customers in 127 countries around the world; a corporation that, despite its universal growth, is still headquartered in Alamance, still owned by the same local family, and still does business with many of the same local customers it has served for more than a century. A corporation that, thanks to its unique approach of market-driven innovation and its ability to meticulously build a global approach to business, continues to fight off the perils of a turbulent textile industry and is sure to remain a part of Alamance for years to come.

This literal rags-to-riches story of success all started four generations and almost thirteen decades ago when John Quinton Gant, a native of Alamance County and a merchant at Company Shops—the community later named Burlington—joined forces with local millwright Berry Davidson to build and open Altamahaw Cotton Mills in 1880.

Right: From luxuriously appointed cabins to rugged covers to high-performance sailcloth fabric, Glen Raven marine fabrics enhance every aspect of the boating world.

Below: GlenGuard protective fabric combines safety with comfort for the utility, petroleum, racing, and industrial apparel markets.

By 1900, Gant had acquired land west of Burlington to build a second mill and village. He chose this location because it was near the railroad and made the cost of transporting goods to the shipping point practically nil, and because commuting from his home in Burlington to Altamahaw had been very difficult prior to the advent of the automobile. Upon acquiring the land and beginning construction, Gant changed the name of the company to Glen Raven Cotton Mills. Though historical accounts say that Gant's wife, Corinna, never liked the name because it reminded her of Edgar Allen Poe's chilling poem *The Raven*, the reason for the name remains a mystery.

One thing that is not a mystery, however, is that John Q. Gant was undeniably the driving force behind Glen Raven. A dynamic man who became known at work and home as simply "The Boss Man," Gant ran both mills for years with all eight of his sons—Joseph, Kenneth, John, Jr., Roger, Edwin, Russell, Cecil and Allen—taking their respective turns working beside him. Upon graduation from college, Joseph, Gant's eldest son, actually supervised the construction of the second mill. Along with Joseph, Gant's next to oldest son, Kenneth, helped open the new mill in 1902. Shortly

thereafter, the company reorganized and was renamed simply Glen Raven Mills. It received its formal incorporation in 1904 with the senior Gant, Kenneth and Joseph named as principals. The company retained the name of Glen Raven Mills until 2000 when it was once again renamed—this time, Glen Raven, Inc.

When John Q. Gant died in 1930, the management of Glen Raven Mills was passed on to sons Roger and Allen, with all of the second generation Gant boys coming on board in different capacities throughout the years. And, like their father before them, they all worked diligently to teach the business to many of their own children—namely Roger, Jr., Kenneth, Jr., Cecil, Jr., Edmund, and Allen, Jr. Many of these third generation Gants, including current President and CEO Allen Gant, Jr., still work in the business and are joined by a fourth generation that are poised and ready to keep the company growing.

Indeed, there have been so many events, people and successes to herald during Glen Raven's more than 125 years that one would need a whole book to list them all. However, a few of the most historical include the fact that not only did John Q. Gant help transform Alamance County and the state of North Carolina from a farming to a manufacturing economy, but he was also instrumental in establishing U.S. Postal Offices at Altamahaw

and Mill Point, which later became the town of Elon, and was responsible for establishing a phone line between Burlington and Altamahaw. Additionally, his company has been a model corporate citizen throughout the years, supporting many local organizations and charities including, but not limited to, Elon University, May Memorial Library in Burlington, the Burlington and Alamance County school systems, the March of Dimes, the American Red Cross, the Habitat for Humanity, and the American Cancer Society Relay for life.

❖

Above: The Industrial Fabrics Association International (IFAI) is one of the many trade shows where Glen Raven provides the marketplace with the latest information on products and services.

Below: Allen E. Gant, Sr., invented pantyhose in 1959, trademarked by the company as Panti-Legs.

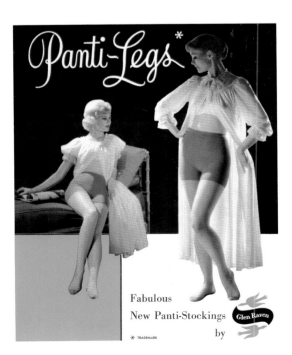

Above: In 1964 an innovative round office was built to house the company executive offices.

Below: Employees involved in Spinning and Carding at the Glen Raven Cotton Mill in 1929.

Business-wise, Glen Raven has had its share of market firsts in parachutes, the invention of panty hose in 1953, and the transition from cotton to acrylic in awning fabrics. Its fabric was used in 1969 to make the flag that flew on the moon.

In addition, it supplied much of the duck cloth used for tents during World War I and was one of the first American companies to begin producing blends of cotton and man-made fibers such as rayon and acetate in the late 1920s. It was a primary supplier of tent canvas, powder bags, and parachute cloth during World War II, and, in 1960, introduced Sunbrella®, the first one-hundred-percent solution-dyed acrylic

outdoor fabric which has become an industry standard and brand model for textiles.

Though recent years have been quite tumultuous for U.S. textile companies, Glen Raven has powered through restructuring, reinventing and reestablishing itself as often as necessary.

The company began to expand on a global scale in 1998 when it acquired Dickson S.A. of France and Elberton, Georgia, a widely recognized leader in branded acrylic fabrics; and in 2003, was reorganized based on markets served, leading to a new subsidiary structure business model. In 2005 it won the coveted Innovation Award presented by internationally-

distributed *Textile World* magazine for its ability to constantly morph itself and its products into whatever its clients need; and in 2006, constructed Glen Raven Asia, a 250,000-square-foot facility in China. In 2007 the company continued in its strategy of growth and innovation when it acquired industrial fabric companies, John Boyle and Company and The Astrup Company.

In addition to the Dickson plant in France and the new China facility, Glen Raven, Inc., has six other production and finishing facilities as well as a logistics and transportation facility and a host of distribution facilities in the United States. The corporation and its subsidiaries employ 2,736 associates worldwide, many of whom work at the company's corporate headquarters, the Technical Fabrics finishing facility and the Custom Fabric plant right in Glen Raven, and all of whom are at the root of Glen Raven's success, according to James M. Borneman, 2005 *Textile World* editor.

"Many talk about innovation, but few companies can respond to the changes innovation demands—Glen Raven is one of those few," Borneman wrote in the magazine's June 2005 issue. "The story inside Glen Raven is about adopting a strategy that fits turbulent times and hinges on each of Glen Raven's associates being heard, unfiltered, and being key to innovation."

Indeed, market-driven to its very core, Glen Raven management utilizes marketing to do much more than support successful brands. They use it to understand markets and help guide company strategy, constantly repositioning assets and making tough decisions on when to enter and exit markets. They use it to invent new products and solutions for their customers, instead of trying to invent customers for their products.

"We've got great customers. We've got customers that have been on the books for 100 years. That's unbelievable—100 years—same customer, same ownership. So what do we do? What do we do to become more valuable to them? That is the whole issue," CEO Allen E. Gant, Jr., told *Textile World*. "True marketing gives you the ability to look into a market and decide whether or not you can add value. It also gives you the ability to determine if you can stay in that market."

"And, sometimes, the decisions we must make are really tough," he said, citing, for example, the panty hose market which, after inventing, was smart to enter, but very difficult to exit. "Making tough decisions and focusing on what our customers want, however, is how our company thrives and is what will hopefully keep us in business for another 125 years."

For more information on Glen Raven, Inc., please visit www.glenraven.com.

From parachutes to packs and OTV/Interceptor shells, Glen Raven has developed fabrics that provide the superior durability and performance a modern soldier needs.

CITY OF BURLINGTON

"Burlington is a community born of the railroad, bred on the loom and built on an ability to turn adversity into opportunity," Burlington's Don Bolden once wrote.

Now a thriving city ideally located between the Triad and Triangle and offering the services of a big metropolis to more than 50,000 residents and a host of burgeoning industrial, retail and residential developments, Bolden could not have been more right.

Indeed, when the railroad left in 1886 after three decades of being the town's heartbeat, the town could have very well just withered away, but instead the citizens faced the challenge head on and turned their community in a whole new direction.

After all they had fought hard to bring the North Carolina Railroad Company to the area in the 1850s, putting together a package of land on which the railroad could build, repair, and maintain its tracks. The new railroad community was officially founded in 1857 and named the "Company Shops." Thirty years later when the railroad decided to leave, the citizens rallied to save the community they helped create. They began by changing its name and, in 1893, the city of Burlington was officially incorporated and chartered by the state's legislature.

With their primary source of employment gone, the citizens of the new Burlington turned their time and attention to a new industry just beginning to blossom. Several small textile plants had begun operations and were soon joined by hosiery manufacturers, many of whom were local entrepreneurs. Soon after the turn of the century, Burlington was known as the "Hosiery Center of the South."

But, in the 1920s, adversity struck yet again when the need for jobs became a major concern for Burlington. Local businessmen began looking for a solution and—with financial help from the local chamber of commerce—Burlington Mills was born.

Though the largest textile maker in the world, this new company, unfortunately, faced adversity almost from the beginning when the demand for cotton goods fell sharply soon after the mill opened. Burlington Mills squashed this adversity by switching to a new manmade fiber called rayon and as a result was propelled into the world of industrial giants. It enjoyed even more success during the Depression years when other mills closed.

However, even with the rise of Burlington Industries as it was now called, Burlington's local leadership was not willing to rest on its laurels. Desiring to never again be reliant on a single industry, they continued to secure the city's future

by diversifying and searching out new industry. First an aircraft factory brought in new jobs during World War II, followed by Western Electric just after the war. And today, while textile employment remains heavy, the largest single employer is actually a medical diagnostic company, LabCorp. LabCorp employs more than three thousand people in Burlington and Alamance County. There is also Honda Aero, Inc., a wholly owned subsidiary of Honda Motor Company, Ltd., which is responsible for Honda's aeronautical engine business and that on July 17, 2007, announced that it was establishing its new corporate headquarters and a state-of-the-art jet engine manufacturing plant at the Burlington-Alamance Regional Airport.

In addition to diversified employment opportunities, Burlington is also known for its water availability and quality. When a critical water shortage hit in the 1950s, posing a real threat to existing industry and business as well as future growth, the city set out to correct the problem and to ensure it would never happen again. A new reservoir was built in the late 1950s and, almost as soon as it was placed in use, plans began for yet another water supply. As a result, present day Burlington has two water treatment facilities and one of the best water supplies in the state—a supply envied by the city's larger neighbors and a tremendous attraction for new industries.

For more information, please visit www.burlingtonnc.gov.

Above: The Burlington City Park Carousel, built in the early 1900s, is a true historical treasure. The Carousel is operational and open to the public from Easter weekend in the spring until the beginning of school each fall.

Below: Alamance Crossing Shopping Center serves as an example of the exciting economic growth being experienced by the Burlington community.
COURTESY OF SAM ROBERTS/TIMES-NEWS, SEPTEMBER 11, 2007.

LONG BROTHERS LANDSCAPING

Poythress Studio

❖

Above: Wesley and wife Melanie.

Below: Company founders Wesley Long (on left) and Marty Long (on right), in the early 1980s with the company's first truck, tractor and trailer.

When brothers John Wesley and Alan Ray "Marty" Long first started their landscaping business in 1984, all they had was $400, a used pickup truck and some borrowed equipment.

Today, Long Brothers Landscaping, Inc., is one of the largest landscaping firms in the country and does more than 6 million dollars in business annually. During peak season it employs up to seventy people with a year-round payroll of fifty. Though Marty has since passed away, Wesley's son Don has stepped up as equal partner and serves as president of the ever-burgeoning company.

And, while both father and son are somewhat modest when it comes to talking about their success, office manager Mimi Cowan is so proud of them she cannot help but brag a little.

"They won't toot their own horns, but I will," Cowan said. "In the same way they nurture the landscapes of our customers, Wesley and Don have fertilized this business with just the right mixture of faith, honesty and genuine hard work. They are the real spirit of this company and the reason we are so highly respected by our customers and our peers."

Ranked in the top one percent of landscaping firms in America, Long Brothers specializes in both commercial and residential landscape services including grading, landscaping, hardscaping, irrigation management and maintenance, landscape design and consultation.

"From shrub and flower installation to tree and boulder placement, we offer it all," said president and co-owner Don. "We pass on the advantages of our good reputation and industry connections to our customers and give each client an array of options. From native plants to exotic species, we have access to just about anything you can dream of."

The company also specializes in hardscapes and has certified professionals who excel at planning and creating patios, walks and walls, which not only add charm and beauty, but value as well.

To assist their clients in spending more time enjoying their landscape and less time working in it, Long Brothers has fine-tuned the installation of irrigation systems. The company features a team of on-staff irrigation system designers and uses professional Hunter Irrigation Systems products with warranty coverage.

In addition to doing all the work and heavy lifting on a project, Long Brothers can also help with landscaping design. The company's team of professionals offers free estimate and consultation services, including the use of Landscape Pro, the most extensive and accurate landscaping computer program on the market; a program capable of showing a client what their new plants will look like in the front of their house five years after planting.

In addition to homes in the Alamance area, some of Long Brothers most visible projects have included the new Alamance Crossing Shopping Center, the Village at Brookwood Retirement Community and the Burlington Depot in Burlington. One can also see the company's handiwork at a host of area apartment complexes including the Lofts at Lakeview, Wolf Creek, Chapel Ridge, The

Terraces, and Summit Overlook as well at businesses such as Johnson Lexus, Chili's, Macaroni Grill, Streets at Southpoint and the Renaissance CenterOffice Complex.

"We've come a long way since that day—with my wife as bookkeeper—Marty and I took our $400 savings and started this business," said co-owner, founder and now vice president Wesley. "There were times when it was really tough, like the first winter when work was slow because the ground stayed frozen. We took jobs sweeping out newly constructed homes for local contractors for $25 a house. We also did snow removal for local businesses, pushing snow from daylight to dark just to make ends meet. But, we made it. With God's help and blessings, we made it."

Both Wesley and Don are also heavily invested in giving back to the community. Wesley and wife Melanie have given countless hours toward the building of the Word of Life Church in Burlington. Many Saturdays would find Wesley grading the church parking lot, and the company donated much of the church's beautiful landscaping.

Both father and son are leaders in their respective churches, always available to listen and respond to the needs of others.

For more information about Long Brothers Landscaping, please visit the company's offices in the Paris Building on Court Square in Graham; call 336-228-7078; or visit its website, www.longbrotherslandscaping.com.

Above: Long Brothers has in-house designers to create patios, walls, walks and water features.

Below: Long Brothers Landscaping Company founder Wesley Long (right) with son Don (left), both dedicated to a tradition of excellence.

ALAMANCE COMMUNITY COLLEGE

Alamance Community College (ACC) celebrates its fiftieth anniversary as an educational institution in 2008—half a century of serving the citizens of Alamance County and their changing needs.

Today's college paves the way for students to earn degrees and certificates in more than forty educational programs crucial for success in the twenty-first century—university transfer, bio-technology, nursing, business administration, machining, and horticulture to name just a few. As one of the premiere community colleges in North Carolina, it is hard to imagine a time when today's Alamance Community College was little more than an idea—the brainchild of a small group of Alamance County businessmen and educators.

In 1958, unemployment was high in Alamance County. The local economy was dominated by Western Electric and the textile industry and skilled labor was desperately needed. Taking action behind the vision of Governor Luther Hodges, some Alamance County business and education leaders saw industrial education as a key to attracting industry and securing a good future for the populace. Behind such local leaders as prominent business leader Wallace Gee and Western Electric engineer J.W. Pierce, the state's first industrial education center—Burlington-Alamance County Industrial Education Center (IEC)—was founded.

In its first year of operation, IEC offered fifteen programs, such as industrial chemistry, yarn and fabric analysis, loom fixing, and

machine shop to meet the demands of local industry. The popularity of IEC grew quickly and by the end of its second year of operation, enrollment figures topped two thousand.

"We were a showplace for the whole Southeastern United States," recalled the late Wallace Gee in an interview a few years ago. "I spent many a day giving tours for visiting educators who came from across the country wanting to see what we were doing so they could adapt it to their needs."

By the early 1960s, with Dr. William Taylor installed as president, IEC was granted full status as a technical institute and changed its

name to Technical Institute of Alamance (TIA). By the 1970s, course offerings had expanded to include computer systems, secretarial skills, drafting, and chemical technology. By this point, physical expansion was a foregone conclusion.

The current campus in Graham came to be through the generosity of Governor Robert Scott and family who donated farmland for construction of a new, larger institution where it stands today. Taking the name of Technical College of Alamance (TCA) in 1979, it ultimately was christened Alamance Community College in 1988 and continued to grow in importance to the local community.

Over the years, the College has pushed ahead of sister institutions when it comes to innovative ideas: the first data processing program in North Carolina; the nation's first two-year biotechnology program; the state's first evening dental assisting curriculum; a multiple award-winning culinary program, to name just a few.

Alamance Community College continues to change according to the needs of the community. With hundreds of local manufacturing jobs lost each year since the early 2000s due to NAFTA, the student population now includes those who have been in the workforce for decades and are taking steps to be retrained in new, exciting careers.

Today's students—children and grandchildren of those first enrollees—have the option of traditional technical courses as well as biotechnology, culinary arts, medical laboratory technology, and a plethora of university transfer courses.

The founders of the College never envisioned that the institution would mature into what it is today—a community college serving more than 17,000 students annually and half a million individuals since its inception.

"As we enter our second fifty years, Alamance Community College remains true to its original mission of training local people to ensure the workforce of Alamance County is second to none," says ACC President Dr. Martin H. Nadelman.

THE ELON SCHOOL

Above: Students in math class.

Below: The girls' soccer team.

With a firm belief that children are the foundation of our future, The Elon School is dedicated to building upon that foundation by offering its students a well-rounded education that not only emphasizes academics, but also focuses on the development of the whole person.

Opened in August 2007, Alamance County's first-ever independent college preparatory school has a four-fold mission: to prepare its students academically with a strong college preparatory and advanced placement curriculum taught by exceptionally qualified and talented teachers; to prepare them aesthetically by helping them to learn appreciation for and develop talents in the fine and performing arts working under the tutelage of professional artists and teachers; to prepare them physically by encouraging them to

practice a healthy lifestyle and participate in interscholastic sports that develop character, sportsmanship and leadership; and to prepare them ethically by allowing them to experience an environment that values a code of honor, respect for others and self, and philanthropy through gifts of service and resources.

The Elon School is open to both boys and girls in grades nine through twelve who demonstrate the ability to succeed in a college preparatory program and who want to contribute to the development of a vibrant learning community. The school specifically looks for talented students with diverse backgrounds, varied experiences, and a respect for community; students who not only have demonstrated scholastic ability, but who also have a promise of future success. Applicants are selected through a process that includes a review of previous school performance, teacher recommendations, admissions testing and personal interview. Need-based financial aid is available for deserving students and Merit Scholarships are also offered.

With a student/faculty ratio of about seven to one and tutorial periods each day for additional academic support, the school fulfills all Standards of Accreditation as set forth by

SAIS/SACS, two regional accrediting associations that cover both public and private schools in the southeast. In addition to academics, the school offers an afternoon program with activities including competitive athletics (the school participates in the Triad Athletic Conference and North Carolina Independent Schools Athletic Association), an Arts Program that includes fine arts and performing arts, and a Service Learning Program that helps students to give philanthropically to the community and to better understand the needs of others in the community.

The Elon School seeks to educate students for the twenty-first century. They are encouraged to think and write analytically and critically, to develop problem-solving skills and to use their creative minds to seek new ideas and solutions to past and present issues. Small class sizes encourage an exchange of ideas and the talented and dedicated faculty work closely with each student, understanding each student's strengths and areas that need improvement.

As students grow at The Elon School they are given more freedom and asked to take on more personal responsibility. Students learn how to better manage their own time and complete long-term assignments.

All students attending The Elon School are expected to also attend a college or university. College counseling begins in the ninth grade and becomes increasingly important throughout a student's career at the school. The college counselor will guide students through the college process, with the student taking increasing responsibility for the process each year.

For more information, please visit www.theelonschool.com or call 336-584-0091.

Above: The Elon School chorus.

Below: Time out at the basketball game.

ALLEY, WILLIAMS, CARMEN & KING, INC.

Audrey W. Garrett Elementary School.

If you have spent time in Alamance County or nearly anywhere else in the Piedmont Triad, chances are you have lived, worked, played, shopped, or continued your education in a project planned, designed or engineered by Alley, Williams, Carmen & King, Inc.

A multi-disciplinary, full-service design firm with offices in Burlington, Kannapolis and Sanford, AWCK has been in business for almost a half century and features a staff of fifty-four architects, civil engineers, registered land surveyors and technical and administrative personnel. Services provided include architecture, civil engineering, surveying, land planning and construction administration services.

The firm has a diverse general practice with emphasis on municipal and local public work and has engineered and designed municipal and public facilities in cities throughout the Piedmont, including everything from town halls, libraries, police stations and fire stations to jails, parks, and recreation centers. They have also designed water and wastewater treatment facilities, distribution and collection systems, and streets and roadways for area governments.

AWCK has designed public schools, additions to the Alamance Community College and over fifty addition and renovation projects for local school systems. They have prepared master plans, preliminary and final subdivision plans for residential, commercial and industrial developments, and have designed manufacturing plants, distribution facilities, commercial retail projects, office buildings, residential condominiums, shopping centers, restaurants, ball fields and churches.

Some of their most recognizable projects include the Mebane Library and Fire Station, Wallace Gee Building at the Alamance Community College, Hawfields Educational Complex for the Alamance-Burlington School System, Glen Raven Mills Corporate Offices, Graham City Hall and Police Station, Mebane Arts and Community Center, Haw River Town Hall and the Gibsonville Town Hall. AWCK also provided engineering for major projects such as Wakefield Development Mackintosh on the Lake, Waterford, Brightwood Farms, Grand Oaks Subdivisions, Rock Creek Industrial Center and Carolina Central Industrial Center.

Alley, Williams, Carmen & King, Inc. is named after the firm's founders and early partners. The original founder and the firm's president 1960 through 1978 was Laurence "Larry" Alley, a University of Virginia graduate and registered professional engineer and land

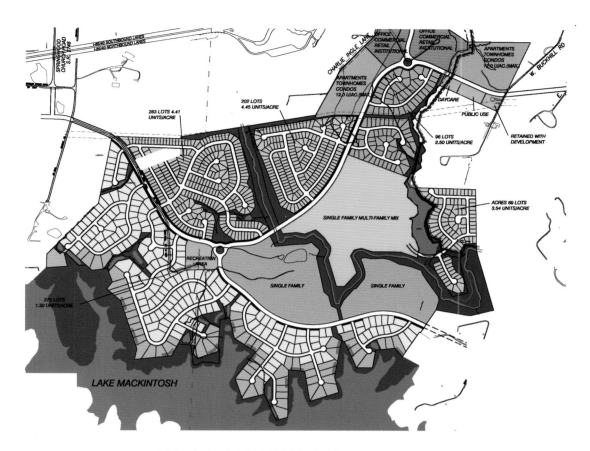

LAKE MACKINTOSH

MACKINTOSH ON THE LAKE

surveyor. Alley, who passed away in 1999, started his own engineering practice in 1954, and later added Williams, Carmen & King.

J. Earl Williams, a civil engineer graduate of North Carolina State University and a World War I veteran, joined Alley in 1955. Williams has also since passed away, but worked with AWCK until December 1970.

Haywood King, a graduate of Chicago Technical College and a registered professional engineer and land surveyor, joined the company in 1958 and became partner in 1960.

The firm was incorporated as AWCK when Herbert "Herb" Carmen, joined the firm in 1960. A graduate of the University of Pennsylvania and a registered architect for over fifty years, Carmen was firm treasurer for twenty years.

Today, all but two of the initial partners have passed on and new qualified professionals have stepped in to continue the tradition established by the founders; professionals such as current Board Chairman Darrell Russell of Alamance County.

A civil engineering graduate from North Carolina State University, Russell joined the

company in 1972 and served as vice president and then president 1993-2005. Since 2005, he has served as chairman and actively works with clients and projects of all sizes.

Franz Holt, also an Alamance native, has served as the firm's president since 2005. A graduate of the University of North Carolina in Charlotte, Holt joined the firm in 1985 and serves as the town engineer for several towns as well as manages other projects.

Serving as vice president is Jeff Moody. Also manager of the Kannapolis office, Moody has been with AWCK since 1987 and is a graduate of the University of North Carolina in Charlotte.

Current company treasurer is Mark Reich, a graduate of North Carolina State University who has been with the firm since 1994. Firm secretary is Alamance resident Kenneth Stafford. A graduate of North Carolina State, Stafford joined the firm in 1989.

For information on Alley, Williams, Carmen & King, call 336-226-5534 or visit the firm's website, www.awck.com.

❖

Mackintosh on the Lake.

BATTLEGROUND TIRE & WRECKER SERVICE, INC.

❖

Above: A photograph of the first fleet, c. 1975.

Below: Two Peterbilt wreckers, c. 2005.

The towing business demands complete dedication and working many long nights, weekends and holidays. It also demands flexibility and the ability to perform diverse and challenging operations far beyond the simple towing of a car.

Battleground Tire & Wrecker Service has experienced numerous diverse and challenging jobs such as airplane recovery and working amidst extremely hazardous materials.

This type of work, which makes a priority out of other's emergencies, became a way of life for Steve Bowman. Having been involved in the business his entire life and regardless of its endless hours and challenges, he says he would not have changed his life's work or chosen another industry in which to work.

Battleground started as a supermarket in the 1960s by brothers Robert and Tony Bowman. Robert and wife, Betty, eventually bought out Tony and expanded the business to include a service station and home heating oil delivery. Steve officially became his father's business partner in 1987 and sole owner in 1998.

The towing aspect of the business that eventually became the company's mainstay came about by accident in 1970 when Robert purchased a wrecker with intentions of reselling it—a 1966 Chevrolet with a ten-ton Stringfellow. After a few months the truck had not sold, so it was decided to keep it to support the service station.

Soon after, the company began offering mobile tire service and, in 1974, a second wrecker was purchased. In 1975 the company incorporated heavy truck repairs creating a need for a larger wrecker and a Holmes 600 was added, one of the largest in the area at that time. In 1977—with the transition to full-fledged tire and wrecker service well underway—a new office, six-bay shop and two-bay tire center was built across the highway from the original location. Though since expanded, it is at this location—6204 South Highway 62 in Burlington—from which Battleground still operates today.

The company received ICC authority in the late 1980s expanding its area of service nationwide, and continues to work closely with a network of reputable vendors providing customer service across the country.

Today, Battleground Tire & Wrecker is a multimillion dollar business with thirty-one employees and a fleet of two roll-backs, five service trucks, and eight wreckers, including five tandem trucks ranging in size up to fifty-ton capacity. It has continuously served Alamance and surrounding counties with a well-trained workforce and the most modern innovations available, such as air cushion recovery.

In addition to air cushion recovery, services include: roadside tire and truck service; light and heavy towing and recovery; inspections; minor and major mechanical work; preventive maintenance programs; and numerous other services. Vehicles served range from lawnmowers and cars to heavy trucks and farm equipment. Customer equipment can be repaired on the lot, on the road, or towed to

Battleground's full-service truck repair center or the repair facility of choice.

With a long history of community support and involvement, Battleground works closely with the State Highway Patrol, local rescue units, and fire, police and sheriff departments and is trained in pin-in accident recovery and underwater recovery.

Battleground has also shown support for local community colleges by helping to implement and participating in the INCITE program to encourage young people to study automotive and diesel mechanics.

Out of dedication to the industry, Steve is actively involved in the North Carolina Trucking Association, Towing and Recovery Association of America and the Towing and Recovery Professionals of North Carolina, the latter of which he was a founding member and continues to serve on the legislative committee.

"Indeed, the industry has experienced many changes over the past forty years and Battleground has kept pace by upgrading equipment and training as it continued to serve the community with a dedication to quality and service," said Connie Bowman, wife of Steve. "And, through these years of growth and change, the Bowman family has worked and sacrificed together to keep

the business both successful and, most importantly, reputable."

After many successful years and working with many long-term loyal employees and customers Steve sold the business in the fall of 2007 to David and Tracy Hardy of Kirk's-Sineath. Merging these two companies created one of the largest and oldest towing companies in the state of North Carolina.

Above: Fifty ton wrecker on another heavy duty recovery.

Below: Steve Bowman (left) and Robert Bowman.

HAYDEN-HARMAN FOUNDATION

"It's not about the foundation. It's not even about the money; it's about helping people," says Dr. Patrick Harman.

And helping people is exactly what the Hayden-Harman Foundation has been doing since his family established it in February 2000 to fulfill the final wishes of his grandmother, Elizabeth Harman.

According to Executive Director and Vice President Harman, his grandmother was always active in charities in High Point where she grew up, and in Alamance County where she moved with her husband, Dave Harman, and lived from the mid-1930s until her death in 1999. She had a special place in her heart for both places and specified that the Foundation should support organizations and projects in these locations through contributions and grants.

Though it was Elizabeth Harman's estate that funded the foundation, the organization's roots actually go back to her own parents, Jesse and Velva Hayden. Her father not only pioneered the first telephone exchange in Thomasville, but in 1899 joined with a partner to also purchase High Point's telephone exchange and, in 1905, officially incorporated it as North State Telephone Company. Hayden steadily expanded the company and remained at the helm until his death in 1952, at which time his wife, Velva, took over and capably led the company until 1974. The company remains in the family today.

Above: David and Patrick Harman.

Below: Phoebe and Pat Harman.

"My great-grandparents and grandparents are the people who really made this possible and it is an honor to fulfill my grandmother's wishes," Harman said, adding that the Foundation gives approximately $500,000 annually to an average of thirty-five organizations. "Our mission is to support good works, good ideas that work, with a focus on promoting social welfare, improving educational outcomes, and supporting historical preservation. We achieve this by assisting and encouraging organizations whose programs have the promise to make a substantial impact on the community and the clients they serve."

Some of the Foundation's many philanthropic deeds have included, for example, a grant which allowed Loaves and Fishes, a local Christian food ministry that had outgrown its facility, to move downtown and combine its storage and distribution center into one place. The Foundation has also contributed to the Norville Breast Care Center of Alamance Regional Medical Center, which opened in 2002. It was named after Phoebe Harman's parents, the late William L. Norville, M.D., and his wife Lil, both of whom served Alamance for years, he as director of public health and she as a teacher. Lil

was also a twenty year breast cancer survivor.

The Foundation has established scholarships at Alamance Community College and Guilford Technical Community College; has helped to create and fund a matched savings program for low-wage workers; has supported capacity-building programs for nonprofit professionals at Elon and High Point Universities; and has encouraged other philanthropists by annually honoring United Way of Alamance County's "Volunteers of the Year" with a $1,000 donation to the charity of their choice.

It has contributed to the building fund for the Positive Attitude Youth Center; to the after-school arts program of the Alamance County Arts Council; to the Alamance-Burlington School system to assist with the development of an early literacy program; to Morgan Place Park for the construction of a walking track; to the May Memorial Library for a Nonprofit Resource Center; and to the Alamance Citizens for Education for the purchase of dictionaries for all of Alamance County's third graders. Another major project in the wings is a children's museum. The brainchild of the Harman family, the future Children's Museum of Alamance County already has a board of directors and a challenge grant from the Foundation for $1 million in matching funds.

In addition to Dr. Harman, the Foundation is capably led by his father, Dr. J. Patrick Harman, president; his brother, David L. Harman, vice president; and his mother, Phoebe Norville Harman who serves as secretary-treasurer.

"I just love this job," Dr. Harman said. "It is so gratifying to give back to the communities that have given us so much. I know Grandmother would be proud."

Above: Patrick and Phoebe Harman at Pink Ribbon Cancer Luncheon.

Below: Loaves and Fishes office and distribution center.

CHANDLER CONCRETE

With a tradition of excellence as solid as their product, Chandler Concrete Company, Inc., is a family owned and operated business that has been supplying quality ready-mixed concrete products to customers for more than sixty years.

When founded by R.F. Kirkpatrick in 1946, the company became the first-ever ready-mixed concrete producer in Alamance County. It quickly laid a sturdy foundation in its home county and was ultimately purchased by Thomas E. "Tom" Chandler in 1973.

Under Chandler's leadership, the company steadily built upon the company's successful foundation in Alamance County and operates over forty ready-mixed concrete plants in North Carolina, Virginia and Tennessee. The company also owns and operates two building supply operations and two concrete block plants.

"Combined, all of these operations give us the flexibility to meet the growing and diverse needs of our customers from the residential do-it-yourself projects to highway construction to large industrial and commercial jobs," said Bob Chandler, son of Tom Chandler and the company's vice president of sales and marketing. "At Chandler Concrete, no job is too big or too small."

According to the Chandlers, the company's growth has been a direct result of its strong

❖

Thomas E. Chandler, Sr.

reputation for providing quality products and outstanding customer service with highly qualified and experienced employees. It is also the result of a long term strategy of steady, but controlled growth through carefully selected acquisitions and expansions.

"While profitability, business success and operating efficiencies are essential, we have

always placed a high value on companies that share similar business interest and principles including a strong focus on quality products, a high level of customer service and dedicated, qualified employees," Chandler said. "We are always looking for ways to better satisfy customers needs and to remain competitive in an industry that is continuously changing."

The company's first presence outside of North Carolina came in 1998 with the purchase of Concrete Ready Mix Corporation, a company with plants in Roanoke, Salem and Botetourt, Virginia. The very next year, Chandler entered the building supply business with the purchase of Home Concrete and Supply of Salisbury, North Carolina, an established company with more than fifty years experience in the concrete and building supply industry. Then, in April 2000, the company purchased Biscoe Supply Company in Biscoe, North Carolina, an operation which included a concrete plant and another building supply store. This purchase—coupled with the company's existing plants in neighboring Randolph and Chatham counties—further established Chandler's presence in central North Carolina as a premier provider of concrete and related products.

The opportunity to expand beyond central North Carolina into the rapidly growing areas of western North Carolina was realized in 2003 with the purchase of Watauga Ready Mixed Concrete based in Boone, North Carolina. With plants in Boone, Blowing Rock, Sparta, Jefferson and West Jefferson, North Carolina, as well as Mountain City, Tennessee, Chandler once again expanded its geographic market providing customers and employees with even more opportunities for growth and development.

In June 2006 the company joined forces with Marshall Concrete Products based in Danville and Christiansburg, Virginia. The purchase included ready-mix concrete plants located in Danville, Alta Vista, Chatham, South Boston, Moneta, Christiansburg, Wytheville, Dublin, and Pearsiburg, as well as two concrete block plants located in Christiansburg and Danville.

This purchase not only gave the company an expanded and greater presence in the southern and southwestern Virginia markets, it also provided it with the opportunity to enhance its product offerings in North Carolina with the addition of concrete block and decorative masonry products.

"Our steady pattern of growth has been possible only because of our dedicated and talented employees who are committed to producing quality products and providing our customers with the high level of service they need and expect," Chandler said, proudly noting that it was because of the company's employees that Chandler Concrete was named a recent recipient of the highly coveted Carolinas AGC Pinnacle Award for Best Supplier/Service Company. "We're proud of our employees and we're proud of having such a strong history to continue building upon as we look ahead to the future."

For more information on Chandler Concrete, please call 336-226-1181 or visit the company at www.chandlerconcrete.com.

WISHART, NORRIS, HENNINGER & PITTMAN, P.A.

The attorneys of Wishart, Norris, Henninger and Pittman, P.A., understand the specific needs and goals of entrepreneurs and owners of closely-held businesses. They understand because they have been there.

"Our partners are, in fact, owners of a closely-held business. Our business just happens to be law," said Wade Harrison, managing partner at the firm's Burlington office. "We have first-hand knowledge of the same challenges faced by our clients as they navigate the various stages of their business."

❖
Davis Street office in Burlington, North Carolina.

Wishart, Norris, Henninger and Pittman, P.A., was founded in 1976 by Charlie Bateman, Robert J. "Bob" Wishart and Robert B. Norris. Bateman left the firm early on and Josh Henninger joined, followed closely by Dorn Pittman. From the very beginning, the firm's focus has been on helping entrepreneurs and owners of closely-held businesses.

"Fresh out of law school, our founding partners looked closely at the legal landscape of Burlington and realized that there were a number of closely-held businesses, primarily in the textile industry, that were seeking legal help in other towns," Harrison said. "They reasoned that, if they could create a specialty law firm capable of providing the same level of service or better in Burlington, there should be enough growth to sustain it."

Turns out they were right as today the firm has grown—without merger—from a practice of four to one of the state's largest law firms with thirty-six attorneys and seventy-five employees. It has transitioned from its humble beginnings in a tiny, upstairs office where Wishart's first desk was a cardboard box to two considerable offices, one in Burlington and one in Charlotte.

Its clientele has grown from just a handful to more than one thousand entrepreneurs and business owners located primarily in North and South Carolina and engaged in all types of business from manufacturing, distribution, textiles and service companies to real estate development, contractors, information technology and a host of professionals. Some clients are large and some are small; some are regional, national and even international. Some are second and third generation, while others are just getting started.

To fulfill clients' needs, the firm has an experienced team highly skilled in all areas essential to closely-held businesses including business planning, mergers and acquisitions, tax planning, adversarial tax representation, estate planning, succession planning, commercial and residential real estate, commercial litigation, debt collection, employment law, divorce and equitable distribution, just to name a few.

What is more, the firm's attorneys are highly respected by not only their clients, but also within the legal profession and the communities they so faithfully serve.

The firm's attorneys include graduates of some of the nation's finest law schools; five have earned MBA degrees; three are licensed Certified Public Accountants; and others are Board Certified Specialists in a variety of areas. A number have chaired various sections of the North Carolina Bar Association, and many are recognized annually by their state peers as "Super Lawyers," and others as among the "Legal Elite." Attorneys from the firm are fellows in national specialty groups and some have been repeatedly recognized as among "The Best Lawyers in America."

The firm is also deeply dedicated to supporting its communities. Many of its attorneys and employees serve on the boards of community and charitable organizations, and the firm itself has created its own charitable foundation to benefit charitable and civic endeavors in both Alamance and Mecklenburg

Counties. The Wishart, Norris, Henninger & Pittman Charitable Foundation regularly supports more than forty charities, with a special focus on children's issues. The firm has been consistently recognized for its good work by organizations such as the Alamance Chamber, March of Dimes, United Way, Burlington City Council, Habitat for Humanity, and Children Resources and Referral.

In 2006, in celebration of its thirtieth anniversary, the firm established a scholarship program and awards a $2,000 scholarship annually to a graduating senior from a public or private school in Alamance County where the firm was born.

For additional information on Wishart, Norris, Henninger & Pittman, please visit www.wnhplaw.com or call 336-584-3388.

Above: Left to right, Robert B. Norris, Josh Henninger, Robert J. Wishart and Dorn Pittman.

Below: Burlington office building c. 2008.

ALAMANCE REGIONAL MEDICAL CENTER

Located on an eighty acre campus on Huffman Mill Road in Burlington, Alamance Regional Medical Center opened in 1995 and was the triumphant result of an innovative and historical merger between a pair of aging community hospitals.

The two hospitals combined by the merger—the first of its kind in the state—were Alamance Memorial Hospital and Alamance County Hospital.

Alamance Memorial's roots date back to 1916 when a local businessman persuaded Dr. Rainey Parker of Goldsboro to open a small hospital in Burlington. Rainey Hospital operated as a private hospital until 1937 when it was turned over to a community board of trustees and renamed Alamance General. The board eventually directed the construction of a new 100-bed facility that opened in 1961 under yet another name, Alamance Memorial Hospital. Additional renovations and improvements followed over the years.

Alamance County Hospital opened in 1951. Hailed as one of the "finest small hospitals in the south," this hospital was owned by the county until the mid-1980s when it became privately owned and financially independent. The facility started out with 100 beds, but increased to 163 over the years.

While both hospitals were successful in their own rights, community leaders and both hospital boards began to realize that healthy growth could not be sustained indefinitely for two hospitals within such a limited service area. The key to future success was obviously cooperation rather than competition.

Alamance Memorial Board Chairman Ralph M. Holt, Jr., and Alamance County Board Chairman D. Earl Pardue, along with other community leaders, initiated that cooperation in

the early 1980s with the two hospitals participating in several joint ventures. By 1985 the boards had begun to meet jointly, and in 1986, passed a resolution making the two hospitals subsidiaries of Alamance Health Services. The two facilities were physically combined in 1995 with the opening of the state-of-the-art medical complex we know today.

At an initial cost of $48 million, the 238-bed, private, not-for-profit Alamance Regional was designed to deliver the ultimate in healthcare. From the patient towers to the soaring "wave" roof line, the new facility was, and still is, both practical and strikingly beautiful.

It is, additionally, one of the county's largest employers with 2,000 employees and a 285-physician medical staff whose unwavering philosophy of respect and compassion for every patient and steadfast pursuit of excellence has not only generated countless satisfied patients, but a healthy dose of recognition and awards as well.

Honors include being named "Microsoft Hospital of the Year" for its use of technology to improve patient care and one of *Business North Carolina Magazine*'s "Top Ten Hospitals for Orthopedics" six years running. The facility's angioplasty outcomes have been publicized as among the highest nationwide by the *American Journal of Cardiology*, and Premier, Inc., a healthcare alliance that measures quality improvement efforts, has lauded it as one of the nation's best facilities for treating heart attacks. Additionally, Alamance Regional is one of only twenty-five percent of the country's hospitals to be accredited by the American College of Surgeons as a Comprehensive Community Cancer Center.

Services provided by the hospital include a wide range of quality inpatient, outpatient, and wellness services. In addition to its highly-respected Cancer Center and Heart and Vascular Center, specialized services at Alamance Regional include a Women's Care Center, which houses the BirthPlace and Level II/III Special Care Neonatal Nursery, internationally-recognized digital imaging services, and complete rehabilitation services.

Satellite facilities include the Mebane Outpatient Center located in Mebane Medical Park; West End Medical Park; Pediatric

Rehabilitation; and outpatient Rehabilitation Centers on South Church Street in Burlington, in the Mebane Medical Park and in Yanceyville.

Additionally, the organization is the creator of the first ever hospital-sponsored retirement community in the Triad. Completed in 2003, The Village at Brookwood's fifty-acre campus is nestled in a beautiful Burlington neighborhood and includes cottages and apartments, which give residents the best of both worlds—the comforts of an independent home life coupled with the security of private assisted living and healthcare accommodations.

For more information about Alamance Regional Medical Center, visit www.armc.com.

Above: Alamance County Hospital opened in 1951 and is one of the two hospitals that merged to create today's Alamance Regional.

Below: Alamance Memorial Hospital opened in 1961 and was also a part of the merger that created Alamance Regional.

BLAKEY HALL & ASSOCIATES

What started out as just a theory is today a successful reality at The Hamlet, Blakey Hall and Henton at Elon, a trio of retirement offerings located adjacent to the beautiful campus of Elon University.

Back in the middle 1980s, while pondering the limited retirement options available to seniors, John Ketcham says he realized that many retirees planned their retirement like most people plan a vacation. And, all too often, those retirees wound up disappointed.

"I knew people who had selected their retirement homes based on the number of tennis courts or golf courses they had access to," Ketcham said in a recent interview. "But, after a year or so, many of them became deeply dissatisfied with their choices. That is when I began to believe that a retiree who continues learning is more likely to have a greater sense of self," Ketcham explained. "Then, I thought, what better place for a retirement community than near a college campus where residents can have the best of both worlds—the ability to enjoy the things they prize in retirement such as leisure activities and, at the same time, have access to educational and cultural opportunities that can stretch their minds."

It simply did not matter that he had no experience in real estate development or that he never even heard of such a retirement community. Ketcham, then a resident of Ohio, so steadfastly believed in his theory that he set out to make it happen. He quickly decided on North Carolina as the location because it had the second greatest inward migration of retirees in the southeast. Second only to Florida, North Carolina was a natural draw for retirees from all over the country because of its mild weather, beautiful scenery and the sophistication of its residents.

Next, he began searching for the right college. He concentrated on the smaller, private institutions as he felt they would be more likely to listen to someone with so little background and capital. An educator friend gave him a list of eight small, private, liberal arts colleges that were regarded as financially and academically sound and Ketcham spoke to the presidents of each. He found them all very open to the idea, but it was Elon College that had the interest and there was a perfect parcel of available land nearby.

"It was beautiful land and I appreciated the location halfway between the Triad and the Triangle," Ketcham said. "It turned out that ours was not the first college-oriented retirement community as some faculty members at the University of Indiana had started a similar project in 1980. That project, however, had floundered and was taken over by new owners in 1989."

Established in 1985, Henton at Elon is today a community of forty single family homes for early end retirees and features a homeowners association, which provides grounds maintenance. Located just up the street from the Henton development is The Hamlet, a rental apartment complex involving forty-two duplex apartments and offering the next level of care for seniors still seeking independent living. Grounds at The Hamlet are maintained as are the buildings. Residents have a community dining room, housekeeping services, transportation and an active social calendar.

Yet even greater care is provided at Blakey Hall, an assisted living residence opened in 1999 and licensed by the state of North Carolina. Blakey Hall has space for seventy-two residents and is located on the same fourteen-acre campus as The Hamlet. The final phase—a secure unit for dementia sufferers who might come to harm from wandering—was completed in 2008.

"I couldn't be more pleased with my choice to locate in Elon," Ketcham said. "It is such a handsome college community with a vigor and vitality that not only energizes our residents, but that also stimulates their minds."

For more information, please visit www.bhhamlet.com or call 336-506-2301.

Above: The Blakey Hall Alzheimer's Unit.

Below: The Hamlet Club House.

WARREN LAND COMPANY

Warren Land Company continues to stake its claim as an integral part of both the history and the future of Alamance County as well as Warren County.

Headquartered in Burlington and founded by the Thomas E. Powell, Jr., family, Warren Land Company has been acquiring and developing land in Alamance and Warren Counties in North Carolina and Mecklenburg County in Virginia for almost a half century. The company primarily focuses on developing land for industrial purposes, but is also engaged in tree farming, growing and harvesting pines on a 550-acre tract of land, which has been owned by the founding family since the Revolutionary War.

One of Warren Land Company's most notable accomplishments is its relationship to Laboratory Corporation of America, which is not only headquartered in Alamance County, but is also the county's largest employer.

One of Warren Land's first acquisitions after its 1960 founding was the Rainey Building,

formerly Alamance General Hospital, located at 1308 Rainey Street in Burlington. The company renovated the building and began leasing space in the early 1960s to several companies, including another of its family businesses—Carolina Biological Supply Company—as well as Bobbitt Laboratories and Granite Diagnostics. And, in April 1969, it was in this building that Biomedical Laboratories was founded by Thomas E. Powell, III, M.D.; John S. Powell, Esquire; James B. Powell, M.D.; and Ernest A. Knesel, Jr., Biomedical Laboratories later became Biomedical Reference Laboratories and was taken public on May 4, 1979, and has since evolved into America's second largest clinical laboratory company known as Laboratory Corporation of America.

Company President Thomas E. Powell, IV, currently heads Warren Land Company. Its headquarter offices are located at 2006 South Church Street in Burlington.

WARREN LAND COMPANY
BOARD OF DIRECTORS
ANNUAL MEETING
NOVEMBER 1, 2007

The Acorn Inn of Elon is the perfect mélange of luxury inn and charming bed and breakfast— a true oasis of tranquility and hospitality for all who pass through its doors.

Nestled in the beautiful town of Elon in Alamance County, just two blocks from Elon University, the Acorn Inn features twelve luxury suites, each complete with whirlpool, king-size bed, fireplace, microwave and refrigerator. In addition to luxury accommodations for about the same cost of a regular hotel room, guests are also treated to true southern hospitality and a complimentary breakfast of fresh-baked bakery items or home-cooked waffles. There is a radiant sunroom and a fabulous front porch where guests can choose to relax year-round or perhaps host their reception or shower. In the summer months, that same charming front porch comes alive with local wine from the Grove Winery and the musical stylings of local musicians such as Mudbone or Wood & Steel.

The unique creation of Jim and Becky Brown and their son and daughter-in-law, Mike and Melissa Brown, Acorn Inn was built new and opened for guests in November 2001. It came about when Mike and Melissa, who both attended Elon University, recognized that—even though many of the college's students were from other states—there were few local accommodations for their out-of-town guests. Since the Browns already had some experience in the hospitality industry with their first property—Affordable Suites of America—opening in June of 1999, and because they had an interest in expanding their hospitality locations, they decided to experiment with a new type of property. And, thus, the Acorn Inn was conceived. All they needed was a place to build it.

"Then, one day while I was jogging from our home in Gibsonville, I came across a vacant lot," Mike said. "There had once been a house there, but it had burned down back in the mid 1990s. After some research to see exactly what could be built there, everything just fell into place and the Acorn Inn came to be."

For more information please visit www.acorninnelon.com or call 336-585-0167.

COMFORT SUITES

With a location as pleasing as its many amenities and its warm, friendly staff, Comfort Suites in Graham is the perfect place to stay while visiting Alamance County.

Conveniently located at 769 Woody Drive at Interstate 85 and Interstate 40, Comfort Suites is nestled just a few miles from area attractions like Elon University, Alamance Community College, Alamance Regional Medical Center, University Commons Mall, Alamance Crossings Mall, Burlington Square Mall, JR Discount Outlet, Graham Historical Museum, Alamance Battleground, Alamance County Historical Museum, Ace Speedway, Challenge Golf Club and Burlington Outlet Village.

Duke University, the University of North Carolina at Chapel Hill, the University of North Carolina at Greensboro and Wet n' Wild Emerald Pointe are just twenty-five miles away. Additionally, a number of local business parks and office complexes are close to the hotel and a variety of restaurants and cocktail lounges are located in the surrounding area.

Opened in May 2002 by longtime residents Jay Patel and son, Hari "Mickey" Patel, some of the hotel's many amenities include a host of complimentary services from high-speed Internet access, a daily hot breakfast, local calls,

the local newspaper delivered to your room each weekday and unlimited access to the exercise room, sundeck, hot tub and indoor heated pool. There is also an in-house business center featuring copy and fax services and complimentary high-speed Internet connections as well as a meeting room that accommodates up to sixty people.

All spacious suites feature upscale furnishings with separate living areas with sofa-sleeper, large working desk, ergonomic chair, two telephones, refrigerator, microwave, coffee maker, iron, ironing board, hair dryer and cable television. Some suites even have whirlpool tubs.

"It was our goal to build a hotel with big city amenities here in our home community," said Mickey. "From the moment you arrive, you'll see why the Comfort Suites is the perfect place to stay while visiting the Graham and Burlington areas. Our friendly staff is ready to greet you with exceptional service."

For reservations or more information, please call 336-221-9199 or you can visit www.comfortsuitesgraham.com.

FAIRCLOTH CONSTRUCTION & REALTY, INC.

Seeing a family enjoying their new home translates into the ultimate job satisfaction for Randy Faircloth, owner and founder of Faircloth Construction & Realty, Inc., in Burlington. The philosophy at Faircloth Construction is that a house is much more than a physical structure. It is an outlet for creativity, and a canvas on which people can create wonderful things and express themselves in unique ways. A house is a place where children grow up and memories are made—it is a home.

As quality custom home builders and developers, Randy and wife Chris live, work and are involved in the local community. Their thirty year-old company takes pride in building a small number of custom homes a year as well as developing unique subdivisions that are designed to take advantage of the beauty of the land on which they are developed.

Randy and Chris and their two children, Sarah and Jacob, are proud to have built over 100 quality custom homes for families in and around Alamance County. Their company has been involved in developing neighborhoods such as Fairfield, Heritage Glen, Buttermilk Creek and Stones Path. These subdivisions have been designed to have a minimal impact on the environment and to utilize green building and developing techniques such as vegetation buffers, minimal environmental invasion and construction using natural materials.

"Professionalism and attention to detail and quality typify every home our company builds," Randy said in a recent interview. "We take pride in knowing that we've made someone's dream of owning a custom home come true and that we handled challenges with confidence and grace, without ever losing track of the importance of the relationship and trust we have with our customers. We consider our profession to be one of the most important and meaningful ways to make a living, and we are proud of the fact that we can drive through our community and see the lasting legacy that we have built."

For more information, you can visit www.fairclothconstruction.com on the Internet or call 336-227-2334.

Above: This impressive brick and stucco home is representative of the many custom homes Faircloth Construction, Inc., builds for families in the central North Carolina area. Note the unique architectural style and attention to detail that is put into this and every custom home built by our company.

Below: Every member of the Faircloth family is involved in this small custom home business. Company owner and President Randy Faircloth and his wife Chris are pictured with children Sarah and Jacob.

JORDAN PROPERTIES/ SAXAPAHAW RIVERMILL

Above: Saxapahaw Rivermill.

Below: (From left) B. Everett Jordan, T. Carter Jordan, John M. Jordan, and John (Mac) Jordan, Jr.

Just as their family legacy—a legacy they shared with an entire community—began to quietly slip away into yesteryear, the John M. Jordan family and their company, Jordan Properties, stepped in to reclaim it.

Today, nearly eight decades after B. Everett Jordan first purchased the textile mill in the center of Saxapahaw and nearly thirty years after it was sold, the next generations of Jordans have repurchased, restored, renovated, and completely revived not just the mill, but the entire historic mill village.

Located along the banks of the Haw River, just a short drive from Chapel Hill, this place where cotton bolls were once spun into yarn is now home to unique loft apartments, town homes, and a diverse collection of retail, office, and studio spaces. Additionally, dozens of cottages that once housed mill workers' families dot the serene landscape and are a perfect blend of modern amenities and vintage detail.

Founded in 1927 by the late B. Everett Jordan, Sellers Manufacturing Company, Inc., owned and operated the Saxapahaw mill as well as three other North Carolina textile mills for fifty-one years. With the help of his sons, Ben E. Jordan, Jr., and John M. Jordan, the senior Jordan, who also served as U.S. Senator from 1958 until 1973, remained at the company's helm for its entire half century in business.

In 1978, Sellers Manufacturing sold three of its mills to Dixie Yarns Inc., but Senator Jordan's two sons and daughter—Rose Ann Jordan Gant—continued the company, changing its name to Sellers, Inc., and operating it as an investment and development company. That same year, John founded Jordan Properties 1978, LLC, as a sister company specializing in the purchase, sale, rehabilitation, development, and management of rural real estate in Alamance and five other surrounding counties. John's sons, John "Mac" Jordan, Jr., and T. Carter Jordan, work at and help direct both companies and were especially instrumental in the renaissance of the historic Saxapahaw mills and village into the beautifully preserved Saxapahaw Rivermill community.

For more information, about what Jordan Properties and Saxaphaw Rivermill have to offer please visit www.jordanproperties.com and www.rivermillvillage.com.

Some might say Jon Lambert was simply following in the footsteps of his forefathers. After all, his grandfather, Jim Lambert, was a part-time auctioneer who owned a small auction barn in the 1950s, and his dad, Jimmy Lambert, himself loved to dabble in the world of antiques.

But, the fact is, while it was indeed his elders who sparked his interest in antiques, Jon did more than just follow along. He jumped in with both feet and is today the owner of Mebane Auction, the largest weekly antique auction in North Carolina.

As just a boy, Jon was going to flea markets and estate auctions with his dad, and, by the age of ten, was studying antique guides. In the late 1970s when he was in his early teens, he started visiting auction barns.

"That's when things really began to change," Jon reminisces. "I fully immersed myself, visiting museums, reading books, and learning as much as possible about identifying and selling pieces."

But, it was not until 1991, after a year or so of selling through another's auction firm, he decided to go it on his own.

Today, his firm hosts hundreds of buyers and phone bidders who purchase an average of nine hundred lots weekly. Buyers range from those looking for $1 items to representatives of museums like the Smithsonian, and private collectors and investors throughout the world. Gross annual sales are above a million and the firm holds a multitude of records. Such records include the state record for highest-dollar amount for a single painting at $750,000, and a world record when it helped a local clock collector sell a Howard for $38,000.

"I love what I do," Jon said, adding that he also does estate walk-throughs and pre-auction estimates. "I love to help families discover treasures they may hold."

As for his location, Jon says that he could not have picked a better place than his native home. "Alamance and the Piedmont are rich in important antiques prized the world over," he said.

Mebane Auction is located at 7607 US 70 West in Mebane. For more information, call 919-536-2424 or visit www.mebaneauction.com.

MEBANE AUCTION

❖

Left: Jon Lambert.

ARMACELL LLC

From the wrestling mats in your school to the construction sites of buildings and homes throughout North America, and even the International Space Station hovering two hundred miles miles above the earth, Armacell LLC's products are everywhere.

The unequivocal world leader in engineered foams, Armacell provides insulation, specialty foam and rubber solutions for a wide range of industries and applications around the globe. In fact, one does not have to look far to see Armacell foam products on the local McDonald's playground, in a building's heating and air conditioning system, in naval vessels maneuvering above and below the water, under the hood of their cars, and in the protective pads worn by athletes.

Insulation products include Armaflex®, the world's leading brand of flexible insulation. It is the product of choice for mechanical insulation, air conditioning and refrigeration, ductwork, and any commercial or residential application that requires prevention of heat loss or gain or protection against condensation. The company also produces special foams for a host of industrial, packaging and electronic applications, as well as the sport and leisure sector under the Ensolite®, OleTex®, ArmaSport®, and Monarch® brands.

A 2000 spin-off from its former parent company, Armstrong World Industries, Armacell is now independently owned and employs 2,500 people at 20 production sites in 13 countries. Five of the company's twenty sites are located in America and include the North American headquarters facility in Mebane. U.S. employees total approximately five hundred, about half of whom are employed locally.

An enormous facility, the Mebane headquarters is a visible example of Armacell's tremendous investment in the North American market. It is located on Oakwood Street Extension where the old Chock Full O' Nuts factory became a manufacturing plant for Armaflex® insulation in 1995. After moving its headquarters to Mebane in 2000, Armacell constructed a state-of-the-art 180,000-square-foot warehouse boasting an electronic nerve center to ensure optimum stock rotation and shipping accuracy on one side of the plant, and acquired an adjacent corporate headquarters building to house corporate staff, research and development, and Armacell customer service.

For more information, visit www.armacell.com.

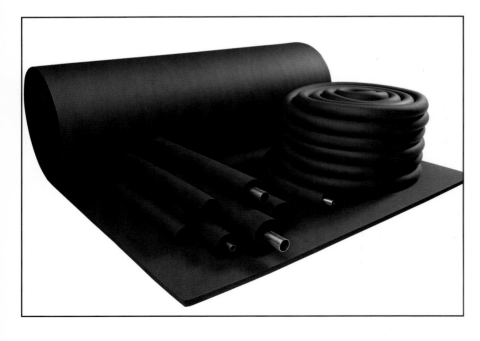

With its centurial birthday just around the corner, the Alamance County Area Chamber of Commerce has much to celebrate.

Indeed, since four local businessmen chartered the organization in 1914, this chamber has been a driving force in the growth and development of Alamance County.

For nearly one hundred years, the Chamber has been involved in building the business base of the county including leading the efforts to bring J. Spencer Love from Gastonia to Burlington where Burlington Industries was born. Historic records also reference the arrival of Western Electric, Honda Power Equipment, GKN, Luxfer, and many more. In addition, the Chamber has weighed in on many of the vital issues, programs, and major initiatives that have molded the community into what it is today.

Now over eight hundred members strong, today's Chamber continues it's roles of building and marketing the community. Chamber President Mac Williams notes that "the Chamber is, essentially, a marketing agency with three distinct, but complementary function areas—Economic Development markets the area as a location for new and expanding industry; the Convention and Visitors Bureau markets the county as a destination for visitors, tourists, and meetings; and the Chamber provides business services to its members and represents business in community development affairs."

Focusing on economic development marketing, the Chamber recently re-branded its new logo and slogan to read "Alamance County, NC—The Carolina Corridor" to better reflect the county's strongest asset, its location in North Carolina on two interstates, between two commercial airports and between two growing metro areas.

"Alamance County has truly evolved into a 'corridor of commerce' and our new branding effort helps better promote that message as we

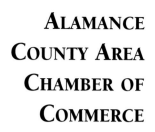

ALAMANCE
COUNTY AREA
CHAMBER OF
COMMERCE

enter the final stretch of our first century in business," said Williams.

For more information, call the Alamance County Area Chamber of Commerce at 336-228-1338 or visit www.thecarolinacorridor.com.

Left: The current office for the Alamance County Chamber is located at the corner of Lexington Avenue and Morehead Street near downtown Burlington.

Below: In this 1958 photo, the Chamber is shown sharing space with the Merchant's Association and Credit Bureau. This building was located at 312-314 West Front Street in downtown Burlington.

ELON UNIVERSITY

❖

*Above: Alamance Building at
Elon University.*

*Below: Elon's 5,500 students come
from 47 states and 45 nations.*

Founded in 1889 by ministers of the Christian Church, Elon University has evolved into one of the nation's premier universities.

From its initial class of seventy-six students, Elon College grew slowly for several decades. Enrollment exceeded 1,000 for the first time in 1955, and J. Earl Danieley was named the institution's sixth president two years later. During Danieley's tenure, Elon opened a new library and student center, and the first class of students studied abroad.

In 1973, J. Fred Young succeeded Danieley as president. Under Young's leadership, the college experienced extensive growth. Dozens of academic and student life programs were added to promote active, hands-on teaching and learning. In addition, the aggressive Elon Vision strategic plan was launched in 1994. Within a decade, Elon had established the Martha and Spencer Love School of Business and opened Dalton L. McMichael, Sr., Science Center, Carol Grotnes Belk Library, Rhodes Stadium and numerous residence halls.

As Elon flourished, Leo M. Lambert was selected as the college's eighth president in 1999. Determined to establish Elon as a national leader in higher education, Lambert guided the institution through an academic reorganization that created Elon College, the College of Arts and Sciences, along with professional schools for communications and education.

In 2001, Elon College became Elon University, with a new strategic plan, NewCentury@Elon, designed to establish Elon as a national model of engaged learning. There were major investments in academic programs, expansion of the faculty, opening of the Ernest A. Koury, Sr., Business Center and the Academic Village, and establishment of the Elon University School of Law.

Today, Elon is ranked among the nation's top universities. About fifty-five hundred students choose from fifty academic majors, and graduate degrees in business administration, education, physical therapy and law. Much of the credit for this transformation can be attributed to Elon's founders' vision of an academic community that transforms mind, body and spirit, and encourages freedom of thought and liberty of conscience.

As a little boy, Mark Crissman remembers proudly carrying his father's big black bag as the two of them made house calls together.

He also remembers watching in awe as his father—the town's much-loved and highly-revered doctor—used his hands, his mind and the contents of that black bag to almost magically heal the sick. He remembers the difference his dad made in the townseople's lives. Even during the segregation era, the elder Crissman did not care what color the patient was nor did he care if they were rich or poor. All he cared about was making them well.

"I was always amazed with the work he did and the love and respect his patients had for him," Mark said of his late father, Dr. Clinton S. Crissman, MD. "Being a doctor was undoubtedly his calling and he continued to answer that call here in Graham for almost a half-century."

Indeed, from the time he hung out his shingle in 1946 to the time of his retirement in 1992, Dr. Crissman not only kept the community healthy, he also helped keep the population growing, delivering thousands upon thousands of babies. With his gentle spirit, immense knowledge and positive attitude, he also inspired people—especially son Mark who himself went on to become a doctor and proudly joined his father at Crissman Family Practice in 1985.

And, though his father has since passed on, Dr. Mark Crissman continues to carry the torch, serving the same community his father served. In fact, Crissman Family Practice is now one of the oldest ongoing medical practices in Alamance County.

But, do not think just because the practice is old that it is out-of-date. Quite the contrary, according to Dr. Crissman, who says the Crissman practice is among the area's most modern, complete with electronic records and extensive diagnostic equipment.

Crissman is joined by two nurse practitioners and a highly trained staff who together continue his father's legacy and offer families the best, most comprehensive medical care possible.

For more information on Crissman Family Practice, call 336-226-2448 or please visit www.crissmanfamilypractice.com.

CRISSMAN FAMILY PRACTICE

214 East Elm Street in Graham, North Carolina.

THE VERY THING, LTD.

Above: Imaginative use of color and furnishings characterize interiors by The Very Thing, Ltd.

Below: Since 1979, The Very Thing has presented a striking floral display at this location on South Church Street.

The Very Thing is more than just the name of their business; it is who they are—interior designers specializing in fine interior design with the abilities and resources to find the "very thing" that makes their clients' homes and businesses more unique and inviting.

Having remained in business for eighty-two years, those at The Very Thing take pride in providing individual and customized services for every client. Searching out the newest and most outstanding textiles, wall coverings and furnishings available in the world has been its consistent goal.

The Very Thing, Ltd. was founded in 1926 as the Neese-Shoffner Furniture Company. With a reputation as the Piedmont area's premier furniture store, Neese-Shoffner sold only the finest in home furnishings and accessories, later branching out into fine china, crystal and gifts, and a wedding registry.

The store was purchased in 1970 by Rose Ann Jordan Gant and Catherine Chandler and, as a reflection of its new owners' interests and tastes, soon became known for its fine antique furnishings and interior design. In 1974 it was reincorporated as The Very Thing, Ltd., and four years later moved to its current location at 2100 South Church Street when Mrs. Gant became sole owner.

Today, The Very Thing serves clients in several states and is renowned for offering custom draperies and upholstery, unique antique furniture, unusual lamps and chandeliers. The company also carries a vast inventory of antique European linens and is the east coast's only dealer for Decadence Down, a line of fine Hungarian goose down pillows and down bedding.

Joining Rose Ann Jordan Gant at The Very Thing is Vice President and Designer Leigh S. Jones, a professional member of the American Society of Interior Designers, and Susan Gant, who works in bookkeeping and sales.

For more information, call 336-226-6066.

There are few businesses more important to the growing success of a farmer than the McBane family business.

Named for the Alamance native who owns it, Paul McBane Farm and Fertilizer Company has been making sure its customers' crops are planted on fertile, pest-free ground and that their animals are well fed and healthy for almost a half-century.

It is a business that is truly a family business as Paul is joined by his son, Steve, who has been working alongside him since he was just a small boy, just as Paul grew up working alongside his own father, Ross McBane. As a matter of fact, the McBane family business of today is actually an offshoot of Ross McBane's business of yesteryear.

"My dad worked for years in the fertilizer business and I worked with him in addition to running a dairy business and milking parlor," Paul said. "When Dad passed away, many of his customers came to me and asked me to continue on with the business so that they wouldn't have to go into town for their farm and fertilizer needs. I decided to oblige them and, in 1963, Paul McBane Farm and Fertilizer was born."

Today, in addition to son Steve who Paul says has been "doing a man's work since he was just eight years old," Paul is joined by his wife, Shelby, who pays the bills, and his daughter-in-law, Cheryl, who keeps the books. Steve and Cheryl's son, Chris, also worked in the business prior to his untimely death in April 2008. The only non-family member currently employed by the company is Miguel Salas. Salas helps run the company's warehouses and has been with the McBanes for more than two decades and is "practically family," Paul said.

Paul and Steve still run the spreader trucks and drive the tractor-trailers that haul commodities to customers. And neither shows any signs of slowing down.

"I learned early on from my father and my grandfather—George Grant McBane—what it is to work hard," said the now seventy-seven years-young Paul. "We enjoy our work and our customers, and that's what makes it all worthwhile."

For more information, call 336-376-3651.

Above: Ross (left) and Paul McBane with a friend about 1944.

Below: Paul McBane in 2007 received service award for serving the Agricultural Community in Alamance County, North Carolina.

ALAMANCE COUNTY HISTORICAL MUSEUM

Views of the Alamance County Historical Museum (clockwise from above): Formal dining room with hand-decorated Limoges china painted by Mary Catherine (Mebane) Holt in 1872; facade of 1875 addition; museum parlor with view of Thomas Day classical revival center table (1838) and Duncan Phyfe settee (1825); period granary and corn crib constructed in 1874 by Emsley and John Coble; pergola with handmade brick columns; interior of summer kitchen set with Enoch Woods "English Scenes" transferware.

Listed in the National Register of Historic Places, the Alamance County Historical Museum was organized in 1975 and opened as a Bicentennial Project in 1976 at "Oak Grove," the birthplace of textile pioneer Edwin Michael Holt. Situated in an attractive rural setting about five miles south of Burlington, North Carolina, the museum consists of the former plantation house, constructed in three stages between 1790 and 1875, and surrounding period outbuildings, including a nineteenth-century granary, barn, corn crib, and carriage house. The site is also enhanced by a reconstructed summer kitchen, pergola, flower gardens, and the Holt family cemetery.

Guided tours of the house museum and grounds are available on a daily basis, excluding Mondays. The museum collection includes furniture and accessories typical of the mid-Victorian era, antique clothing, portraits and paintings, vintage quilts, and early forms of transportation, such as an 1870 Phaeton carriage, a Conestoga wagon, and a 1907 Ford Runabout. Examples of the "Alamance Plaid," the first commercially woven colored cotton fabric manufactured in the American South, are also prominently displayed.

Rotating exhibits have included Civil War artifacts, Piedmont North Carolina pottery, Victorian paper ephemera, and textile memorabilia. The museum collection also includes Native American artifacts and items recovered from several local archaeological sites.

The Alamance County Historical Museum is made available for wedding receptions, civic club luncheons, and other private functions. For further information please visit the museum's website, www.alamancemuseum.org, or contact us at the following e-mail address: achm@triad.twcbc.com.